*The original letters from which these excerpts
were taken are on file at Newcastle Publishing Co., Inc.*

I just read your incredible double volume . . . the *Best ever
written* on the subject.

> —*Michael Timothy Cassett*, radio show host,
> author-numerologist, Los Angeles

I have been studying the numbers for some time now and have
never seen a more "complete" or "thorough" set of books with
which to work.

> —*Rose M. Uhlhorn*, numerology student, Glenview, Illinois

Your work is outstanding! By far the finest work on numerology
I've yet to come across. Sophisticated and quite involved but
clearly and simply explained. Beautifully, beautifully done.

> —*Ann Walker, R.N.*, numerology student, St. Louis

It is the most fantastic work of its kind—on any Occult subject
I have come across in the past seven or eight years. I could not
believe that any person would ever write a work on any Occult
subject as thorough and complete as you have managed to do. It
has certainly been one of the biggest thrills going thru your
presentation—I love the systematic and logical way in which you
present this subject.

> —*Roberta Strain, AMAFA*, astrologer, numerologist,
> music teacher, Bound Brook, NJ

The most detailed and yet comprehensive treatment of this subject I have yet to find! . . . Your book . . . cannot be surpassed,
and will be treasured in the years ahead.

> —*Sharla S. Breger*, astrologer-numerologist, Chicago

The book is synergy—putting all aspects of the subject together
—making a powerful tool.

> —*Jeanne Silk, R.N., M.A.C.S.*, nurse, psychotherapist,
> numerologist, Tempe, Arizona

NUMEROLOGY
The Complete Guide

VOLUME ONE

NUMEROLOGY
The Complete Guide

VOLUME ONE

THE PERSONALITY READING

Matthew Oliver Goodwin

NEWCASTLE PUBLISHING COMPANY, INC. • NORTH HOLLYWOOD, CALIFORNIA • 1981

For additional information on readings and classes, write:

Matthew Goodwin
P.O. Box 2204
Culver City, CA 90231

A NEWCASTLE BOOK
First printing October 1981
7 8 9 10
Printed in the United States of America

Design: Riley K. Smith
Typography: Freedmen's Organization

Printed by Delta Lithograph • Van Nuys, CA

TO ARLENE

ACKNOWLEDGMENTS

I would like to acknowledge the many people who helped.

Thanks—
> to the special friend (who prefers to remain anonymous) who first introduced me to numerology,
>
> to Naomi Weisman, who shared her insights,
>
> to Dana Holliday, who contributed her unique awarenesses,
>
> to Kelley Jeane Younger, for helping to make this project a reality and for consulting on the book,
>
> to Anne Brenden Monkarsh, for her gracious special help,
>
> to Pam Cisneros, who typed so much of the mountain of manuscript,
>
> to Judy Yerman, whose contribution when needed was so important,
>
> to Mary Leipziger, who contributed the back-cover photograph (and the pastries to help my occasionally lagging spirit).

Thanks to those whose encouragement for my special project was so meaningful:
> Ida Goodwin, Jean Brill, Miriam Miller, Harvey Yerman, Elliot Brill, Susan Brill, Bill Brill, Helen Brill, Antonino Bruno, Lenore Goldman, Bernie Weisman, Audrey Simmons, Neil Perlmutter, Boris Marks, Julian Hanberg, Gerta Farber.

And, of course, thanks to Josh Goodwin for his support, to Lisa Goodwin for her encouragement from around the world, to Adam Chess for his concern—and especially to Arlene Goodwin who was always there to listen, discuss and lend loving sustenance.

Los Angeles, 1981

CONTENTS

PART II: CHARACTER DELINEATION—THE CORE

THE REFERENCE CHARTS

PART I:
INTRODUCTION

CHAPTER 1

A BEGINNING

Numerology is the study of the occult significance of numbers. It's probably the simplest of the occult fields to learn and master. Using numerology, you can discover a person's strengths and weaknesses, deep inner needs, emotional reactions, ways of dealing with others, talents. You can help yourself by becoming aware of your own character and learning to understand and deal with others—family, friends, lovers, employers, employees. You can find out what kind of potential energy and what type of stress are currently existing in your life and in the lives of those about you. You can determine the best times to marry, change jobs, move, speculate, take a trip.

How is all this information derived? In all the occult fields, observers have found correlations between certain clearly observable physical phenomena and the inner workings of people. In other words, the universe seems to have provided many keys which, when understood, provide superb tools for the understanding of human nature. In astrology, the key relates the planets' positions at a person's birth with the person's traits; in palm reading, the key relates the lines and bumps of the hand with a person's characteristics; and, in numerology, the key relates a person's name and birthdate with that person's nature. Significantly, all the readings are consistent with each other—the different readings often have similar information or cover different, but related, aspects of a person's traits.

Why does numerology work? There are many explanations in the literature—discussions of psychic energy, the God force, the vibratory effect of numbers. These explanations have not clarified anything for me. Frankly, *I* don't know why numerology works. I don't know whether the numbers are merely a descriptive code or representative of a force determining people's behavior. Numerology, like the other occult fields, does not, at this time, allow for scientific explanation. I can only attest to the fact, confirmed by other numerologists and their clients, of the consistent congruence between a person's numbers and that person's characteristics and life experiences.

Some numerologists feel that the field can be traced back over 10,000 years. The centuries-old Hebrew Kabbala, for instance, deals with the subject. Pythagoras in Greece some 2600 years ago is even credited with giving this field new life, along with his other mathematical studies. It is delightful to be carrying on a tradition with such a long history. Although some people are comforted in the knowledge that numerology has so many thousands of years of study behind it, the link between modern numerology and the ancients is a somewhat tenuous connection.

The modern phase of numerology was started by L. Dow Balliett, an American woman in Atlantic City, N. J., who published several books on the subject at the turn of the century. Later, Dr. Julia Seton helped publicize the field. Since then, the work of these two women has been extended by Florence Campbell, Juno Jordan and others, so that there now exists a small literature on the subject. Unfortunately, much of the literature is abstruse, archaic or fragmented.

This book is a presentation of the entire field of numerology in a manner which will allow a beginner to easily assimilate the material and an advanced student to quickly master the craft. The individual elements making up a reading are fully defined and analyzed and many examples are included showing how the elements are combined into a delineation. Throughout, the emphasis is on clarity and completeness.

Each section of the book forms a complete unit of the subject. When you've finished Part II, for instance, you'll be capable of giving simple character readings which will be correct as far as they go. Completion of Part III will add considerable depth to the readings and Part IV will develop your advanced delineation skills. Part V covers progressed delineations—determining the potential energies and events for any time in a person's entire life.

Much of the reference material required by a numerologist is presented in a unique format at the end of each volume: charts specially designed for easy cross-reference. The charts are available for reference in giving readings after the subject has been mastered.

I hope you'll find numerology as exciting and satisfying as I have. I expect that if you study the field at all, you'll be fascinated by your new understanding of yourself and others. In addition, you'll probably be surprised to find your awareness of the universe and its structure significantly broadened.

CHAPTER 2

THE BASICS

THE BASIC NUMBERS

The study of numerology is the study of the symbolism of numbers. Each number represents one large area of human awareness and experience; all the numbers together cover all possible awarenesses, experiences, talents and characteristics. Only the single digits—1, 2, 3, 4, 5, 6, 7, 8, and 9—and the Master Numbers 11 and 22 are used. The Master Numbers, the only numbers not reduced to a single digit, represent a special higher level of potential than the other numbers.

As a beginning step, think of each number as a lesson to be learned. We'll list each number along with its "keywords," the simplest expression of the number's lesson, and then describe the lesson more completely in an accompanying paragraph or two. Think of the lesson as the heart of each number, the essence to which all the experiences and characteristics relate.

In this introductory chapter, each number is described briefly. As your study advances, additional aspects of each number will be discussed. Your own observation and experience will broaden your understanding. Later on, in the advanced Chapter 22 in Volume 2, we'll summarize the myriad characteristics of all the numbers.

1

INDIVIDUATION
INDEPENDENCE
ATTAINMENT

The lessons
of the
numbers

A person must distinguish himself from other people and acknowledge his own INDIVIDUATION. The individual has to develop the capability of standing on his own and going from dependence to INDEPENDENCE. Once independent, the person becomes aware of his potential for ATTAINMENT as an individual—for creating and pioneering when working alone, for leading and managing when working with others.

2

RELATION
COOPERATION

Independence is important but has its limitations. There *are* other people all about, and another lesson involves being a meaningful part of a group—a small group like family or friends, a larger group like a business or community. The person must learn adaptability, service, consideration for others, i.e., the meaning of a RELATION with others, the idea of COOPERATION.

3

EXPRESSION
JOY OF LIVING

A person must discover, both as an individual and as a group member, his capability of EXPRESSION: (1) artistic expression—writing, painting, sculpting, singing or any of the many other means of expressing inner thoughts and emotions, and (2) expression of feelings toward others—friendship, affection, love. The JOY OF LIVING can be expressed with optimism and enthusiasm. There can be a purity, even a naiveté here. (This is, perhaps, the most enjoyable lesson of all the numbers.)

4

LIMITATION
ORDER
SERVICE

Life doesn't always present opportunities for singing and laughing. Life doesn't always appear expansive or yours for the taking. Often, it feels just the opposite. The individual must learn the difficult law of LIMITATION. Everyone has limitations—limitations presented by the environment, by the physical body, by the restrictions of the individual's viewpoints. Rather than struggle against these limits, it is necessary to learn to live with them, to accept them and to make a meaningful existence, not in spite of the limitations, but *because* of the limitations. It is a difficult lesson. The individual embarking on this course must learn system and organization, ORDER on a practical level. He must be prepared to be of SERVICE to others.

5

CONSTRUCTIVE FREEDOM

There is a time for expansion, for dealing with change, unexpected happenings, adventure. This lesson usually gives a person an abundance of talents in every direction, the capability of accomplishing almost anything for which an opportunity is presented—and many opportunities *are* presented. With the freedom that this abundance of talent and opportunity brings, life can be exciting. But the lesson is more difficult: the individual must learn the CONSTRUCTIVE use of FREEDOM. The individual must not waste his many talents or misuse his ongoing opportunities; he must not get lost in solely physical desires—food, sex, alcohol, drugs. He must not scatter his potential and end up with frustration. He must make a meaningful existence by using freedom productively.

6

BALANCE
RESPONSIBILITY
LOVE

A person must learn to give the beauty of love and harmony, sympathy and understanding, protection and BALANCE. Along with the balancing, the lesson of RESPONSIBILITY can be a meaningful one. The individual may find himself responsible for more than what rightly seems his share. Others will recognize his strength, and he may be expected to help them if they are in need and cannot help themselves. He will probably be the one who holds the family together, who harmonizes and adjusts difficult situations. He may choose to limit himself to his family, his friends, possibly the close community. The friendship and LOVE the individual expresses to others will come back to him from those he helps. He can bask in the glory of a job well done and the quiet reward of friendship and love returned.

The individual's capability at harmony and balance may also be expressed creatively—there is the possibility of artistic achievement.

7

ANALYSIS
UNDERSTANDING

There's a time for introspection, a time to subject all an individual knows to mental ANALYSIS, so that eventually a person possesses much of knowledge and UNDERSTANDING.

Spiritual awareness is employed, and emphasis on material matters avoided. Desire for material accumulation will probably lead the individual off the track, for this is a time for study and meditation, a time to know oneself—in the deepest way.

There will be much time spent alone—the person must learn to be alone and not feel isolated. Often, the individual will appear "different" to others—his way of thinking or doing may be very much his own and may seem inexplicable to his fellow man. He must accept that he *is* on a different wavelength and find satisfaction in that. In a world where materialism rates so highly, the road for the counselor, the professor, the pure researcher may be a difficult one.

8

MATERIAL SATISFACTION

The individual must learn to deal with the material things of life, the practical matters. He will find himself at home in the business world—with much capability as an efficient administrator or executive. He will learn how to handle money—how to accumulate it, how to spend it wisely. The individual will work for MATERIAL SATISFACTION. This may mean emphasis on money to buy the best in houses, cars, furnishings, trips. (Perhaps, if he can reach the highest level of this lesson, he will see that material freedom can mean relying very *little* on money or material matters. Few ever gain this insight.)

The individual will be very conscious of status in relation to material things and will work to satisfy his need for status to prove his superiority. He may appear single-minded, rigid or stubborn to others. Striving for power and high material goals may make him aware of the limitations of his ability or the restrictions of his circumstances.

9

SELFLESSNESS
HUMANITARIANISM

There's a time to learn the satisfaction of giving to his fellow man. This is a difficult lesson. The satisfaction comes from the giving. There is little reward—the love and friendship are sometimes returned, the obligation often not repaid. The person must place all others before himself, must give for the sheer pleasure of giving, because he has learned the ultimate satisfaction of SELFLESSNESS and HUMANITARIANISM. The individual gives (1) by helping others or (2) by giving of himself in some form of creative expression.

11
ILLUMINATION

The master numbers exist on a higher spiritual plane than the single digits. The first master number, the 11, must work to develop intuition, to tune into psychic forces not available to those with lower numbers. He must stand ready to be a channel with a message from above. In his life, he must inspire by his own example, living in the way revealed to him, spreading his ILLUMINATION for others to absorb and benefit. This number is as difficult as it is rewarding.

Often, particularly at an early age, the individual is aware of his special powers yet unable to synthesize them for his own use or for the good of his fellow man. He is often a relatively impractical idealist, far more a dreamer than a doer. There is an undercurrent of nervous tension always present from the high power sources to which the individual is attuned. He has to learn to live with his special powers, to set himself aside from the world of material accumulation in order to better understand the powerful forces which can reveal a higher guidance.

22
MASTER BUILDER

The second master number, the 22, is potentially capable of combining the idealism of the first master number, the 11, with the ability to put these ideals into a concrete form. Enormous power is available to him to produce on a significant scale, for the benefit of humanity. When this potential can be realized, the individual becomes a MASTER BUILDER, capable of feats well beyond all others.

Few with this number can marshal their forces to reach anywhere near the ultimate potential. The individual is aware of the forces within him, aware also of the nervous tension that accompanies these forces. He spends his time grappling with powers that are difficult to comprehend and use. Often, he is seen by his fellow men as a person with enormous potential who has not, for some unexplained reason, been able to fully use his capabilities. The highest potential is also the most difficult to reach.

Odd/even
numbers

The numbers are related to each other in many different ways. The odd numbers, for example, have somewhat different qualities than the even.

ODD NUMBERS	EVEN NUMBERS
1 INDIVIDUATION INDEPENDENCE ATTAINMENT	2 RELATION COOPERATION
3 EXPESSION JOY OF LIVING	4 LIMITATION ORDER SERVICE
5 CONSTRUCTIVE FREEDOM	6 BALANCE RESPONSIBILITY LOVE
7 ANALYSIS UNDERSTANDING	8 MATERIAL SATISFACTION
9 SELFLESSNESS HUMANITARIANISM	
11 ILLUMINATION	22 MASTER BUILDER

The odd numbers can be thought of as dealing with the *individual* alone—the individuation of the 1 or the selflessness of the 9; the even numbers, on the other hand, involve the relation of the individual *to the group*—the cooperation of the 2, the love of the 6.

The odd numbers relate to relatively *abstract* concepts—the joy of living of the 3, the illumination of the 11, while the even numbers are concerned with more *practical* matters—the service of the 4, the material satisfaction of the 8.

The odd numbers involve more *idealistic* endeavors—the constructive freedom of the 5 or the understanding of the 7; the even numbers relate to more *mundane* affairs—the responsibility of the 6 or the order of the 4.

Other
number
relations

There are other relations besides the odd and even.

Each number can be viewed as the next logical development following the stage represented by the previous number. The independence of the 1, for instance, is followed by the cooperation with others of the 2; the constructive freedom of the 5 is followed by the balance and responsibility of the 6.

From a different perspective, each number represents the opposite of the previous number: the limitation of the 4 is followed by the constructive freedom of the 5, the material satisfaction of the 8 is followed by the selflessness of the 9.

Number groups

Although it's not obvious from the brief descriptions, some numbers seem to group naturally with other numbers because of the similarity of the characteristics expressed.

For instance, 2, 6 and 9 all deal with different aspects of how people get along with each other. The number 2 represents the less personal relation of people in a business or some other group situation associating and cooperating with each other. The number 6 represents the relation of people in a family or other small community group—6 deals with friendship, affection and love. The number 9 represents the giving quality of a humanitarian or philanthropist—a person who gives feelings, time or money to others with little concern with return.

Another example of a group is 1, 4 and 8, all representing different aspects of self-centeredness. The number 1 involves the potential to become independent, to break with any prevalent bonds of dependency. A person working on independence is likely to be most concerned with his own needs to the partial or complete exclusion of others' needs. The number 4 may concern a person with his own real or imagined limitations. A person may strive to break through the feelings of limitation or may, although rarely, attempt to learn to live with the strong restrictions imposed. In either case, the concern with limitation is likely to make a person extremely aware of his own needs and his struggle to fulfill the needs despite the restrictions, leaving little room to be concerned with others' needs. The 8 may well feel more power than the 4, but usually, because of this power, the 8 will work hard to take care of his material needs with the traits and power he possesses. An 8's material needs tend to be a large and significant area of his life, so that the needs of others are likely to go wanting.

The group of numbers 2, 6 and 9 stand for many traits besides the relation of people to each other and 1, 4 and 8 involve many characteristics besides self-centeredness. But, awareness of the different number groupings gives you a potent tool for a delineation. If you find a person with strong 2's, 6's or 9's, the likelihood is strong that this is a person with a friendly, loving, giving approach. Or, if you find a person with strong 1's, 4's or 8's, this is likely to be a relatively self-centered person.

Positive/ negative energy

Most people express positive energy most of the time. That's why all the keywords define potential achievements: the achievement of independence with 1, the achievement of cooperation with 2, all the way to the achievement of a master builder with 22. But, although there's mostly positive potential being used, there's also, unfortunately, negative energy available, too. Since the numbers represent all possible traits and characteristics, they symbolize negative as well as positive potentials.

Each number can be thought of as part of a single continuum extending from 1 to 22, and each keyword (and each awareness, experience, talent or characteristic) can be viewed, not as an isolated phenomenon, but as one step of an infinite number of steps along its own continuum. The keyword represents the positive potential of the number, but the continuum includes the entire range from the negative potential to the positive.

When we use the 1 keyword INDEPENDENCE, we really mean the continuum on which independence represents the ultimate positive potential. The negative end of the continuum would be lack of independence, i. e., dependence. In between the two extremes would be passivity, resignation, subservience.

Similarly, the 6 keyword LOVE is one end of a continuum, with the other end being inability to relate. From inability to relate, other steps along the continuum would be association, friendship, affection and eventually love.

Each number, then, must be thought of as representative of the total continuum. The keyword is handy for memorization, but it only states one end, the positive end, of the continuum. At the beginning of your study, it will be useful to fall back on the keyword and the brief description, but your awareness of the symbolism will rapidly expand as you begin to relate the keyword to the continuum it represents.

Chart 1: The Numbers— Basics

Turn to CHART 1: THE NUMBERS—BASICS, on page 222. The paragraphs describing the numbers are repeated here in a different format, a format designed to make it easier to see the relations between the numbers. If you thumb through the other charts grouped at the end of each volume, you'll see that they follow a format similar to Chart 1. There's a page for each number in each chart, with the number and its keywords at the top of the page. The first page of each chart is headed with the element which the specific chart explores, and, on the second page, the make-up of this particular chart is described and explained. Because of this repeating format, it's easy, first, to compare different numbers for the same element in one chart, and second, to compare the descriptions of a particular number in different charts.

THE BASIC DATA

Only two simple pieces of information are needed as a basis for delineation: the birthdate, and the name given at birth. If either is not available, a reading is not possible.

The birthdate is usually readily available. The birthname may, at times, be more difficult to determine. When there's any doubt, check the birth certificate if at all possible. Many people change the spelling of their name or add or subtract middle names. It's not uncommon to find a person surprised at either the name or the spelling on the certificate. Even if the name on the birth certificate has never been actively used, this name is still one of the determinants.

(Neither the birthdate nor the birthname is accidental or arbitrary. The soul comes to earth in a physical body to learn lessons that can only be learned while in a material form. The birthdate and birthname are determined for the soul. Your birthdate was the best time to reappear on earth—with your birthname—to learn the lessons your soul has chosen to learn. Whether your parents searched long and hard for your name, or came upon it in a flash, the name came to your parents through universal wavelengths they probably didn't know existed.)

Different alphabets

The numerology described in this book is based on the twenty-six letter Roman alphabet used in English and French speaking countries. The same numerology system also applies if similar alphabets, such as the twenty-eight letter alphabet used in Spanish-speaking countries or the twenty-one letter Italian alphabet, are used. (The number values assigned to these different alphabets are given later in this chapter.) If a person were named in an alphabet using other than Roman letters—Russian, Japanese, Hebrew or Greek, for instance—the transliterated name (the name as written in the Roman alphabet) will provide the same accurate numerology reading.

Special names

Some names have to be slightly adjusted for use in a delineation, as follows:

1. In some cultures, a person may be given seven or eight different names. A reading based on this long a name would be diffused and give an inaccurate picture. Use birthnames, as given, up to a maximum of four names. If a person has more than four names, use only the first and last as the birthname.

> Carolyn Emily Annette Crown is used as Carolyn Emily Annette Crown.
> Maria Luisa Juliana Aida Basile is used as Maria Basile.

2. If a name is hyphenated, eliminate the hyphen and use as two separate names.

> Betty-Jane Mosher is used as Betty Jane Mosher.
> Richard Pettingbone-Wilson is used as Richard Pettingbone Wilson.

3. Combine a compound last name into one name.

> Arthur van der Kalen is used as Arthur Vanderkalen.
> Anna della Reese is used as Anna Dellareese.

4. Omit Jr. or Sr. or II, III, IV following the birthname.

> Henry McAnn, Jr. is used as Henry McAnn.
> Neil Harold Lewis III is used as Neil Harold Lewis.

Adopted child's name   There is one significant exception to the use of the birthname. In the case of adoption, use the name the child is given by the first family with whom the child resides on a *permanent* basis. The soul's linkage here is with the permanent adoptive parents rather than with the foster parents or natural parents.

THE BASIC OPERATION

To start a delineation, we convert the birthdate and birthname into single digits or master numbers using the BASIC OPERATION: Simply *reduce the numbers by addition*. For example:

$$34 = 3 + 4 = \underline{7}$$

$$50 = 5 + 0 = \underline{5}$$

$$48 = 4 + 8 = 12$$

12 is not a single digit or master number. Repeat the addition process.

$$12 = 1 + 2 = \underline{3}$$

$$29 = 2 + 9 = \underline{\underline{11}}$$

(If a master number—11 or 22—is reached, *don't* reduce it to a single digit.)

To find the basic number corresponding to a year, use the same process:

$$1952 = 1 + 9 + 5 + 2 = 17$$
$$= 1 + 7 = \underline{\underline{8}}$$

$$1972 = 1 + 9 + 7 + 2 = 19$$
$$= 1 + 9 = 10$$
$$= 1 + 0 = \underline{\underline{1}}$$

$$1975 = 1 + 9 + 7 + 5 = \underline{\underline{22}}$$

(22 is a master number. Don't reduce it to a single unit.)

Names are similarly reduced by addition. Each letter in the name is assigned a number based on its location in the twenty-six letter English alphabet.

A, the first letter, is 1

B, the second letter, is 2

C, the third letter, is 3

J, the tenth letter, is 1 $(10 = 1 + 0 = \underline{1})$

K, the eleventh letter, is 2   (In assigning number values to letters, *all* numbers are reduced to a single digit. Although K is the eleventh letter, and will be used as a master number in other contexts, for these purposes K is a 2.)

$(11 = 1 + 1 = \underline{\underline{2}})$

L, the twelfth letter, is 3 $(12 = 1 + 2 = \underline{3})$

S, the nineteenth letter, is 1 $(19 = 1 + 9 = 10$
$10 = 1 + 0 = \underline{1})$

T, the twentieth letter, is 2 $(20 = 2 + 0 = \underline{\underline{2}})$

U, the twenty-first letter, is 3 $(21 = 2 + 1 = \underline{3})$

Z, the twenty-sixth letter, is 8 $(26 = 2 + 6 = \underline{\underline{8}})$

The number value of letters

The number values of the twenty-six letter English alphabet are summed up in this chart. (The French alphabet uses the same twenty-six letters.)

1	2	3	4	5	6	7	8	9
A	B	C	D	E	F	G	H	I
J	K	L	M	N	O	P	Q	R
S	T	U	V	W	X	Y	Z	

The number values of the twenty-eight letter Spanish alphabet are:

1	2	3	4	5	6	7	8	9
A	B	C	D	E	F	G	H	I
J		L	M	N Ñ	O	P	Q	R RR
S	T	U	V		X	Y	Z	
	CH				LL			

The number values for the twenty-one letter Italian alphabet are:

1	2	3	4	5	6	7	8	9
A	B	C	D	E	F	G	H	I
		L	M	N	O	P	Q	R
S	T	U	V				Z	

To find the basic number corresponding to a name, assign each letter its number and reduce, by addition, to a single digit or master number. For example:

$$\begin{array}{cccccc} A & R & T & H & U & R \\ 1 + & 9 + & 2 + & 8 + & 3 + & 9 = 32 \end{array}$$
$$= 3 + 2 = \underline{\underline{5}}$$

$$\begin{array}{ccccc} K & E & V & I & N \\ 2 + & 5 + & 4 + & 9 + & 5 = 25 \end{array}$$
$$= 2 + 5 = \underline{\underline{7}}$$

$$\begin{array}{ccccc} K & A & R & E & N \\ 2 + & 1 + & 9 + & 5 + & 5 = \underline{\underline{22}} \end{array}$$

With the completion of Part I, we've laid the foundation on which to build your readings. In Part II, we'll use the BASIC OPERATION—reducing the numbers by addition—to convert the BASIC DATA—birthdate and birthname—into BASIC NUMBERS with their symbolic meanings and proceed with the beginnings of character delineation.

PART II:
CHARACTER DELINEATION—
THE CORE

THE CORE

There are approximately twenty numerology components which are derived from a person's birthdate and birthname. A complete character delineation evolves from the synthesis of these many pieces. The core of a reading involves only four of these elements. The core expresses the essence of a person—his direction, his strengths and weaknesses, his potential for change and development.

If we think of a complete character delineation as comparable to a full-color portrait, the core would be equivalent to a slightly fuzzy black-and-white reproduction of the portrait. The core would be as rough and incomplete as the reproduction—but it would be accurate, and it would give us the major characteristics just as the reproduction does. The reproduction might show that the person has large almond-shaped eyes, but until the color is added, you wouldn't know if they're black or blue or brown, and until the focus is sharpened, you can't really know if there's an especially lively glint in the eye. Similarly, the core may tell you that the person is systematic and orderly. But when color is added and the focus is sharpened (or in numerology terms, when the modifiers are added) the person may be systematic to the point of stubbornness or rigidity.

The core, then, is the major determinant in the character delineation, and its power is diffused throughout the entire reading. The core, while only part of the picture, *is accurate as far as it goes.*

The core consists of the following elements:

1. Life Path
2. Expression
3. Soul Urge
4. Birthday

CHAPTER 3

THE FIRST ELEMENT
OF THE CORE:
THE LIFE PATH

THE LIFE PATH IS THE MAJOR LESSON TO BE   **Definition**
LEARNED IN THIS LIFE, THE CENTRAL FOCUS OF A
PERSON'S EXISTENCE. The Life Path is at the heart of the
core.

Let's look, for a moment, at the world in terms of reincarnation. Simply stated, reincarnation explains that the soul re-
turns to earth in physical form again and again, each time to
concentrate on a specific lesson. When the soul has absorbed all
the lessons, it no longer needs to return to earth, but can move
on to a higher plane. The specific lesson, determined by the
soul prior to assuming physical form, is the Life Path. Whether
you believe in reincarnation or not, the Life Path is still the
central focus of the life.

The Life Path (sometimes called the Birthforce, Birthpath or
Destiny) determines other related matters. It describes the opportunities available in order to learn the major lesson, as well
as the environment—the people and places—in which these opportunities are likely to be found. Some of a person's attitudes
and characteristics are determined by the Life Path, for these
traits are prescribed as an aid to the study of the main lesson.

Visualize the Life Path as a broad channel or highway running through all the possible activities a person may encounter
in a lifetime. The route holds the environment and all the opportunities for the study at hand. The channel is extremely
broad. People with the same Life Path may have different approaches to pursuing their study, but the channel is wide

enough to accommodate all comers. As long as a person stays on the course, he will be contributing the maximum to his own growth and development. Most people wander out of the channel from time to time; some people have difficulty finding the channel (and a numerology reading may help them get their bearings); and some few people choose to head off in some other direction.

Calculation

THE LIFE PATH IS DERIVED BY FINDING THE SUM OF THE MONTH, DAY AND YEAR OF BIRTH AND REDUCING THAT SUM TO A SINGLE DIGIT OR MASTER NUMBER.

1. Determine the number representing the month, day and year. Determine each separately.

MONTH:

January, the first month, has a value of 1
February, the second month, has a value of 2
March, the third month, has a value of 3
April, the fourth month, has a value of 4
May, the fifth month, has a value of 5
June, the sixth month, has a value of 6
July, the seventh month, has a value of 7
August, the eighth month, has a value of 8
September, the ninth month, has a value of 9
October, the tenth month, has a value of 10 = 1 + 0 = . . . 1
November, the eleventh month, has a value of 11
(master number, not reduced)
December, the twelfth month, has a value of 12 = 1 + 2 = 3

DAY:

Add the numbers and reduce to a single digit or a master number. For example:

If the birthday is the 1st, the value is 1
2nd 2
9th 9
10th = 10 = 1 + 0 = ... 1
11th 11
(master number, not reduced)
12th = 12 = 1 + 2 = ... 3
20th = 20 = 2 + 0 = ... 2
21st = 21 = 2 + 1 = ... 3

$$22\text{nd} \ldots\ldots\ldots\ldots\ldots\ldots\ldots\ldots\ldots\ldots 22$$
(master number, not reduced)
$$23\text{rd} = 23 = 2 + 3 = \ldots\ldots\ldots\ldots 5$$

YEAR:

Add the numbers and reduce to a single digit or a master number. For example:

$$1918 = 1 + 9 + 1 + 8 = 19$$
$$= 1 + 9 = 10$$
$$= 1 + 0 = 1$$
$$1940 = 1 + 9 + 4 + 0 = 14$$
$$= 1 + 4 = 5$$
$$1975 = 1 + 9 + 7 + 5 = 22$$
(master number, not reduced)

2. Add together the numbers representing the month, day and year. Reduce to a single digit or a master number.

Example: May 28, 1935

Month: May is the fifth month. Therefore, May = 5.

Day: $28 = 2 + 8 = 10$
$$= 1 + 0 = 1$$

Year: $1935 = 1 + 9 + 3 + 5 = 18$
$$= 1 + 8 = 9$$

Write the numbers directly below the date:

$$\text{May} \quad 28, \quad 1935$$
$$5 \ + 1 \ + \ 9 \ = 15$$
$$= 1 + 5 = 6$$
The Life Path is 6

Example: November 4, 1975

Month: November is the eleventh month. Therefore, November = 11

Day: 4

Year: $1975 = 1 + 9 + 7 + 5 = 22$

Write the numbers directly below the date:

$$\text{November} \quad 4, \quad 1975$$
$$11 \quad + 4 + \ 22 \ = 37$$
$$= 3 + 7 = 10$$
$$= 1 + 0 = 1$$
The Life Path is 1

Always add the numbers after *separately* determining the number representing the month, day and year. If you add them all at once, you may end up with a master number that doesn't apply or lose a master number that should apply:

Example: March 12, 1940

> Month: March is the third month. Therefore,
> March = 3
>
> Day: 12 = 1 + 2 = 3
>
> Year: 1940 = 1 + 9 + 4 + 0 = 14
>
> $$= 1 + 4 = 5$$

Write the numbers below the date:

March   12,   1940
  3   + 3 +   5   = 11

The Life Path is 11

Adding the numbers all together would have been incorrect:

March   12,   1940
  3   +   1 + 2   +   1 + 9 + 4 + 0   = 20
                                      = 2 + 0 = 2
                                      Incorrect.
                                      The master number
                                      has been lost.

With just a little practice, you can do most of the work in your head, and the first step of your numerology calculation would look like this:

November   4,   1975
  11   + 4 +   22   = 37 = 10 = 1 Life Path

Chart 2: The Life Path

Turn to CHART 2: THE LIFE PATH on page 236. Here you'll find discussions of the salient points of all the Life Paths.

Central Focus

The upper horizontal division, labeled "Central Focus," contains discussions of the main lesson of each Life Path. The essence of the lessons are the keywords appearing adjacent to the number at the top of the table. The discussion in this upper division is an elaboration on the keywords. Read the central focus of your own Life Path and relate it to the keywords. Compare the central focus of your Life Path with the basic lesson of your Life Path number shown on Chart 1. Make this comparison with a few Life Path numbers of people you know well. You should begin to experience the simple relation between the charts, as well as the complex meanings of the keywords and the numbers they represent.

The lower the number of the Life Path, the less complex and more direct is the lesson to be assimilated. Life Paths 1 through 6 deal with fundamental concepts. Life Paths 7, 8, and 9 are dealing with more advanced understandings; in a sense, a higher level of some of the lower numbered lessons. And 11 and 22 are concerned with most complex manifestations. The higher the number of the Life Path, the greater the ultimate potential and the more difficult the possibility of reaching that potential.

Each soul determines its own Life Path before coming to earth in a physical manifestation. The lessons are not learned in consecutive order. Each lesson must usually be studied over a period of many, many lifetimes.

Characteristics

The second horizontal division of Chart 2, labeled "Characteristics," describes the traits and attitudes found with each Life Path. All the traits are not developed to the same degree of intensity in a person, though they are all usually apparent. Some of the traits are seemingly assets—the warmth and friendliness of 3, the enthusiasm of 5. Some of the traits are seemingly liabilities—the self-centeredness of the 1 or the lack of adaptability of the 7. But, as you work with these traits, you'll see that they are not fixed assets or liabilities at all—each trait can be thought of as a continuum of traits which run the gamut from positive to negative. The enthusiasm of 5, for instance, can range from the positive pole of enthusiasm which can make a vital contribution, to the negative pole of enthusiasm for every new exciting awareness, an enthusiasm which makes it difficult for some 5's to stick to any project for any length of time. The self-centeredness of the 1 can range from the negative pole of complete self-centeredness to the exclusion of all others' interests, to the positive pole of self-concern denoting a person's belief in himself or his work strong enough to to push forward a project that would not succeed without this added strength.

As we proceed with the development of the art of character delineation, it will sometimes be possible to clarify the extent to which the various traits are positively or negatively expressed for each person. For now, we must content ourselves with only the awareness of the characteristics.

Negative Expression

Most people are using their lives in a constructive manner. In numerology terms, we would say that they are expressing the positive side of their Life Path, the side of the Life Path discussed under "Central Focus." Everybody, from time to time, and some few people almost all the time, express the negative side of the path instead and live in a non-constructive (rarely destructive) way. The "Negative Expression," the third horizontal division, defines the facets of this side of the character. A person expresses negatively (a) when he exaggerates the lesson of the Life Path to the point of unproductivity, or (b) when he denies the lesson of the Life Path to express the very opposite of the intended lesson.

Later on, we'll see how, in some cases, you can determine whether this negative approach is stressed to the detriment of the major lesson. Even when a person is following this negative expression, he still possesses the traits noted in the "Characteristics" division, but he is apt to be emphasizing the negative end of the continuum of some of the traits, at least.

Commentary

The lower horizontal division of Chart 2 provides a "Commentary" on some of the subtleties involved on each Life Path. As you gain experience in numerology, these discussions should help clarify some of the complexities you're likely to meet.

Sample reading

With an understanding of the Life Path, you now possess the single most important element of a character delineation. The information you have is accurate, *as far as it goes*, but must be couched in careful terms to allow for the ample modifications as you synthesize the many additional elements.

A sample reading with this limited information, might read as follows:

The central focus of your life is the learning of _____ _____ _____.

Fill in with "Central Focus" information.

Here are some of the attitudes and traits you're likely to express: _____ _____ _____.

Fill in with "Characteristics" information.

Like most people, there are times when you aren't always expressing the best that's in you. Sometimes,

Fill in with "Negative Expression" information: first,

you're probably struggling with ____

_____

or with _____

_____.

the exaggeration of the lesson, and second, the denial of the lesson.

Life Paths of some famous people

When you begin doing delineations, you'll find that some people, although they recognize their characteristics quickly, complain that they'd prefer a different Life Path to the one they now have. You may want to remind them that it's possible to lead a full, meaningful and productive life with a Life Path of any number.

Here, for instance, are the Life Paths of some famous people. (The lesson of the Life Path in the examples chosen is most visible to the public, but this isn't necessarily the case with the Life Paths of all celebrated personalities.)

Martin Luther King (Michael Luther King), born January 15, 1929, with a Life Path of 1.
A life devoted to INDEPENDENCE and ATTAINMENT.

Henry Kissinger (Heinz Alfred Kissinger), born May 27, 1923, with a Life Path of 2.
The quintessence of diplomacy, a master of RELATION and COOPERATION.

Boris Pasternak (Boris Leonidovich Pasternak), born February 10, 1890, with a Life Path of 3.
The Nobel Prize winner, who made the most of EXPRESSION.

Sigmund Freud, born May 6, 1856, with a Life Path of 4.
The father of psychoanalysis, his contribution consisted of using ORDER and SERVICE.

Abraham Lincoln, born February 12, 1809, with a Life Path of 5.
His name is almost synonymous with CONSTRUCTIVE FREEDOM.

Dwight Eisenhower (David Dwight Eisenhower), born October 14, 1890, with a Life Path of 6.
He handled the Allied forces in World War II with BALANCE and RESPONSIBILITY.

Eleanor Roosevelt (Anna Eleanor Roosevelt), born November 11, 1884, with a Life Path of 7.
A life of accomplishment based on ANALYSIS and UNDERSTANDING.

Andrew Carnegie, born November 25, 1835, with a Life Path of 8.
A self-made millionaire, who learned about MATERIAL SATISFACTION.

Mahatma Gandhi (Mohandas Karamchand Gandhi), born October 2, 1869, with a Life Path of 9.
The leader of India's independence drive was immersed in ideas of SELFLESSNESS and HUMANITARIANISM.

Peter Hurkos (Peter Van Der Hurk), born May 21, 1911, with a Life Path of 11.
This psychic detective involved himself in the spiritual realms of ILLUMINATION.

Joseph Kennedy (Joseph Patrick Kennedy), born September 6, 1888, with a Life Path of 22.
The multi-millionaire head of the Kennedy clan was a MASTER BUILDER.

The Life Path is fixed and unchangeable. No one can change his birthdate and therefore no one can change his Life Path. Acceptance of the Life Path allows for full growth and productive development. Confidence in himself and his direction allows a person to move forward to a positive destiny.

CHAPTER 4

THE SECOND ELEMENT
OF THE CORE:
THE EXPRESSION

THE EXPRESSION IS A PERSON'S POTENTIAL NAT-
URAL ABILITIES. The Expression is second in importance of
the four core elements.

Definition

All of us are gifted, in one direction or another, with our
own natural talents and capabilities. The Expression, describing these abilities, is usually the part of a person which is most
visible to others. Because the Expression is often so apparent, it
should not be mistaken for the essence of a person. These
natural abilities are what we have to work with as we move
along the broad channel of the Life Path, and, as such, they are
less important than the central focus of the Life Path. When
the Expression and the Life Path are harmonious, the visible
Expression may also reflect, to a large extent, the main lesson
delineated by the Life Path. When the Expression and the Life
Path are not harmonious, the Life Path may come as a surprise
to the observer who sees only the more obvious Expression.

A few numerologists feel that the Expression is the single
most important element in a reading. In my experience, I have
found that the Life Path holds the key to the understanding of
a person's nature in a way that the Expression does not. The
Life Path is fixed (since the birthdate can't be changed) but the
Expression, derived from the *name, can* be altered by changing
the name. To my way of thinking, this adds additional weight

to the importance of the Life Path over the Expression. As you go along in your study, examine your own numbers and the numbers of other people you know well. Compare the importance of the Life Path and the Expression in providing an awareness of a person and draw your own conclusion. (If your conclusion favors the Expression, consult the bibliography for a view favoring this understanding.)

The Expression often describes the abilities used in the type of work the person enjoys. For instance, a 6 Expression, with its emphasis on balance and responsibility, may well indicate a teacher, nurse or counselor. (People often fit their Expressions into a broader spectrum of occupations than you might expect, though, because they concentrate on that part of the work which is emphasized by their Expressions. That same 6 Expression may be used by an administrator running a small private school, a bookkeeper in a clinic, or the head of the production department in an engineering office. These people are expressing the helpfulness and conscientiousness, the balancing and adjusting abilities, the responsibility capabilities of the 6 in the performance of their jobs. The job description doesn't stress the 6 talents as much as the job description for the teacher, nurse or counselor, but the administrator, bookkeeper and production head choose to stress their 6 abilities in carrying out their work. It's usually more helpful to describe a person's abilities in a reading, rather than to list vocations which seem to fit the Expression.)

Along with these abilities, the Expression also describes the kinds of attitudes which are usually to be found with these talents. These attitudes are usually as visible as the abilities.

Calculation

THE EXPRESSION IS DERIVED BY FINDING THE SUM OF THE NUMBER VALUES OF ALL THE LETTERS IN EACH NAME, REDUCING THIS SUM TO A SINGLE DIGIT OR MASTER NUMBER, THEN ADDING THE SUMS OF ALL THE NAMES TOGETHER AND REDUCING THAT TOTAL TO A SINGLE DIGIT OR MASTER NUMBER.

1. Consult the table on page 18 to find the numerical value of each letter. Place this numerical value below each letter:

LOUISE   KAREN   CASPER
363915   21955   311759

2. Add the numbers in each name together. Reduce this sum to a single digit or master number.

LOUISE $3 + 6 + 3 + 9 + 1 + 5 = 27$
$= 2 + 7 = \underline{9}$

KAREN $2 + 1 + 9 + 5 + 5 = \underline{\underline{22}}$
(Master number, not reduced)

CASPER $3 + 1 + 1 + 7 + 5 + 9 = 26$
$= 2 + 6 = \underline{\underline{8}}$

3. Add the numbers obtained for each name together. Reduce this sum to a single digit or master number:

$9 + 22 + 8 = 39$
$= 3 + 9 = 12$
$= 1 + 2 = 3$
The Expression is 3

4. On a numerology chart, the calculation would look like this: (The numbers in parentheses represent subtotals which are further reduced.)

```
L O U I S E     K A R E N     C A S P E R
3 6 3 9 1 5     2 1 9 5 5     3 1 1 7 5 9
 (27) 9    +      22     +     (26) 8     = 39
                                          = 12
                                          = 3 Expression
```

Here are a few additional examples:

```
HOWARD     JOSEPH       SNYDER
8 6 5 1 9 4  1 6 1 5 7 8  1 5 7 4 5 9
 (33) 6   +  (28)(10) 1  +  (31) 4      = 11 Expression
```

```
S Y L V I A   ANNE      P A S E T T A
1 7 3 4 9 1   1 5 5 5   7 1 1 5 2 2 1
 (25) 7   +   (16) 7  +   (19) 1        = 15
                                        = 6 Expression
```

Always add the numbers of each name *separately*, then add these totals together. If you add all the numbers of all the names all together at once, you may end up with a master number that doesn't apply or lose a master number that should apply.

Turn to CHART 3: EXPRESSION on page 250. Here you'll find discussions of the different Expressions.

Chart 3: The Expression

Abilities

The upper horizontal division of this chart, labeled "Abilities," describes the capabilities and talents possessed by each Expression. Some of these may be latent, but most of them are operating and are apparent.

Positive attitudes, negative attitudes

The middle and lower divisions of the chart, labeled "Positive Attitudes" and "Negative Attitudes," describe the harmonious and discordant extremes of all the Expressions. For example, a person with a 1 Expression may be ambitious and determined (positive attitude) or too aggressive (negative attitude). A person with a 4 Expression may be systematic and orderly (positive attitude) or have a rigid, stubborn approach (negative attitude). Each of these examples expresses the extremes of one particular attitude. Although the chart lists the extremes for ease in syntheses to be developed, begin to be aware of the continuums which are present. The knowledge of the continuums will help as you become more experienced in delineating.

Later, when we synthesize all four of the elements of the core, we will often be able to see which attitudes a person is more likely to express, and, sometimes, whether the positive or negative side is expressed. Since the delineation describes attitudes in effect throughout a person's life, we must be aware that, at different periods in life a person may express different parts of the range of a particular attitude. A person with a 3 Expression may, when young, be something of a dilettante in scattering his forces (negative attitude). As he matures, he may express the joy of living instead, colored with optimism and enthusiasm (positive attitude). It's also possible that he may start out in life expressing the joy of living and regress to something of a dilettante.

We cannot know precisely at what point a person will be along the range of a particular attitude at any specific time, but the synthesis will clarify the basic attitudes and the probable thrust of that attitude. The art of delineation will allow us to read the Expression for any time in a person's life and provide an interpretation most useful to the person at the time of the reading.

Sample reading

The reading of the Expression, without any additional information, provides some awareness of a person's abilities. The information is accurate, *as far as it goes*, but must be worded to allow for the changes which are likely to take place as we combine the Expression with the other elements.

A sample reading might read as follows:

You probably have most of the following abilities: _____ _____ _____.

Fill in with "Abilities" information.

When you put your best foot forward, you're likely to _____ _____ _____.

Fill in with "Positive Attitudes" information.

At times, like all of us, you're not always expressing your positive potential. At these times, you're likely to be _____ _____ _____.

Fill in the "Negative Attitudes" information.

The abilities and attitudes described by the Expression derived from your birthname are likely to be with you all your life. When your name changes—by marriage, by deleting your middle name, by using a nickname—the given Expression remains but the abilities and attitudes may be modified by the Expression derived from the new name. (We'll discuss all the ramifications of name changes later on in Volume 2, Chapter 24.) The basic talents are usually there for the whole life, though sometimes overlaid by new and different emphases and additions.

CHAPTER 5

THE THIRD ELEMENT
OF THE CORE:
THE SOUL URGE

THE SOUL URGE IS A PERSON'S INNER MOTIVA-
TION, WHAT HE WANTS TO BE, TO HAVE AND TO DO.
The Soul Urge is third in importance of the four core elements.

The Soul Urge (sometimes known as the Heart's Desire, the
Motivation or the Ideality) is concerned with deep inner longings. These longings express those matters which seem most
important to the person, and these important matters are influ-
ential in determining the person's point of view, the principles
on which he acts, his general approach.

Occasionally, when the Soul Urge is harmonious with other
parts of the core, it may be visible so that others are aware of it.
For most people, the Soul Urge is below the surface, rarely expressed openly. Many people seem almost unaware of their
own Soul Urge, although they can readily identify with it when
it is described. To the outside observer, the delineation of the
Soul Urge often serves as a key to an understanding of a person,
clarifying the person's actions and approaches in a most reveal-
ing way.

As we proceed along the broad channel of the Life Path, we
are guided by the motivations of the Soul Urge. If our longings are easy to satisfy within our own broad channel, we are
apt to benefit from the available possibilities. If we want something which we perceive as unavailable on our channel, or

Definition

more available on another channel, we may be subject to conflict in deciding on which channel we choose to operate. When we synthesize the core elements, we will become familiar with how these disparate elements may be joined for positive development.

Calculation

THE SOUL URGE IS DERIVED BY FINDING THE SUM OF THE NUMBER VALUES OF THE VOWELS IN EACH NAME, REDUCING THIS SUM TO A SINGLE DIGIT OR MASTER NUMBER, THEN ADDING THE SUMS OF ALL THE NAMES TOGETHER AND REDUCING THAT TOTAL TO A SINGLE DIGIT OR MASTER NUMBER.

There is at least one vowel in every syllable.

A, E, I, O, U are *always* vowels. Their value, from the table on page 18, is:

A = 1
E = 5
I = 9
O = 6
U = 3

Y is *sometimes* a vowel. Its value is 7. Y is a vowel when there is no other vowel in a syllable.

Example: Yvonne, Sylvia, Larry

Y is a vowel when it is preceded by A, E, I, O, U and sounded as one sound.

Example: Hayden, Doyle, Raymond

W is *sometimes* a vowel. Its value is 5. W is a vowel when it is preceded by A, E, I, O, U and sounded as one sound.

Example: Bradshaw, Matthew, Lowell

1. Place the numerical value of each vowel above the vowel:

```
   1     3      5     9 6
ARTHUR  TRENT  WILSON
```

2. Add the numbers in each name together. Reduce this sum to a single digit or master number.

$$\text{ARTHUR} \quad 1 + 3 = \underline{\underline{4}}$$
$$\text{TRENT} \qquad\quad = \underline{\underline{5}}$$
$$\text{WILSON} \quad 9 + 6 = 15$$
$$\qquad\qquad\qquad = 1 + 5 = \underline{\underline{6}}$$

3. Add the numbers obtained for each name together. Reduce this sum to a single digit or master number.

$$4 + 5 + 6 = 15$$
$$= 1 + 5 = 6$$
$$\underline{\text{The Soul Urge is 6}}$$

4. On a numerology chart, the calculation would look like this: (The number in parentheses represents a subtotal which is further reduced.)

4	5	(15) 6	= 15 = 6 Soul Urge
1 3	5	9 6	
ARTHUR	TRENT	WILSON	

Here are a few additional examples:

(16) 7 +	11 +	8	= 26 = 8 Soul Urge
6 5 5	1 91	3 5	
LOWELL	ADRIAN	HUNTER	

(14) 5 +	(17) 8 +	9	= 22 Soul Urge
1 6 7	7 91	6 3	
CAROLYN	SYLVIA	YOUNG	

Always add the numbers of the vowels of each name *separately*, then add these totals together. If you add the vowels of all the names together, you may end up with a master number that doesn't apply or lose a master number that should apply. For instance, in the name Carolyn Sylvia Young above, if the vowels are added together, you get $1 + 6 + 7 + 7 + 9 + 1 + 6 + 3 = 40 = 4$ Soul Urge, and the 22 Master Number has been lost.

Chart 4: The Soul Urge

CHART 4: THE SOUL URGE, on page 264, discusses the different Soul Urges.

The upper horizontal division of this chart, labeled "Motives," describes the person's inner motivation. The middle and lower divisions of the chart, labeled "Positive Attitudes" and "Negative Attitudes," describe the most harmonious and most discordant extremes of the attitudes just as Chart 3 did for the Expression.

Sample reading
The reading of the Soul Urge without any additional information provides some awareness of the person's inner motivation. The information is accurate, *as far as it goes*, but must be expressed to allow for the modifications which will take place when the synthesis of the core elements proceeds.

A sample reading might read as follows:

You are apt to want _____ _____ _____.

Fill in with "Motives" information.

You are probably _____ _____ _____ _____,

Fill in with "Positive Attitudes" information.

but you can also be _____ _____ _____ _____.

Fill in with "Negative Attitudes" information.

The motivations and attitudes described by the Soul Urge derived from your birthname are with you all your life. When a person changes his name, the primary motivations and attitudes remain, but are often modified by new and different emphases derived from the Soul Urge of the new name. (We'll discuss the effect of name changes in Volume 2, Chapter 24.)

CHAPTER 6

THE FOURTH ELEMENT OF THE CORE: THE BIRTHDAY

THE BIRTHDAY IS A SUB-LESSON TO BE LEARNED IN THIS LIFE, A SUB-FOCUS ON THE LIFE PATH. The Birthday is fourth in importance of the four core elements.

The Birthday is one of the numbers added together to derive the Life Path—or, in numerology terms, the Birthday is one of the numbers *behind* the Life Path. Later on, we will see that all the numbers behind the Life Path, Expression and Soul Urge are sub-influences. The Birthday is the only sub-influence important enough to be part of the core.

Definition

THE BIRTHDAY IS DERIVED BY REDUCING THE DAY OF BIRTH TO A SINGLE DIGIT OR MASTER NUMBER.

If you're born on the 1st of any month, for instance, your Birthday is 1; on the 16th, your Birthday is 7 (1 + 6 = 7); on the 23rd, your Birthday is 5 (2 + 3 = 5).

Calculation

In Chapter 3, we visualized each Life Path as a broad channel or highway. Now, visualize the highway of each Life Path divided into eleven lanes, one for each Birthday: 1 through 9, plus the master numbers 11 and 22. Everyone on the particular

Chart 5: The Birthday

highway is learning the same major lessons, but the lane occupied by each person presents an additional sub-lesson modifying the main focus of the Life Path.

If we look at the 3 lane, for example, we see it further subdivided into four divisions, one representing a day of birth on the 3rd, one a day of birth on the 12th (1 + 2 = 3), one a day of birth on the 21st (2 + 1 = 3), and one a day of birth on the 30th (3 + 0 = 3). These four all have the same sub-lesson of 3, but each has slightly different traits and attitudes because of the different numbers *behind* the sub-lesson number.

The highway of each Life Path, then, is actually divided into 31 divisions, each representing the sub-focus, traits and attitudes determined by the day of the month on which a person is born.

CHART 5: THE BIRTHDAY, on page 278, provides readings for each of the Birthdays.

The sub-lessons are the keywords related to the single digit or master number of each Birthday and are found at the top of each page of the chart adjacent to the large number. The attitudes and abilities for each day of birth are listed under the appropriate day of the month.

Let's, for example, look at the different numbers on the 3 Birthday page.

A birthday on the 3rd of any month:

> Sub-lesson: Expression. Joy of living.
> Emphasis on 3 attitudes and abilities only.
> No sub-emphasis on other energies.

A birthday on the 12th of any month:

> Sub-lesson: Expression. Joy of living.
> Emphasis on 3 attitudes and abilities.
> Sub-emphasis on 1 and 2 attitudes and abilities (1 and 2 are the numbers behind the birthday of 12).

A birthday on the 21st of any month:

> Sub-lesson: Expression. Joy of living.
> Emphasis on 3 attitudes and abilities.
> Sub-emphasis on 2 and 1 attitudes (2 and 1 are numbers behind the birthday of 21).

A birthday on the 30th of any month:

> Sub-lesson: Expression. Joy of living.
> Emphasis on 3 attitudes and abilities. Similar to 3 Birthday but the energy is more strongly expressed here. (30 is a higher octave of 3, meaning that the 3 traits are intensified. The "good conversationalist" ability

of the 3, for instance, is replaced by "excellent conversationalist" of the 30; the "affectionate and loving" 3 is replaced by the "very affectionate and loving" 30. 20 is, similarly, a higher octave of 2, and 10 a higher octave of 1.)

No sub-emphasis on other energies.

As you look over Chart 5, you'll see that several days show a special emphasis. The 11th is a master number with traits relating not only to 11 but also to its reduced level 2. The 22nd is a master number with traits relating not only to 22 but also to its reduced level 4. (In Chapter 8, we'll discuss the master numbers in detail.) The 13th, 14th, 16th, and 19th are birthdays related to karmic influences, and there's a negative emphasis here. (In Chapter 11, we'll discuss the karmic influences in detail.)

Relative importance

The sub-lesson of the Birthday is of much less importance than the major lesson of the Life Path. The sub-focus should be considered primarily as an influence on the central focus. A 6 Life Path is always focused on balance, responsibility and love, for instance, but a 4 Birthday would assist the balance and responsibility part of the main lesson with a sub-lesson of limitation, order and service, while a 5 Birthday is apt to hinder the main lesson with the 5's focus on constructive freedom.

Sample reading

The reading for the Birthday would be used as an adjunct to the reading for the Life Path. A sample reading might be as follows:

Your major lesson of _____
_____ is modified by

Complete with Life Path keywords.

a minor lesson of_____
_____.

Complete with Birthday keywords.

Here are some of the attitudes and traits you may express: _____
_____
_____
_____

Complete with information derived from the Birthday description.

Like the Life Path, the Birthday is fixed and unchangeable. The influence of the sub-focus is sure to be felt, no matter how the traits involved are used or allowed to remain latent.

CHAPTER 7

SYNTHESIS OF THE CORE ELEMENTS

The core, as we mentioned previously, is the major determinant in a character delineation. In this chapter, we'll first examine the principles involved in synthesizing the elements into the core. Then we'll proceed, step-by-step, in the delineation of a complete core synthesis, clarifying the way in which each portion of the synthesis is developed using the above principles. Finally, we'll explore some of the assumptions underlying these guiding principles.

Four simple principles are involved in core synthesis:

Principles of core synthesis

1. The relative power of the elements.
2. The modifying abilities of the elements.
3. The harmony or discord among the elements.
4. The effectiveness of the combined elements.

We'll explore each of these principles, then put them to work.

1. The Relative Power of the Core Elements

Relative power

Here's a diagram of the core, showing the relations of the elements:

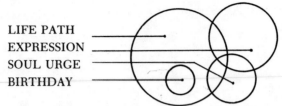

LIFE PATH
EXPRESSION
SOUL URGE
BIRTHDAY

It's apparent that each core element has a different size, representing their different relative powers. The Life Path has the most power. It provides approximately fifty percent of the power of the core. The Expression is responsible for about thirty percent of the power while the Soul Urge provides only about twenty percent. The force of the Life Path is approximately equal to the forces of the Expression and Soul Urge combined. The Birthday strength is far less than the other elements. It represents about a fifth the power of the Life Path (1/5 x 50) or ten percent of the strength of the core. The Birthday, then, is only about a third as strong as the Expression and about half as strong as the Soul Urge. (As the diagram shows, the Birthday is always treated as an integral part of the Life Path.)

Perhaps this drawing shows the relative power of the core elements even more dramatically:

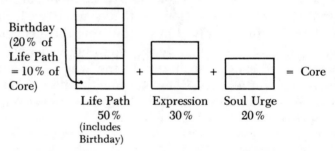

The synthesis, of course, must reflect the relative power of the elements. For instance, a core with a 3 Life Path and a 22 Soul Urge would produce an emphasis on the 3. Half the strength of the core would be related to the 3 potential and only about one-fifth of the strength to the 22, so that the 3 potential would govern. If the situation was reversed, with a 22 Life Path and a 3 Soul Urge, the emphasis would, of course, shift to the 22 potential.

In numerology terms, the relative power is expressed in relation to the *position* of the number. A number is most powerful in the Life Path position, less powerful in the Expression position, and weaker yet in the Soul Urge position. The position of the number, therefore, determines how strong an influence it represents in the core. The relative power is expressed in a core delineation by devoting an amount of writing (or speaking) to each element proportional to the power of that element.

2. The Modifying Abilities of the Elements

Looking back at the first core diagram, on page 46, the overlapping of the circles representing the elements indicates that the potentials of the elements modify or alter the potentials of the other elements. Referring to the diagram:

> The Life Path is modified by the Expression, Soul Urge and Birthday.
> The Expression is modified by the Life Path and Soul Urge.
> The Soul Urge is modified by the Life Path and Expression.
> The Birthday modifies the Life Path.

The core relations translate into relations in a person's life. The central focus of a life, for instance, is altered by the person's abilities and motivations, as well as by his sub-focus. This is just another way of expressing the other core elements acting on the Life Path. The other elements can be expressed in a similar manner.

How do we determine how the elements are altered? Let's look to the other two principles.

3. The Harmony or Discord Among the Elements

Suppose you have two core elements, one with a 6 potential, the other with a 2 potential. The 6 force is involved with handling responsibility, creating balance, providing love and harmony, sympathy and understanding. The 2 energy is concerned with adaptability, consideration, relating and cooperating with others. The forces of the 6 and 2 work well together with mutually beneficial energies. The 6 potential and the 2 potential are, in general, a harmonious combination.

What happens when we deal with a combination of 6 and 7 energies? The 6 force is, as before, involved with caring for others, expressing love and friendship, working to balance and harmonize relations. The 7 force is introspective, focused on studying, learning, analyzing, developing wisdom and spiritual awareness. Can you see that the concerns of the 6 involve relations with others, usually in everyday, down-to-earth situations, while the 7 grows inwardly, quietly, possibly spiritually, somewhat apart from practical affairs? These two forces are traveling in different directions, working toward different goals. The 6 potential and the 7 potential are, in general, a discordant combination.

In the same way, we can analyze the relations between all

the combinations of potentials. We'll find, though, that the harmony or discord of many combinations are far less obvious than the examples just shown.

Look, for example, at a blending of a 1 potential with a 5 potential. The 1 is working to acknowledge its individuality, to express its independence, to attain as a leader or creator, while the 5, with many talents and many opportunities, is developing the constructive use of freedom. If the 1 has advanced to the point of attainment as a director or pioneer and can fuse this energy with the 5 potential to harness the available talents and opportunities, there can be an extremely harmonious combination. But suppose, instead, that the 1 is struggling just to become independent while the 5 is being overwhelmed by the change and variety in his life, the constant flux in the environment. The attempted stability of the 1 is at odds with the emphasis on the instability of the 5—a very discordant merger.

The 1·5 combination is, therefore, sometimes harmonious and sometimes discordant. That seems somewhat harder to handle than our first examples. In reconsidering that harmonious 6·2 combination, suppose the 6 potential is so responsible for family and friends that his own needs are virtually submerged while the 2 force is concentrating on helping everyone cooperate, again to the exclusion of his own needs. There's a good chance that the over-responsible 6 fused with the overzealous 2 will be reduced to a doormat in the name of helping others, producing a discordant blending rather than the previous harmony.

The fact is that the combination of *any two* potentials can produce a harmonious *or* a discordant resultant. This corroborates my own experiences with numbers—and most people's experiences with other people. As you work with the numbers, I expect you'll draw the same conclusion. This is quite a complex situation! *An understanding of this complexity is a vital link in producing delineations.* I've dealt with this matter at length so you won't be apt to forget it or neglect it or attempt to reduce it to some simple formula when it is, in reality, sprawling and untidy.

Let's accept that either harmony or discord can be produced by combining any two energies. But, let's also recognize that a given combination USUALLY produces one or the other. Some fusions are more consistent than others. The 6·2 combination is *almost always* harmonious, and so is 3·6. The 6·7 combination is *almost always* discordant, and so are 4·5 and 8·11. The 1·5 combination is harder to predict. So are 6·9 and 2·3.

For our beginning syntheses, we'll assume that the *usual* resultant is the *only* resultant. We can produce a reasonably good delineation with that assumption, although we can delineate a more meaningful reading (as we will later on) by accepting the complexity which exists.

Turn to CHART 6: THE ASPECTS, on page 292, and you'll find the usual resultants of all the combinations. The word "usually" is stressed, as you can see, and most combinations are noted as USUALLY harmonious or USUALLY discordant. There's one other resultant shown: The combinations of identical numbers, 1·1, 2·2, 3·3, are labeled USUALLY very discordant. Chapter 9 is devoted to this special case. Hold off on delineations with these combinations until after we've developed the general case.

Some of the combinations or aspects in Chart 6 show the opposite resultant in parentheses below the usual resultant. Become familiar with these possibilities as you begin working on delineations.

Chart 6 is different than any other chart in the book. It's the only chart which compares a combination of potentials. But, as you use it, remember that these resultants and the discussions which follow them are meant primarily to assist you in the beginning. These comparisons are based on my experience with numbers, and the discussions are limited by the available space. But there's nothing sacred about the discussions. Your experience in delineation will provide you with your own resultants and reasons. Probably, many of your conclusions will be similar to mine, but if you see the world and the resultants differently, and you are gaining and giving insight with your readings, then, by all means, follow your own instincts.

It might seem that the best core would be one where all the combinations of elements are harmonious. When this does occur, the lack of discord may make for a comparatively comfortable use of the energies involved, but may tend to inhibit growth and development.

I rarely think of "best" or "worst" in the context of numerology. Each life is developed from its own potentials and each of us can deal only with the potentials we possess. You can only express, at best, the highest level of your own potentials. It will not benefit you to compare yourself (or anyone else) with others. People have their own potentials and are operating only within those contexts.

We have been dealing with the harmony or discord of combined energies. Harmonious *energies* do not guarantee harmonious *lives*, just as discordant *energies* do not necessarily produce discordant *lives*. Along with the energies a person possesses, he still has the free will to determine how to use these forces, and

Chart 6:
The Aspects

he operates in an environment which exerts its own effect. Free will and environment play a large part in determining the harmony or discordance of lives, as we'll see when we discuss these important factors at the end of this chapter.

Effectiveness 4. The Effectiveness of the Combined Elements

Imagine that Bertha and Eddie are contemplating starting a business together. Bertha is full of creative ideas and Eddie is a superb organizer, capable of dealing with people, money and all the other details that are involved in a business. Clearly, these two people have harmonious energies.

Eddie is very dynamic. He rises at dawn and is energetic until late at night, demanding a great deal quickly and efficiently from himself and his associates. Bertha is a different type—very quiet and contemplative. She may spend weeks alone, honing an idea to perfection. She doesn't like to be interrupted when she is working creatively—she wants to complete her project before discussing it with others. The harmony of *her* creativity and *his* organizational abilities will be severely tested by the effectiveness (or in this case, ineffectiveness) of their combined energies.

Harmony or discord, then, is only one way of looking at a combination of elements, and effectiveness, or workability, is another. In a character delineation, effectiveness is a measure of the relative levels of the opportunities (the Life Path), the abilities (the Expression) and the motivations (the Soul Urge). By determining the effectiveness, you can recognize whether a person possesses enough abilities and motivations to take advantage of his opportunities, and enough motivation to use his abilities. (The Birthday is treated as part of the Life Path and is not compared in effectiveness with the other elements.)

Think of the Life Path as a pitcher, with the size of the pitcher determined by the number of the Life Path. A 1 Life Path is the smallest pitcher, a 2 somewhat larger, a 22 the largest of all. Imagine filling the pitcher with a liquid representing the Expression. A 1 Expression would represent just a little bit of liquid while 22 would portray the largest quantity of liquid.

Consider a subject with a 22 Life Path and a 1 Expression. We have then, in the analogy, a large pitcher with almost nothing in it. The subject will be hard pressed to use his abilities to take advantage of the substantial opportunities which are present. This is a combination lacking in effectiveness.

Looking at the other extreme, we have a similar ineffective blend. If we attempt to fill a 1 Life Path pitcher with 22 Expression liquid, we have a small, full pitcher with most of the liquid wasted. A subject with this combination would have difficulty finding suitable opportunities to use his abilities.

The most effective combination is represented by a comfortably filled pitcher. A 5 Life Path with a 3 or 4 Expression is effective, as is a 6 Life Path with a 7 or 8 Expression. Again, we'll leave the combination where the elements are the same number to Chapter 9.

When we imagine the Life Path as the pitcher with the Soul Urge the liquid, we can determine the effectiveness of the opportunities combined with the motivations. Similarly, the relation between motivation and ability uses the Expression as pitcher with the Soul Urge as liquid.

Let's examine the effectiveness of the different combinations. The combinations are listed by the number of spaces between the elements under consideration.

a. If both elements are 9 or below, subtract the lower from the higher.

For example, with an 8 Life Path and a 5 Soul Urge, there are 3 spaces (8 minus 5) between the elements. Or, with a 2 Expression and a 9 Soul Urge, there are 7 (9 minus 2) spaces between.

b. If either or both elements are 11 or 22, assume one space between 9 and 11, and one space again between 11 and 22.

With a 6 Expression and an 11 Soul Urge:

$$\underbrace{3}_{6\ 7\ 8\ 9} + \underbrace{1}_{11} \quad = 4 \text{ spaces between 6 and 11}$$

With a 4 Life Path and a 22 Expression:

$$\underbrace{5}_{4\ 5\ 6\ 7\ 8\ 9} + \underbrace{1}_{11} + \underbrace{1}_{22} \quad = 7 \text{ spaces between 4 and 22}$$

TABLE OF EFFECTIVENESS

Table of
Effectiveness

LIFE PATH/EXPRESSION

LIFE PATH HIGHER THAN THE EXPRESSION BY 6 OR MORE SPACES (Opportunities substantially outweigh abilities.)

You will have to work to find just the right environment to make use of your natural talents. It may be frustrating when some of these aptitudes don't mesh with your opportunities in the ways you expect or aren't appreciated in circumstances which seem appropriate to you. You may be impatient. Your growth and development, no matter how fast, is apt to proceed too slowly for your own satisfaction. Learn to pursue your main lesson at the natural pace that presents itself.

(When the Life Path is higher than the Expression by 7 or more spaces, the ineffectiveness of the combination, with its attendant frustrations and disappointments, will form a strong part of the subject's core.)

LIFE PATH HIGHER THAN THE EXPRESSION BY 3, 4 OR 5 SPACES (Opportunities outweigh abilities.)

The opportunities are there, but you will have to work to take advantage of them. You must stretch your talents to meet your experiences. The expansion of your natural capabilities can lead to growth, to the realization of higher conditions of life for yourself. Expend time and effort appraising your strengths and weaknesses. A realistic awareness and acceptance of these potentials will be significant in your positive development. Be especially realistic in examining the available opportunities.

LIFE PATH HIGHER OR LOWER THAN THE EXPRESSION BY 1 OR 2 SPACES (Effective balance of opportunities and abilities.)

You have the potential to take advantage of the opportunities presented with relative ease, to make the most of the experiences which come your way. Your natural abilities will probably find ample field for expression. The environment will allow your talents to be displayed and appreciated. As your capabilities find the opportunities to expand to meet their potential, your development will progress in a manner which may bring you much satisfaction.

LIFE PATH LOWER THAN THE EXPRESSION BY 3, 4 OR 5 SPACES (Abilities outweigh opportunities.)

The opportunities are present, but not as many as you would like, and often in an unclear or deceptive form. Learn to evaluate your opportunities and to perceive when more is promised than can be delivered. If you have deceived yourself or been deceived, don't continue but move to another lead. You will probably have to develop your talents primarily on your own— the people and surroundings will only rarely provide help. Develop faith in your own capabilities rather than expecting aid from outside yourself. Have patience even though your development proceeds more slowly than you would prefer.

LIFE PATH LOWER THAN THE EXPRESSION BY 6 OR MORE SPACES (Abilities substantially outweigh opportunities.)

You will have to study your environment with care to find opportunities to take advantage of your natural talents. The people and situations you meet often don't present the potential for growth you are seeking. Often, the development you are expecting does not materialize, even though you have performed well. It may be frustrating to be aware of your capabilities and yet have to work so hard to find a satisfactory path for their use. Learn not to demand more of the world around you than is realistically there. Pursue your main lesson at the natural pace that presents itself.

(When the Life Path is lower than the Expression by 7 or more spaces, the ineffectiveness of the combination, with its attendant frustrations and disappointments, will form a strong part of the subject's core.)

LIFE PATH/SOUL URGE

LIFE PATH HIGHER THAN THE SOUL URGE BY 6 OR MORE SPACES (Opportunities substantially outweigh motivations.)

Although you may or may not have a clear understanding of your inner needs, these needs are rarely strong enough to act as your primary motivating force. Your reactions to the people and situations in which you come in contact will direct the course of your development to a greater extent than your need to fulfil your inner urges. Because these experiences are not an integral part of you, you may find yourself driven by motivations which are often unclear to you and do not necessarily bring the satisfaction of growth.

(When the Life Path is higher than the Soul Urge by 7 or more spaces, the ineffectiveness of the combination, with its compulsive motivation based on experience, will form a strong part of the subject's core.)

LIFE PATH HIGHER THAN THE SOUL URGE BY 3, 4 OR 5 SPACES (Opportunities outweigh motivations.)

Although you are able to recognize your opportunities, you don't always feel the need to pursue them. Sometimes, you do follow your inner urges and take advantage of the possibilities. But, probably just about as often, you develop the experience at hand and follow where the experiences lead. You may have difficulty understanding or dealing with people pushed by strong inner needs or desirous of pushing you to advance yourself. Most of the time, you are likely to be content with the natural pace of your development.

LIFE PATH HIGHER OR LOWER THAN THE SOUL URGE BY 1 OR 2 SPACES (Effective balance of opportunities and motivations.)

You are well motivated to recognize and take advantage of your opportunities with relative ease. You make the most of the experiences which come your way. You are usually on the lookout for ways to best develop yourself, ways to satisfy your inner desires. Your environment probably reinforces your motivations to allow them full play. You are apt to find much growth in the satisfaction of your inner urges.

LIFE PATH LOWER THAN THE SOUL URGE BY 3, 4 OR 5 SPACES (Motivations outweigh opportunities.)

Although you are able to recognize your opportunities, you find somewhat fewer possibilities than you would like to advance your inner development. The experiences at hand, while not necessarily presenting opportunities to fulfill your inner needs, are apt to act as a secondary motivating force. Make the most of these experiences. Learn to accept the natural pace of your development.

LIFE PATH LOWER THAN THE SOUL URGE BY 6 OR MORE SPACES (Motivations substantially outweigh opportunities.)

Although you have a strong sense of your inner needs, you may have to search diligently to satisfy these desires. Your reactions to the people and situations in which you come in contact will direct the course of your development to a greater extent than the available opportunities. Use the opportunities when they appear. Make the most of the experience when the opportunities you would like are not available. Your development is likely to proceed more slowly than you would like. Be patient and grow at the natural pace which you find.

(When the Life Path is lower than the Soul Urge by 7 or more spaces, the ineffectiveness of the combination, with its attendant frustrations, will form a strong part of the subject's core.)

EXPRESSION/SOUL URGE

EXPRESSION HIGHER THAN THE SOUL URGE BY 6 OR MORE SPACES (Abilities substantially outweigh motivations.)

You are little motivated to put your natural talents into play. You are probably not completely aware of your inner urges. You're apt to drift along with only occasional displays of your potential abilities. Sometimes, long after your peers have made their mark, you will begin to express your motivations.

(When the Expression is higher than the Soul Urge by 7 or more spaces, the ineffectiveness of the combination, with its marked lack of motivation, will form a strong part of the subject's core.)

EXPRESSION HIGHER THAN THE SOUL URGE BY 3, 4 OR 5 SPACES (Abilities outweigh motivations.)

At times you have the incentive to display your talents. Mostly, though, you show a good part of your capabilities without feeling a need to push yourself to use more of those natural abilities. Your development may proceed slowly because of the small motivational emphasis, but, in general, you are satisfied with your growth.

EXPRESSION HIGHER OR LOWER THAN THE SOUL URGE BY 1 OR 2 SPACES (Effective balance of abilities and motivations.)

You are aware of your capabilities and have the incentive to use these talents to aid in your own development. You know how to fit your capabilities in where you can shine. You are motivated to display and develop your abilities with much advantage to yourself.

EXPRESSION LOWER THAN THE SOUL URGE BY 3, 4 OR 5 SPACES (Motivations outweigh abilities.)

Your motivation sometimes seems to outrun your abilities. Although you have many ideas, your natural talents don't necessarily help to advance these ideas. Learn to be content with the realization that it will take more time than you would prefer to fulfill your inner desires.

EXPRESSION LOWER THAN THE SOUL URGE BY 6 OR MORE SPACES (Motivations substantially outweigh abilities.)

You have many ideas that motivate you, but you often find that your natural abilities aren't of much help in fulfilling your inner desires. Although some of your inner urges may be satisfied, you have a tendency to overlook the realized satisfactions and push forward where your needs have not been met. Learn to accept your natural pace of development.

(When the Expression is lower than the Soul Urge by 7 or more

spaces, the ineffectiveness of the combination with its imbalance of motivation, will form a strong part of the subject's
core.)

Now that we've explored the principles, we're ready to proceed with a core synthesis. We're going to go slowly, step by
step, pointing out where the information we use is obtained.
This first synthesis is apt to appear somewhat fragmented and,
in part, a trifle repetitious. But remember that right now we're
primarily concentrating on the procedure. Later on, we'll polish the delineation, remove the repetitions and produce a co-
hesive whole.

The steps in core synthesis

THE 22 STEPS INVOLVED IN THE CORE SYNTHESIS

1. Derive the elements of the core.
2. Express the central focus of the Life Path.
3. Express the sub-focus of the Birthday.
4. Express the harmony or discord of the Life Path/Birthday aspect.
5. Determine the harmony or discord of the Life Path/Expression and the Life Path/Soul Urge aspects.
6. Express the characteristics of the Life Path.
7. Express the characteristics of the Birthday.
8. Discuss the negative expression of the Life Path.

Life Path and Birthday as modified by the other elements.

9. Express the abilities of the Expression.
10. Express the harmony or discord of the Life Path/Expression aspect.
11. Express the effectiveness of the Life Path/Expression combination.
12. Determine the harmony or discord of the Expression/Life Path and the Expression/Soul Urge aspects.
13. Express the positive attitudes of the Expression.
14. Express the negative attitudes of the Expression.

Expression as modified by the other elements.

15. Express the motives of the Soul Urge.
16. Express the harmony or discord of the Life Path/Soul Urge aspect.
17. Express the effectiveness of the Life Path/Soul Urge combination.
18. Express the harmony or discord of the Expression/Soul Urge aspect.
19. Express the effectiveness of the Expression/Soul Urge combination.
20. Review the harmony or discord of the Life Path/Soul Urge and Expression/Soul Urge aspects.
21. Express the positive attitudes of the Soul Urge.
22. Express the negative attitudes of the Soul Urge.

Soul Urge as modified by the other elements.

We're going to delineate a fictitious subject named Harlan William Allen, born on May 12, 1941. Let's imagine Mr. Allen has just walked in and asked us for a reading. We see that he's tall, muscular, nicely dressed, with a handsome face, wavy blonde hair and blue eyes. There's probably little else we can determine about him just from a visual inspection. We'll turn to the numbers—and see what we can find.

In the analysis that follows, we'll first list each step, followed by a *general* explanation when necessary. We will then indicate, in italics, precisely where the information for Harlan's *specific* delineation is to be found, and then show that portion of his synthesis derived by following the instructions. The actual delineation will be shown indented. When we complete the 22 steps, we should re-read all the indented paragraphs which make up Harlan's total core synthesis.

STEP 1

DERIVE THE ELEMENTS OF THE CORE.

From the calculation instructions in Chapters 3 through 6:

Typical core
synthesis,
step by step

$$\begin{array}{cccccc}
\text{May} & 12, & 1941 & & & \\
5 & + 3 & + 6 & = 14 = 1 + 4 & & = \underline{\underline{5 \text{ Life Path}}} \\
& & 12 & = 1 + 2 & & = \underline{\underline{3 \text{ Birthday}}}
\end{array}$$

$$\frac{2}{1 \quad 1} \quad + \quad \frac{(19) \ 1}{9 \quad 9\,1} \quad + \quad \frac{6}{1 \quad 5} \quad = 9 \ \text{Soul Urge}$$

HARLAN   WILLIAM   ALLEN

$$\frac{8\,1\,9\,3\,1\,5 \quad\quad 5\,9\,3\,3\,9\,1\,4 \quad\quad 1\,3\,3\,5\,5}{(27) \ 9 \quad + \quad (34) \ 7 \quad + \ (17) \ 8}$$

$$= 24$$
$$= 2 + 4$$
$$= 6 \quad \text{Expression}$$

STEP 2

EXPRESS THE CENTRAL FOCUS OF THE LIFE PATH.

The central focus remains the same irrespective of the other core elements.

From CHART 2: THE LIFE PATH *copy the central focus of the 5 Life Path shown in the upper horizontal division.*

> The central focus of your life is learning the exhilaration of the *constructive* use of freedom. Life is full of exciting opportunities for you—there can be much variety, change, unusual happenings, unusual people, unforeseen adventure. You will find that you are capable at almost any task, that you are talented in a number of directions. The world is your oyster—there are exciting things to do at every turn—and that undoubtedly is the difficulty. You must learn how to pick and choose, how to seek experiences which will be of benefit, how to discard those activities that are not working, how to profit from every experience. You must learn not to waste your time or scatter your forces, not to get lost in purely physical delights—food, sex, drink or drugs. It can be sheer delight to be a rolling stone, but the frustration of moving from place to place, from person to person, from opportunity to opportunity may eventually overwhelm the delight.

STEP 3

EXPRESS THE SUB-FOCUS OF THE BIRTHDAY.

The Birthday represents only twenty percent of the Life Path. Express the relative strengths of the elements by the relative amount of space devoted to them. The Birthday sub-focus, then, should be only about one-fifth as long as the Life Path focus. In this step, express the keywords of the sub-focus, possibly with some slight elaboration.

From CHART 5: THE BIRTHDAY *use the keywords for the 3 Birthday. To elaborate on these keywords, read the central focus of the 3 Life Path found in Chart 2. These energies are operating, but in a much reduced manner, since the energies are being applied here to the Birthday rather than the Life Path itself.*

> While you're learning how to use freedom, learn the joy of expressing yourself. Give of yourself, openly, warmly, with delight. Learn, too, to express yourself, using your imagination, your artistic abilities, but especially, your ability with words.

STEP 4

EXPRESS THE HARMONY OR DISCORD OF THE LIFE PATH/BIRTHDAY ASPECT.

From CHART 6: THE ASPECTS *read the 3·5 aspect—usually harmonious. The 3·5 aspect, as written, discusses the enhancement of the 3 energy by the 5 energy. Since the 5 Life Path is, in our example, being modified by the 3 Birthday, rewrite the aspect to express the enhancement of the 5 energy by the 3 energy.*

> Your ability to give of yourself in social situations as well as with creative expression—most likely with words—will help in working toward an awareness of the constructive use of freedom.

STEP 5

DETERMINE THE HARMONY OR DISCORD OF THE LIFE PATH/EXPRESSION AND THE LIFE PATH/SOUL URGE ASPECTS.

Although we have not yet delineated the Expression and the Soul Urge, we must, at this point, determine the aspects relative to the Life Path because that harmony or discord will modify the Life Path characteristics and negative expression expressed in Steps 6 and 7.

From CHART 6: THE ASPECTS:

The 5 Life Path/6 Expression is usually discordant. The strong personal desire of the 5 for freedom conflicts with the potential of the 6 for responsibility and concern for others.

The 5 Life Path/9 Soul Urge is usually discordant. The strong personal desire of the 5 for freedom conflicts with the potential of the 9 for giving to others.

From CHART 3: THE EXPRESSION *read the 6 Expression and from* CHART 4: THE SOUL URGE *read the 9 Soul Urge to become familiar with the reading for these elements.*

In this example, the 5 Life Path energies (along with the Birthday energies) represent fifty percent of the core and are opposed by the combined 6 Expression and 9 Soul Urge, representing the other fifty percent of the core. The 6 and 9 are, in some ways, similar energies. The 6 keywords of balance, responsibility and love, may be thought of as expressed on a higher level in the 9 keywords of selflessness and humanitarianism. In Harlan, the giving qualities of the 6 and 9 will conflict with the carefree, self-centered traits of the 5, but will, at the same time, tend to alleviate the excesses of the 5 and produce a more workable blending than the unmodified 5.

STEP 6

EXPRESS THE CHARACTERISTICS OF THE LIFE PATH.

Modify the Life Path characteristics based on the aspects found in Step 5.

From CHART 2: THE LIFE PATH *list the characteristics of the 5 Life Path from the second horizontal division. Study each trait to determine if it is affected by the discord with the 6 Expression and 9 Soul Urge. Modify the characteristic to express this effect.*

> You are probably versatile and active and can do almost anything with superior talent. Although you are interested in the new, different or progressive, you usually proceed here with awareness of your responsibilities and concern for others.

The 5·6 and 5·9 aspects tone down the 5 Life Path desire to jump into new things.

> You are apt to be clever, with an inborn ability to accomplish what you want. You may be a quick thinker with a good ability to analyze, although that ability isn't always used to further your best interests.

This trait is expressed as indicated on Chart 2. The 5·6 and 5·9 aspects don't add or subtract.

> Although you sometimes have feelings of restlessness, impatience and the desire to try something new, these feelings are tempered by your desire for balance in your life and those around you as well as your concern for giving to others.

The 5·6 and 5·9 aspects strongly affect the basic 5 Life Path characteristic. The 5 trait still exists, but with substantial modification.

> Although you love change and enjoy travel and adventure, you are also capable of routine tasks demanded by your sense of responsibility. At times, these traits may produce feelings of conflict.

This trait, like the last, is strongly modified. The balancing effect of the aspects, as well as the potential conflict, are both expressed.

> You are probably a delightful companion and can inspire and delight with your enthusiasm. You may occasionally have to temper your sudden impulses to change direction.

The 6 and 9 tone down the erratic nature of the 5.

> You are enthusiastic. You tackle each new experience with renewed enthusiasm.

This trait is expressed as indicated on Chart 2. The 6 and 9 do not add or subtract.

> You tend to express eternal youth. The excitement of life keeps you young.

This trait is expressed as indicated on Chart 2. The 6 and 9 do not add or substract.

STEP 7

EXPRESS THE CHARACTERISTICS OF THE BIRTHDAY.

Read the characteristics of the Birthday in CHART 5: THE BIRTH-DAY. Summarize these traits in the delineation. The relative strength would be expressed by having the Birthday traits about one-fifth as long as the Life Path traits. Express the harmony or discord of the Life Path/Birthday aspect.

From CHART 5: THE BIRTHDAY summarize the characteristics of the 12 Birthday. Remember, from Step 4, that the 5 Life Path/3 Birthday is usually harmonious. Modify the traits as required.

> You are probably good with words. You work well, using your original strongly creative approach. You usually express the joy of living. People are likely to see you as cheerful, friendly and sociable, a good conversationalist, full of energy. You're

likely to be affectionate, loving and sensitive. Your
strong feelings may cause occasional rapid ups
and downs. You usually have many interests, so
you're likely to scatter your energy.

*The 5·3 aspect would stress strong creativity, noted in the sec-
ond sentence. The 5 has a self-centered side, so that the "very
affectionate, loving" in Chart 5 is changed to "affectionate,
loving."*

STEP 8

DISCUSS THE NEGATIVE EXPRESSION OF THE LIFE PATH.

The negative expression is determined, to a strong extent, by
the free will and the environment, but it is also related to the
aspects the Life Path makes with the Expression and the Soul
Urge. It's occasionally possible, just from the numbers, to determine if a person will tend to express negatively (particularly
in the special cases discussed in Chapter 9). It is important,
however, to warn the subject of the potential problems inherent in the negative expression.

From CHART 2: THE LIFE PATH *read the negative expression of
the 5 Life Path in the third horizontal division. If this subject
expresses negatively at all, he will tend to express the second
negative expression, the denial of the lesson, because of the
strength of the 6 and 9 discord. There is still the possibility of
the first negative expression, the exaggeration of the lesson, so
it, too, must be mentioned.*

When you are hesitant about using your freedom,
it may seem easier to retreat into a safe and stable
situation. When you do this, the changes and uncertainty will still be there, but you will probably
have difficulty dealing with them.

There's a chance that you'll be so exhilarated with
the opportunities before you, that you'll jump
from thing to thing with maddening speed, lost in
overindulgence or erratic behavior. This is apt to
bring much frustration.

These negative expressions are unproductive. They
should be avoided in order to proceed constructively with your development.

STEP 9

EXPRESS THE ABILITIES OF THE EXPRESSION.

The abilities remain the same irrespective of the other core elements.

From CHART 3: THE EXPRESSION *copy the abilities of the 6 Expression shown in the upper horizontal division.*

> You are probably a responsible, helpful and conscientious person. You have the ability to rectify and balance inharmonious situations and you would be available to give help and comfort to those in need. You would work well where the care of the old, young or sick is involved. You probably show concern for the betterment of the community. In addition, you are apt to possess creative and artistic talents.

Although Harlan possesses these potential abilities, it's probable that all aren't being used. The delineation should indicate these possibilities.

> It's possible that you're not using or developing all of these capabilities at this time. Some of your talents may have been used in the earlier part of your life and some may still be latent. Be aware of your capabilities, so that you can make use of them at appropriate times.

STEP 10

EXPRESS THE HARMONY OR DISCORD OF THE LIFE PATH/EXPRESSION ASPECT.

From CHART 6: THE ASPECTS:

The 5 Life Path/6 Expression is usually discordant. The strong personal desire of the 5 for freedom conflicts with the potential of the 6 for responsibility and concern for others.

The Life Path represents about half the core while the Expression represents about a third. The 5 Life Path will govern the 5·6 aspect, but Harlan will have to deal with the conflicting energies of the 6 Expression.

> You are probably exhilarated by all the exciting opportunities and adventures so often present in your life. It may be difficult, at times, to give up this excitement to satisfy your responsibilities.

There may even be times when you want to shirk these responsibilities or give them up altogether to enjoy the excitement of freedom.

Ignoring your responsibilities will probably not be very satisfying for you. You have to find some way to satisfy the adventurous side of your nature and, at the same time, enjoy the pleasures you receive when you express your responsible, conscientious side. You may find that an out-of-the-ordinary job may be helpful in balancing the quiet stability you may desire in a close family. Or, you might plan exciting trips or follow some unusual avocations to offset the solid, respectable job which gives you satisfaction.

STEP 11

EXPRESS THE EFFECTIVENESS OF THE LIFE PATH/EX-PRESSION COMBINATION.

Copy the effectiveness from the appropriate paragraph in the Table of Effectiveness in this chapter.

Harlan has a 6 Expression and a 5 Life Path; 6 – 5 = 1 space. Copy the paragraph describing the Life Path higher or lower than the Expression by 1 or 2 spaces.

You have the potential to take advantage of the opportunities presented with relative ease, to make the most of the experiences which come your way. Your natural abilities will probably find ample field for expression. The environment will allow your talents to be displayed and appreciated. As your capabilities find the opportunities to expand to meet their potential, your development will progress in a manner which may bring you much satisfaction.

STEP 12

DETERMINE THE HARMONY OR DISCORD OF THE EX-PRESSION/LIFE PATH AND THE EXPRESSION/SOUL URGE ASPECTS.

The harmony or discord of the aspects relative to the Expression will modify the Expression positive attitudes and negative attitudes expressed in Steps 13 and 14.

From CHART 6: THE ASPECTS:

As we've expressed in Step 10, the 6 Expression/5 Life Path is usually discordant. The strong personal desire of the 5 for freedom conflicts with the potential of the 6 for responsibility and concern for others.

The 6 Expression/9 Soul Urge is usually harmonious. The potential of the 6 for responsibility and concern for others is enhanced by the potential of the 9 for giving to others. The potential for creative self-expression of both the 6 and 9 enhances the expressive capabilities.

We have, to this point, explored the Life Path and the abilities of the Expression. From CHART 5: THE SOUL URGE *read the 9 Soul Urge. In this example, the 6 Expression, representing thirty percent of the core, is opposed by the 5 Life Path (with the Birthday), representing fifty percent of the core, and enhanced by the Soul Urge, representing twenty percent of the core. In Harlan, the balance and responsibility of the 6 will be in conflict with the free, adventurous spirit of the 5. At the same time, the balance, responsibility and love of the 6 will be enhanced by the selfless, humanitarian outlook of the 9, and the creative self-expression of the 6·9 provides a stronger potential than the creativity of the 6 by itself.*

STEP 13

EXPRESS THE POSITIVE ATTITUDES OF THE EXPRESSION.

Modify the positive attitudes of the Expression based on the aspects found in Step 12.

From CHART 3: THE EXPRESSION *list the positive attitudes of the 6 Expression from the middle horizontal division. Study each trait to determine if it is affected by the discord with the 5 Life Path or the harmony with the 9 Soul Urge.*

> When you are involved closely with people, you are probably most loving, friendly and appreciative of others, as well as very sympathetic, kind, generous and understanding. There may be times, though, when you prefer not to be involved at all.

The 6·5 discord is expressed by the possibility of sometimes being involved and sometimes not. The 6·9 harmony enhances the attitude expressed, and accounts for the "most loving, friendly, etc." and "very sympathetic, kind, etc."

Although you may well be involved in domestic activities, you may feel the pressures of these responsibilities conflicting with your own need for individuality. The resolution of this conflict (or the lack of resolution) will determine how good a husband and parent you are.

The 6·5 discord substantially affects this attitude. The 6·9 harmony effect is not specifically mentioned. Its effect would be present as noted in the previous attitude.

You are probably extremely open and honest with others.

The 6 openness and honesty is reinforced by the similar 9. The free-spirited 5 tends to be open and honest also, although its openness and honesty may be self-centered and not necessarily work to forward its best interests.

STEP 14

EXPRESS THE NEGATIVE ATTITUDES OF THE EXPRESSION.

Modify the negative attitudes of the Expression based on the aspects found in Step 12.

From CHART 3: THE EXPRESSION *list the negative attitudes of the 6 Expression from the bottom horizontal division. Study each trait to see if it is affected by the discord with the 5 Life Path or the harmony with the 9 Soul Urge.*

There is the possibility that you may be too exacting of yourself and willing to sacrifice yourself (or your family) for the welfare of others, but your strong individual needs will probably mitigate this attitude.

The 6·5 discord substantially modifies this characteristic.

At times, you may have substantial difficulty distinguishing helping from interfering.

The 6·9 harmony intensifies this trait.

Although you may express worry and anxiety, you are apt to try and cover these feelings and look at the bright side instead.

The free spirit of the 5 resists the negativity of the 6 and 9.

The expression of your individual needs will probably keep you from becoming a drudge because

of excessive involvement with your responsibilities.

The 6·5 discord strongly modifies this attitude.

STEP 15

EXPRESS THE MOTIVES OF THE SOUL URGE.

The motives remain the same irrespective of the other core
elements.

From CHART 4: SOUL URGE *copy the motives of the 9 Soul Urge
shown in the upper horizontal division.*

> Your inner nature wants to give of itself to others,
> usually in a humanitarian or philanthropic man-
> ner. You probably want to give friendship, affec-
> tion, love. You may want to give your knowledge
> and experience. You may also want to share with
> others your artistic or creative talents. It's possible
> that these talents are of considerable magnitude.

STEP 16

EXPRESS THE HARMONY OR DISCORD OF THE LIFE
PATH/SOUL URGE ASPECT.

From CHART 6: ASPECTS:

*The 5 Life Path/9 Soul Urge is usually discordant. The strong
personal desire of the 5 for freedom conflicts with the potential
of the 9 for giving to others.*

*The Life Path represents about half the core while the Soul
Urge represents only a fifth. The 5 Life Path will govern the
aspect, but Harlan will have to deal with the conflicting
energies of the 9 Soul Urge.*

> Although your inner nature feels the need to give
> to others, you may often feel torn between this
> need and your stronger need to explore the exhil-
> arating opportunities that present themselves for
> your personal development. You must learn to
> balance these opposing energies to avoid the frus-
> tration of missing an adventure or the sadness of
> not being available to those in need of your help.

STEP 17

EXPRESS THE EFFECTIVENESS OF THE LIFE PATH/
SOUL URGE COMBINATION.

Copy the effectiveness from the appropriate paragraph in this chapter.

The subject has a 9 Soul Urge and a 5 Life Path. 9 – 5 = 4 spaces. Copy the paragraph describing the Life Path lower than the Soul Urge by 3, 4 or 5 spaces.

> Although you are able to recognize your opportunities, you find somewhat fewer possibilities than you would like to advance your inner development. The experiences at hand, while not necessarily presenting opportunities to fulfill your inner needs, are apt to act as a secondary motivating force. Make the most of these experiences. Learn to accept the natural pace of your development.

STEP 18

EXPRESS THE HARMONY OR DISCORD OF THE EXPRESSION/SOUL URGE ASPECT.

From CHART 6: ASPECTS:

The 6 Expression/9 Soul Urge is usually harmonious. The potential of the 6 for responsibility and concern for others is enhanced by the potential of the 9 for giving to others. The potential for creative self-expression of both the 6 and 9 enhances the expressive capabilities.

The Expression represents about one-third the core while the Soul Urge represents only one-fifth. The 6 Expression will govern the aspect, but will be aided by the harmonious energies of the 9 Soul Urge.

> Your natural talent at being helpful and able to balance inharmonious situations will be substantially aided by your inner need to give to others, often without thought of yourself. You may be much concerned with the betterment of the community and capable of assisting in that betterment.
>
> You are apt to be strongly motivated to develop your creative expressive talents.

STEP 19

EXPRESS THE EFFECTIVENESS OF THE EXPRESSION/SOUL URGE COMBINATION.

Copy the effectiveness from the appropriate paragraph in this chapter.

The subject has a 9 Soul Urge and a 6 Expression. 9 − 6 = 3 spaces. Copy the paragraph describing the Expression lower than the Soul Urge by 3, 4 or 5 spaces.

> Your motivation sometimes seems to outrun your abilities. Although you have many ideas, your natural talents don't necessarily help to advance these ideas. Learn to be content with the realization that it will take more time than you would prefer to fulfill your inner desires.

STEP 20

REVIEW THE HARMONY OR DISCORD OF THE LIFE PATH/SOUL URGE AND EXPRESSION/SOUL URGE ASPECTS.

The harmony or discord of the aspects relative to the Soul Urge will modify the Soul Urge positive attitudes and negative attitudes expressed in Steps 21 and 22.

Review the usually discordant 5 Life Path/9 Soul Urge aspect discussed in Step 16. Review the usually harmonious 9 Soul Urge/6 Expression aspect discussed in Step 18.

For Harlan, the 9 Soul Urge, representing twenty percent of the core is enhanced by the 6 Expression, representing thirty percent of the core, and opposed by the 5 Life Path (with the Birthday), representing fifty percent of the core. The selfless humanitarian outlook of the 9 will be bolstered by the balance, responsibility and love of the 6. The 6 and 9 will also provide a strong potential for creative self-expression. At the same time, the potential of the 9 for giving to others will meet strong resistance from the personal desire of the 5 for freedom. Since the 5 has so much strength relative to the 9, the conflicts between the 5 and 9 will be more strongly influenced by the 5 than the 9.

STEP 21

EXPRESS THE POSITIVE ATTITUDES OF THE SOUL URGE.

Modify the positive attitudes of the Soul Urge based on the aspects discussed in Step 20.

From CHART 4: THE SOUL URGE *list the positive attitudes of the 9 Soul Urge from the middle horizontal division. Study each trait to determine if it is affected by the discord with the 5 Life Path or the harmony with the 6 Expression.*

> When you are concerned about others, you are very sympathetic, generous and kind. At these

times, your sensitive nature expresses much love, compassion and tolerance. There may be times, though, when you prefer not to be involved at all.

The 9·5 discord is expressed by the possibility of sometimes being involved and sometimes not. The 9·6 harmony enhances the attitude expressed, and accounts for the "very sympathetic, etc.," and the "much love, etc."

You possess a deep, intuitive understanding of life, innate wisdom, good intuition and a broad point of view.

These traits are expressed as indicated in Chart 4. The 5 and 9 do not add or subtract.

You are capable, at times, of expressing high ideals and an inspirational approach. You are capable of being self-sacrificing, but this trait is apt to conflict with your love of freedom.

The 9·5 discord indicates the conflict between self-sacrifice and freedom.

You can give freely without being concerned about any return, although your desire to give may cause conflicts with your self-centered needs.

The 9·5 discord indicates the conflict between giving and self-centered needs.

STEP 22

EXPRESS THE NEGATIVE ATTITUDES OF THE SOUL URGE.

Modify the negative attitudes of the Soul Urge based on the aspects discussed in Step 20.

From CHART 4: SOUL URGE *list the negative attitudes of the 9 Soul Urge from the bottom horizontal division. Study each trait to determine if it is affected by the discord with the 5 Life Path or the harmony with the 6 Expression.*

You may be far too sensitive, extremely emotional with your emotions expressed very strongly.

The 9·6 harmony intensifies the sensitivity and the emotions.

You probably suffer from the conflict between your high spiritual aims and your need for freedom and personal expansion.

The 9·5 discord intensifies the conflict.

> At times, you probably resent the necessity of giving. At times, when your giving conflicts with your own needs, you may not give, but you'll be dissatisfied anyway.

The 9·5 discord intensifies the problem.

> Sometimes you're disappointed in the lack of perfection in yourself and others.

The trait is expressed as indicated on Chart 5. The 5 and 6 do not add or subtract.

> Your tendency to be quite moody and critical at times is usually offset by your freedom-loving delight.

The 9·6 harmony may intensify the moodiness, but the 9·5 discord tends to balance the negativity.

Summary of the core synthesis

When we started the core synthesis we knew only Harlan's birthname and birthdate. Amazingly enough, we now have a reasonably detailed idea of his character. When we started our discussion of the core, we compared it to a slightly fuzzy black-and-white reproduction of a full color portrait. We now have that fuzzy reproduction.

A summary of the core synthesis might read like this:

> Harlan William Allen, born May 12, 1941, is an active, versatile, freedom-loving person with much excitement and adventure in his life, enhanced by his expression of the joy of living. He has the capability of being responsible, loving and giving. He must learn to balance the somewhat self-centered exhilaration he finds in freedom with his inner need to give much to others in the way of friendship, love and affection. He has the potential for artistic or creative endeavor.

But just how accurate is the picture? There is, of course, no way to check on the fictitious Harlan, but, from my experience, I'd expect we'd come pretty close. But don't just take *my* word for it. Follow the 22 steps and delineate your own core synthesis. Do a few others—your parents, spouse, children, close friends. IF THERE'S A MASTER NUMBER OR REPEATED

NUMBERS AMONG THE CORE ELEMENTS, SET THAT
READING ASIDE UNTIL YOU'VE READ THE NEXT
CHAPTERS. I expect you'll be as astonished as I was when I
began to be aware of the mysterious power of numbers.

If you've carefully followed Harlan's core synthesis and if
you do a few delineations of your own, you'll be developing
your own numerology skills. The synthesis, as outlined, certainly requires patience in the enfolding. The 22 steps are
specifically designed to make you aware of the manner in
which the various energies are blended. As you grow more
familiar with the numbers and the idea of synthesis, the delineation process will become second-nature. When we discuss advanced reading, you'll see how we can simplify the 22 steps and
produce even better readings.

Let's go back now and examine some assumptions underlying
the basic principles of delineation.

Potentials

IN A CHARACTER DELINEATION, WE ARE DEALING
ONLY WITH POTENTIALS. We have no way of knowing
exactly how an individual will use these potentials.

In a core reading, there are 11 different possible Life Paths,
11 different possible Expressions, 11 different possible Soul
Urges and 31 different possible Birthdays. There are, then, over
40,000 different cores possible ($11 \times 11 \times 11 \times 31 = 41,261$).
Somewhat over 4 billion people are living in the world at this
time. If we assume that the different cores are spread around
more or less evenly, there are about 100,000 people with the
same core.

By the time we take all the modifiers (Part III) into account,
we'll have well over 4 billion possible combinations, confirming
our feeling of the uniqueness of each individual. But, let's look
only at the core—the essence, as it were. Surely, we're *not* saying that those 100,000 people with the same core are similar.
We *are* saying that those 100,000 people have the same potentials. That is a far different prospect.

Potential, by the dictionary definition, means,

> 1. possible as opposed to actual;
> 2. capable of coming into being or action.

A potential, by its very nature, is not a fixed or finite characteristic. It's in constant flux, modifying the free will and environment and being, in turn, modified by them. The potential

is a moving force, shifting direction, expressing, at different times, a positive, negative or neutral side.

Let's look more closely at a few of the 100,000 people who share one core. Remember that Harlan William Allen, our fictitious subject, had a 5 Life Path, a 6 Expression, a 9 Soul Urge and a 3 Birthday. Now, coincidentally (actually, not so coincidentally—I really planned it all along) Abraham Lincoln was born on February 12, 1809, which gives him the same core as Harlan. Though we have no idea what the fictitious Harlan might do with his potentials, we can easily check on Honest Abe. You might want to re-read Harlan's delineation now that you know it also represents Lincoln. The core synthesis is a good description of our sixteenth President's potentials.

Lincoln's great achievement was the freedom he brought to the slaves (5: freedom, 6: concern for betterment of community, 9: humanitarian). In his early life he had many jobs—he built and navigated a steamboat down the Mississippi, worked in a store, managed a mill, spent some time as a surveyor as well as a village postmaster, served in the Black Hawk War (5: rolling stone). He had a troubled courtship with Mary Todd, with many breaks and reconciliations (5·6 conflict). He was an extraordinary stump speaker, went on to give some of the finest speeches in American history (3: verbal ability, 6·9 creative potential). He had a reputation for uncommon sociability (6: caring, 3: social).

The great naturalist, Charles Darwin, was born Charles Robert Darwin on February 12, 1809, the same day as Lincoln. Darwin has the same core as Lincoln.

Darwin's reputation as a great scientist and writer rests particularly on his *Origin of the Species* and *Descent of Man*, books which are monuments not only in biology but also in English literature (5: constructive expansion of knowledge, 6·9: creative potential, 3: writing ability). His life was dramatically changed, his life course set by his five-year round-the-world cruise as naturalist on the *Beagle* (an ultimate expression of the 5 freedom and opportunity). Although his scientific writing made him famous, he enjoyed the excitement of his experimental work far more than the writing (5: exciting opportunities, 3: writing ability). He was a devoted husband and father, a born teacher, was sympathetic, genial, courteous and kind, with a quiet naturalness arising from a complete absence of pretension (all expressions of 6 qualities enhanced by the 9 energy).

Both Lincoln and Darwin contributed to the world by a superb use of their potentials. But, as you can see, their lives were extremely dissimilar. There are other factors besides the potentials which account for a person's development. We'll discuss them shortly.

Delineation for the entire life or any specific time period in the life

A CHARACTER DELINEATION IS A READING FOR THE ENTIRE LIFE OR FOR ANY SPECIFIC TIME PERIOD IN THE LIFE. The potentials in a reading must be expressed in broad enough terms so they can, indeed, make sense for the entire span of years from birth to death. The subject, the person receiving the reading, must be able to easily relate the broad description of the potential to his particular place along the continuum of that potential at the time he receives the reading.

Let's study this point in more detail. An old friend of mine— let's call her Emily—with a Life Path of 1, would be a good subject. Let's look at her life in relation to her Life Path potentials—individuation, independence and attainment.

Emily grew up as the youngest child in a large family and enjoyed much comfort and support. When she married in her mid-twenties, she was content with her passive housewife's role. When her husband was seriously injured in an industrial accident, Emily was forced to take a full-time job to support him and their three young children. For over ten years, until her husband's early death, Emily was breadwinner, nurse, housewife and mother. Although she was indeed the head of the household, she felt totally dependent for love and support on those who were, in actuality, dependent on her.

After her eldest children had married, Emily centered her needs on her youngest boy. The child was uncomfortable with her efforts to keep him in a subordinate role. As soon as he was old enough, he found employment in a distant city. Despite a close relation with a nearby brother and sister, Emily felt alone and defeated. Although she had friends and visited her children and grandchildren frequently, she felt that no one needed her.

Now in her early sixties, Emily has at last accepted the unavailability of someone on whom she can lean. She has learned to make decisions capably, to spend her time enjoyably with friends, family and activities. She has begun to learn the meaning of independence.

Emily's life expresses her use of her potentials. Her delineation would reflect the changes in her life as she aged. The delineation would be expressed so that it is meaningful to Emily and points the way to future development no matter how old she is when she receives the reading.

Read the central focus and the commentary of the 1 Life Path in Chart 2. This might serve as a brief, but complete, reading which satisfies the above points. It encompasses Emily's lack of individuation in childhood, her dependence in young adulthood, her independent actions and subservient feelings when her husband was injured, her reliance on her young son when the other children married, her inability to accept being independent when her youngest child left, the eventual positive experience of independence, even her potential for attainment in the years to come.

A CHARACTER DELINEATION INDICATES THE POTENTIALS—ABOUT A THIRD OF THE INFORMATION DESCRIBING A PERSON. THE FREE WILL AND ENVIRONMENT—INFORMATION DESCRIBING THE OTHER TWO-THIRDS—ARE NOT CONTAINED IN THE DELINEATION.

Potentials, free will, environment

Look at Emily again. Her environment—the large family into which she was born, her husband's work and accident—were major factors in her life. Her free will was responsible, in her particular case, for her limited progress. Her role as passive wife, her years as head of her family without any feelings of independence, her dependence on her young son, her ultimate beginning understanding of her life lesson were all acts of her will which determined the directions of her life. If she had been a less subservient wife, if she had chosen to lead her family as an independent woman might, if she had not centered her needs on her son, her life would have taken significantly different directions.

Some people are disappointed that *all* the information isn't available in a reading. We have to recognize that the universe is structured by the potentials, but the potentials are operating within a field of freedom.

As you proceed with numerology, you may be amazed at how much you do learn about people, using only the potentials. You'll begin to understand subtleties which you didn't even see before, become aware of motivations previously hidden, gain insights which you cannot gain in any other way. Many subjects will provide part of the missing two-thirds. Most enjoy filling in at least portions of the information for your understanding.

THE CHARACTER DELINEATION, LIKE THE LIFE IT REPRESENTS, IS COMPOSED OF POTENTIALS WHICH ARE SOMETIMES HARMONIOUS, SOMETIMES DISCORDANT, SOMETIMES CONFLICTING, OFTEN AMBIGUOUS OR INCONSISTENT. The task of the numerologist is to express, as clearly as possible, exactly what is present in a manner which will be of most use to the person receiving the reading. It is important to express conflicts, ambiguities or in-

Ambiguity in delineations

consistencies just as the numbers describe them, so that the subject will understand the forces within. Don't attempt to tidy up a reading by making all the pieces fit together neatly and consistently. Although this may satisfy a desire for order, it does the subject a disservice by distorting the information he receives.

Particularly with your first readings, you're apt to be concerned because the parts of a delineation may feel as if they don't go together. I've often prefaced parts of a delineation with some remark like: "I don't understand how you can be —————— and —————— at the same time, but that's what the numbers say." You'll find that the subject will almost invariably understand the forces and their relation, and usually be happy to explain it to you.

Express the potentials positively

ALWAYS EXPRESS THE DELINEATION IN THE MOST POSITIVE MANNER POSSIBLE. *Don't* give a reading from a negative point of view. It may fix a subject's mind with the difficulties of his life and make it harder for him to resolve whatever discords or conflicts are present. (If you were dealing, in an extreme case, with a chart replete with conflicts, you would express the least difficult conflict as the most harmonious force available, the second least difficult conflict as the next most harmonious force, and so forth.)

Suppose, for instance, a chart shows a person who prefers to spend much of his time alone, has difficulty communicating with others and reticence in expressing emotions. If you said "Marriage is not recommended because you seem to have problems getting along with others," you would be stating the information in a damaging way. It would be better to express the information positively: "Marriage will require you to work at increasing your skills in getting along with others."

You must stay constantly alert to the powerful forces with which you are dealing. Handle with care!!!

CHAPTER 8

CORE SYNTHESIS WITH MASTER NUMBER ELEMENTS

The numbers 11 and 22 are master numbers. They represent the potential for heightened levels of awareness and understanding and the possibility of achievements of great significance. They are always accompanied by substantial charges of nervous tension. This combination of potential power and nervous tension does not make for easy going. The high level of energy can be extremely taxing.

It isn't possible to operate at the high level of the master number all the time. For many people, it's hardly possible to *ever* work at that level. Now, since 2 is the reduced form of 11 (1 + 1 = 2), the 11 energy devoted to illumination can be interpreted as a higher form of the 2 energy dedicated to relation and cooperation, with illumination and the dissemination of the products of the illumination implying working with others on a spiritual rather than a mundane level. Similarly, the 22 energy related to becoming a master builder can be understood as the higher level of the energy given to order and service of the 4, the reduced form of 22 (2 + 2 = 4). With an 11 element, you can choose to operate with the higher 11 energy or the reduced 2 energy, just as with the 22, you can use either the 22 or the 4 energy. I always write 11 as 11/2 and 22 as 22/4 to indicate the choice conferred *only* by the master numbers. (If the core element is 2 or 4, 2 or 4 energy alone is available and cannot be raised to 11 or 22.)

The choice we're talking about is not always a conscious one. A child with a master number element is *always* operating on the reduced level. Although the child would have some occasional glimpses of higher awarenesses, he would probably be more aware of the tensions he feels. Often, the tension and the latent power of the master number will be so difficult to live with that the child, or even the young adult, will express the reduced element with negativity. The 22 youngster is apt to feel frustrated by his limitations, by his rigid approach, by his concentration on details to the exclusion of the bigger picture. Instead of being able to use the 22 power, the youngster is expressing an overbalance of the 4 energy. The youngster with an 11 element often expresses negatively by denying the 2 energy. Instead of being sensitive, cooperative, considerate, the subject may be too sensitive, shy, uncertain, sometimes apathetic or indifferent.

As a person grows older, the power and awarenesses of the master number are more readily understood and used. Some mature adults may operate on the master level a good deal of the time, use the reduced level only occasionally. Many adults have difficulty with the power. They prefer to operate on the reduced level most of the time. Some adults, only somewhat in touch with their latent powers, prefer to stay almost exclusively on the mundane level.

The master number energy is there to be used if and when a person is ready. The master number tension is present whether or not the power is used. A subject with an 11 or 22 element reminds me of a moon rocket on the launching pad—enormous energy to be used—and the possibility of a premature fizzling out.

Birthday with master number

If the Birthday is a master number, the delineation proceeds in the same manner as shown in Chapter 7. The 2 energy of the 11/2 Birthday and the 4 energy of the 22/4 Birthday are already included in the description on CHART 5: THE BIRTHDAY, along with an emphasis on nervous tension.

Life Path, Expression or Soul Urge with master number

When the master number appears in the Life Path, Expression or Soul Urge, the same delineation steps are followed as in Chapter 7, but the master number energies must be read on the higher level of 11 or 22 and the lower level of 2 or 4. The harmony/discord and the effectiveness comparisons must be related to 11 and 2—or 22 and 4.

Look at CHART 6: THE ASPECTS. The aspect 1·22 is usually discordant but 1·4 is usually harmonious. The higher level aspect is often at odds with the lower level aspect. The effectiveness is apt to vary, too. While 2·3 is an effective combination, 11·3 is relatively ineffective. The subject will feel a degree of tension because of these different relations of the high and low level energies with the other elements. You can imagine the difficulties when you're operating with two related energies, both an integral part of you, with one producing harmony and effectiveness, while the other tends to conflict and ineffectiveness.

Following is a partial core synthesis for Grandma Moses, the legendary artist. The step-by-step delineation that follows (the individual steps are similar to those in Chapter 7) presents the special way a reading is handled if the Life Path, Expression or Soul Urge is a master number. In this example, Grandma Moses has a master number Life Path. But a similar method would be used if the Expression or Soul Urge was the master number.

Step-by-step partial core synthesis with a master number element

In the analysis that follows, we'll proceed as we did in Chapter 7. We'll first list each step, followed by a *general* explanation when necessary. We will then indicate, in italics, precisely where the information for Grandma Moses' *specific* delineation is to be found, and then show that portion of her synthesis derived by following the instructions. The actual delineation will be shown indented.

STEP 1

DERIVE THE ELEMENTS OF THE CORE.

From the calculation instructions in Chapters 3 through 6:

> Grandma Moses was born Anna Mary Robertson on September 7, 1860. Therefore, she has:
>
> > 22/4 Life Path
> > 6 Expression
> > 9 Soul Urge
> > 7 Birthday

STEP 2

EXPRESS THE CENTRAL FOCUS OF THE LIFE PATH.

The central focus remains the same irrespective of the other core elements.

From CHART 2: THE LIFE PATH *copy the central focus of the 22 Life Path and the 4 Life Path shown in the upper horizontal division.*

22 Life Path

> Learn the ultimate mastery of combining the highest spiritual ideals with the enormous power to achieve the largest of material goals. With this master number, you have added perceptions, added awarenesses. . . .

Provide an explanation of the special choice available with a master number.

> Your lesson in life, just outlined, is a high level lesson, indeed. Along with this high level lesson, there is an additional lesson on a mundane level. The potential of the higher lesson is available when you feel capable of handling the energy, but you may choose to spend some or a good deal of your time on the mundane lesson. I would suspect that, as a child or young adult, you found it far easier to operate on the lower level. As you grew older, you probably found yourself better able to handle the higher level power.

4 Life Path:

> On the mundane level, learn the advantage of order and service in accomplishing your work. You will probably be involved in practical, down-to-earth work. You must learn the rewards of service. You will have to determine where your duty lies. . . .

STEP 3

EXPRESS THE SUB-FOCUS OF THE BIRTHDAY.

From CHART 5: THE BIRTHDAY *use the keywords for the 7 Birthday. To elaborate on these keywords, read the central focus of the 7 Life Path found in Chart 2.*

> While you're learning to be a master builder and learning the lesson of limitation, order and service, learn also how to use analysis and understanding. . . .

STEP 4

EXPRESS THE HARMONY OR DISCORD OF THE LIFE PATH/BIRTHDAY ASPECT.

From CHART 6: THE ASPECTS *read the 7·22 aspect—usually discordant. The aspect, as written in the chart, expresses the conflict of the 7 energy with the prevailing 22 energy.*

> Your introspective ways conflict with your potential for working toward substantial material achievement.

From the same chart, read the 4·7 aspect—usually harmonious. Rewrite the aspect to express the enhancement of the prevailing 4 energy by the 7 energy.

> Your capability at study and research will help in working toward an awareness of system and order.

STEP 5

DETERMINE THE HARMONY OR DISCORD OF THE LIFE PATH/EXPRESSION AND THE LIFE PATH/SOUL URGE ASPECTS.

From CHART 6: ASPECTS:

The 22 Life Path/6 Expression is usually harmonious. The potential of the 6 for responsibility and concern for others is enhanced by the potential of the 22 for substantial material achievement, but the nervous tension of the 22 will be a partial detriment to the 6 approach.

The 22 Life Path/9 Soul Urge is usually harmonious. The potential of the 9 for giving to others is enhanced by the potential of the 22 for significant material achievement.

The 22 Life Path, 6 Expression and 9 Soul Urge are usually all working together in a harmonious manner. Although the 22 represents a potential difficult to achieve, Grandma Moses will find the additional harmonious energy of great help.

The 4 Life Path/6 Expression is usually harmonious. The potential of the 4 for system and order enhances the potential of the 6 for responsibility and concern.

The 4 Life Path/9 Soul Urge is usually discordant. The potential of the 4 for fixity of approach conflicts with the potential of the 9 for giving to others.

The 4 Life Path and 6 Expression, representing eighty percent of the core's energy, are in conflict with the 9 Soul Urge, representing twenty percent of the core's energy. The 4 potential for system and order works along with the balance and responsibility of the 6 (and the humanitarianism of the 9, although it is not specifically mentioned in the chart). The 4 rigidity conflicts with the giving qualities of the 9 (and the flexibility of the 6, again not specifically mentioned in the chart).

STEP 6

EXPRESS THE CHARACTERISTICS OF THE LIFE PATH.

Modify the Life Path characteristics based on the aspects found in Step 5.

From CHART 2: THE LIFE PATH *list the characteristics of the 22 Life Path from the second horizontal division. Study each trait to determine if it is affected by the harmony with the 6 Expression and the 9 Soul Urge. Modify the characteristic to express this effect.*

> You are probably extremely capable at whatever work you choose, with the possibility of rising to the top of your profession. Even when you are not accomplishing, your latent capability is most obvious.

The 6 balance and the 9 universality add to this characteristic, but it is already so strongly stated that any addition would be superfluous.

> You are probably practical. You have an innate understanding of the forces involved in material problems.

This trait is expressed as indicated on Chart 2. The 22·6 and 22·9 do not add or subtract.

> Although you have an unorthodox way about you, this is apt to be expressed in a reasonably balanced manner. Your significant perceptions of universal matters will provide you with avenues not available to others or often not understandable to others. You may well operate on a different wavelength than others, but you probably know how to make yourself understood.

The balance of the 6 and the universality of the 9 offset the unorthodox 22 tendencies.

You're likely to have a charismatic personality. The glow of your inner fire will probably be visible to all. Even when you're not accomplishing all that might be expected, others will be drawn by the excitement, balance and humanity expressed in your activities.

The balance of the 6 and the humanitarianism of the 9 are noted in the last sentence.

Your special awarenesses and capabilities are usually accompanied by an almost electric field of nervous tension which can rarely be hidden.

This trait is expressed as indicated on Chart 2. The 22·6 and 22·9 do not add or subtract.

From CHART 2: THE LIFE PATH *list the characteristics of the 4 Life Path from the second horizontal division. Study each trait to determine if it is affected by the 4·6 harmony or the 4·9 discord. Modify the characteristic to express this effect.*

You are probably practical and capable of systematizing and managing. You can produce order where little exists.

This trait is expressed as indicated on Chart 2. The 4·6 doesn't add and the 4·9 doesn't subtract.

You are willing to work long and hard and have much patience with detail. You are very conscientious and often seem to do better with difficult problems than with simpler work. Occasionally, you may seem to make the work harder by your peculiar approach, but you are, nevertheless, capable of completing the work.

The 9 energy tends to somewhat modify the 4 fixity. Therefore, the addition of the "occasionally" at the beginning of the last sentence.

You have a serious approach, express honesty and sincerity and are extremely responsible.

The 6 responsibility adds to the responsibility of the 4 energy.

You have fairly strong likes and dislikes and express what you feel is right and wrong with some strength.

The 6 and 9 flexibility tones down the 4 rigidity.

At times, you have a somewhat fixed approach.
This may express as strength to accomplish a task
or as stubbornness.

The 6 and 9 flexibility tones down the 4 rigidity.

STEP 7

EXPRESS THE CHARACTERISTICS OF THE BIRTHDAY.

From CHART 5: THE BIRTHDAY *summarize the characteristics of
the 7 Birthday. Remember, from Step 4, that the 22 Life
Path/7 Birthday is usually discordant while the 4 Life Path/7
Birthday is usually harmonious. Modify the traits as required.*

You aren't particularly adaptable. You often prefer
working alone but feel isolated. You need time to
rest and meditate, particularly after you've been
working with others on any substantial project.

*Although the 4·7 is usually harmonious, the 4 here adds to the
lack of adaptability. The effect of the 22·7 is noted in the last
sentence.*

You're likely to be introspective. . . .

Continue with the rest of the Birthday characteristics.

STEP 8

DISCUSS THE NEGATIVE EXPRESSION OF THE LIFE PATH.

Remember that the negative expression is determined,
to a strong extent, by the free will and environment. This section warns of the potential problems inherent in the negative
expression.

From CHART 2: THE LIFE PATH *read the negative expression of
the 22 Life Path in the third horizontal division. If she expresses
negatively at all, Grandma Moses will tend to express the
second negative expression, the denial of the lesson. The first
negative expression is unlikely because of the added harmony of
the 6 and 9 energies, but it, too, must be mentioned.*

If you feel overwhelmed by your powers, you may
retreat from using them. You will then accomplish
little, feel frightened by the world around you and
uncomfortable with your nervous tension.

There's a slight chance that you'll use your substantial powers for your own selfish ends, but, con-

sidering your sense of balance and your concern for others, this isn't very likely.

From CHART 2: THE LIFE PATH *read the negative expression of the 4 Life Path in the third horizontal division. If Grandma Moses expresses negatively at all, she will tend to express the first negative expression, the exaggeration of the lesson. The second negative expression is unlikely because of the added balance of the 6 and 9 energies, but it, too, must be mentioned.*

If you feel overwhelmed by feelings of limitation, these feelings may stem from your own stubborn and obstinate manner and your rigid approach, but you probably would be hard pressed to see that you are causing your own problems.

There's a slight chance that you'll be disorganized and irresponsible, but considering your sense of balance and your concern for others, this isn't very likely.

Indicate the unproductivity.

These negative expressions are unproductive. They should be avoided in order to proceed constructively with your development.

The delineation would continue with Steps 9 through 22 as outlined in Chapter 7. The aspects and effectiveness would relate to *both* the 22 Life Path and the 4 Life Path.

Birthday and one additional element with master numbers

Let's examine some special situations involving master numbers. Let's assume a subject with a master number for a Birthday (born on the 11th, 22nd or 29th) and the other master number as one of the other elements. (If the Birthday and the other element are the same master number, read Chapter 9 before proceeding with the core synthesis.)

Suppose we find a person with an 11/2 Birthday and a 22/4 Expression. The Birthday reading is found on CHART 5: THE BIRTHDAY, and the 22/4 Expression would be delineated like the Grandma Moses example with both the 22 Expression and the 4 Expression described and compared to the other energies. The existence of two master numbers in the core would produce heightened perceptions and power potential along with a high level of tension. This is a difficult combination to handle and will take much maturity to handle wisely. A child or young adult, particularly, with this configuration is likely to have hard going. The delineation should express the difficulty and the struggle, but also emphasize the very special gifts involved and the significant possibilities.

Two elements other than Birthday with master numbers

A more powerful combination exists with a subject having two elements, other than the Birthday, with two different master numbers. (If the master numbers are the same, read Chapter 9.)

Paul McCartney, born James Paul McCartney on June 18, 1942, has a 22/4 Life Path, an 11/2 Expression, a 5 Soul Urge and a 9 Birthday. *Seventy percent of his core consists of master energy potential.* If a person with one master number can be compared to a moon rocket on the launching pad, you can imagine the energy level with two master numbers. A most difficult combination with which to come to grips! The potential is enormous, but these people, beset with nervous tension, often wonder why they accomplish so little with so much latent ability. Paul McCartney seems to have managed to focus his potentials for significant development. He represents a subject who may be said to have overcome the difficulties inherent in his master number potential. I would assume that he is bristling with energy, awareness and tension.

McCartney's synthesis is a more complicated affair than when only one master number is present. In his delineation, the 22 Life Path energy must be related to the 11 Expression as well as the 2 Expression. The 4 Life Path energy must also be related to the 11 and 2 Expression energies. The 5 Soul Urge must be related to the 22 and 4 Life Paths as well as the 11 and 2 Expressions. The procedure is similar to the Grandma Moses delineation, but the number of combinations is increased. All of these energies are active in the subject and have to be described.

A master number in the core calls special attention to the subject. It indicates the *possibilities* of significant perceptions and powers. It *always* indicates nervous tension. More often than not, you'll find a person struggling to understand and release the enormous energies he feels but has not learned to master. Occasionally, you'll find a subject bewildered or overwhelmed by these forces. Many times, the person will endeavor to make life easier by depressing the master number and operating primarily on the lower level, leaving only glimpses of the potent latent energy. The individual with a master number may choose to ignore or forget the higher potential, but, if you look closely, the tension is almost always visible. The master number is, indeed, a mixed blessing.

CHAPTER 9

CORE SYNTHESIS WITH REPEATED NUMBER ELEMENTS

Charlie has a core with a 1 Life Path
        2 Expression
        3 Soul Urge
        4 Birthday.

We can see that Charlie has many different potentials: leadership potential from the 1, sensitivity from the 2, artistic expression from the 3, self-discipline from the 4—to name just a few. It's clear at a glance that Charlie has all sorts of energies he can develop, many directions in which to grow and develop.

Charlie's friend, Amy, has a core with a
        2 Life Path
        3 Expression
        6 Soul Urge
        9 Birthday.

Amy has many different potentials, too: the diplomatic potential of the 2, the social and artistic potential of the 3, the responsible, loving and creative potential of the 6, the humanitarian potential of the 9. Although she has all sorts of energies, they seem to fall together in two groups. Amy is likely to do well with people: she is likely to combine the diplomatic, social, responsible, loving and humanitarian potentials. And Amy can also develop another side: her artistic and creative potentials. Amy's energies are probably easier to focus than

Charlie's, but both friends have many exciting avenues to explore.

Amy's friend, Jill, has a different kind of core. She has a

6 Life Path
1 Expression
6 Soul Urge
5 Birthday

Instead of the usual core with four different numbers, Jill has a core with only three. Now, she still has much potential to develop: the responsible, loving and creative potential of the 6, the leadership potential of the 1, the adaptable and imaginative potential of the 5—but—and this is a big BUT—the potential is poorly balanced. While thirty percent of Jill's core is devoted to 1 potential and ten percent is devoted to 5 potential, a substantial *sixty percent* is devoted to 6 potential. You might assume that it would be desirable to have all that loving, responsible, creative energy. It *can* be desirable, but only after Jill learns how to handle the problems created by the imbalance.

If Jill had only one 6 core element, she'd tend to be a balanced person—loving and responsible. With the two 6 core elements, she has an excess of loving potential and an excess of responsibility potential. In her young years, Jill is likely to express *much* love and *much* responsibility. She can probably handle any and all responsibility, so her friends and family are always asking her to help—and she does help, willingly, lovingly, no matter how much time it takes.

So what's the problem? Dear, sweet Jill is *so* loving, *so* giving, *so* helpful, she probably never has time for her own needs, may even feel she has few personal needs that are important. She's so busy helping others that she doesn't realize she's become a drudge, a doormat, a virtual slave. Jill is undoubtedly giving a great deal, but, in the process, she isn't growing and developing—she's fallen victim to her unbalanced core.

At some time in her life, Jill is likely to get tired of the heavy burden she's assumed. She's likely to begin to decide which responsibilities are legitimately hers, which people she cares to help. With some practice in becoming more discriminating, Jill's life can change for the better. She'll no longer be taken for granted or be treated like a doormat. In addition, she'll be willing and able to take care of her own needs, have time to explore the closeness of relations with others, and begin to develop new depths of feeling and understanding. Jill will have succeeded in changing the imbalance into a dynamic positive force.

IF TWO CORE ELEMENTS HAVE THE SAME NUMBER, THE SUBJECT WILL PROBABLY *START OUT IN LIFE*

EXPRESSING ONE (OR BOTH) NEGATIVE EXTREMES OF THE POTENTIAL INSTEAD OF THE POSITIVE PO-TENTIAL:

1. USING THE ENERGY ALMOST EXCLUSIVELY SO THAT IT BECOMES THE FOCUS OF A DISBAL-ANCED APPROACH. POSITIVE POTENTIAL *MAY* BE EXPRESSED AT THE SAME TIME.
2. ALMOST COMPLETELY IGNORING THE POTEN-TIAL.

Jill, of course, was using the first extreme. She concentrated on being loving and responsible to the detriment of her own development. Although she suffered as a consequence, she was using the 6 energy in an unbalanced manner—even though it included the expression of the 6 positive potential.

Ninety-eight out of a hundred people with 6·6 energy express that first extreme. Sometimes, that first extreme is tempered by short periods of the second extreme—in the 6·6 case, periods of irresponsibility and coolness. In rare cases, you'll find the 6·6 energy expressed completely by the second extreme: a person who is almost always aloof, unloving, unwilling to handle re-sponsibilities.

The doubled core element usually presents substantial obsta-cles to development—but ALL OBSTACLES ARE CAPABLE OF BEING OVERCOME. Only the individual involved can decide when he or she wants to shift from the negative to the positive potential.

One path to a balanced approach is found by adding the doubled numbers and expressing the positive potential of the sum. A way out of the 6·6 difficulties is to express the positive 3 potential: (6 + 6 = 12, 1 + 2 = 3)—trade in the heavy approach of the doormat for the lighter expression of the joy of living of the 3.

Turn to CHART 6: THE ASPECTS and study the negative ex-tremes associated with each pair of doubled numbers. For each number, the first description indicates the overuse of the energy while the second description expresses the ignoring of the energy. A path to a more balanced approach is included after the description of the extremes.

(If we're dealing with 9·9 energy, a path to a more balanced approach is not as simple to derive, since 9 + 9 = 18 and 1 + 8 = 9. The path here is defined as the positive potential of the 1 and 8.)

Chart 6: The Aspects

Examples of doubled core elements

We can look at the lives of some well-known people to better understand the problems of the doubled elements as well as the contributions possible either because of, or in spite of, the imbalance. (Included are a few infamous individuals who were unable to use their free will to overcome their problems.) Compare the descriptions in CHART 6: THE ASPECTS with the energies actually expressed.

The people we're using as examples are often expressing VERY EXTREME examples of the energies we've been describing. I've purposely picked these extreme examples to graphically illustrate the dynamics involved. (In most of these cases, the energies of the doubled core elements are directly related to the fame—or infamy—of the subject.) Obviously, most people are not expressing anything like these extremes.

John L. Lewis (John Llewellyn Lewis) was born on February 12, 1880.

The charismatic leader of the coal miners union had a 1 Expression and a 1 Soul Urge. Lewis was known for his hard-headed negotiations with the mine owners, his unwillingness to back down. He used his forceful, dominating stance to achieve constructive ends. Rather than change the 1·1 negative energy to positive, he found a fulfilling way of making the negative energy work for him. A highly unusual, but successful, approach.

Jack Ruby (Jacob Rubenstein) was born on March 23, 1911.

The nightclub owner who killed Lee Oswald had an 11/2 Life Path and an 11/2 Soul Urge. The culminating act of his life was an extreme negative expression of the distorted idealism associated with 11·11 energy. Ruby compounded the confusion surrounding the Kennedy assassination, a negative expression of the 2·2 energy. He was unable to come to grips with either the high or low level energy of the master number.

Richard Speck (Richard Benjamin Speck) was born on December 6, 1941.

This mass murderer had a 3 Expression and a 3 Soul Urge. He was unable to express his deep-seated anger through normal channels. Speck's senseless killings were related, in an extreme manner, to his inability to come to grips with his difficulties with self-expression, a negative expression of the 3·3 energy.

John Mitchell (John Newton Mitchell) was born on September 15, 1913.

Nixon's Attorney General has a 22/4 Soul Urge and a 4 Expression. He went to prison because of his involvement with Watergate. His stubborn attitude (overuse of the 4 energy) and his lack of feeling of accountability (ignoring the 4 energy) were some of the traits responsible for his problems. Mitchell's undoing was a result of his inability to cope with both extremes of the negative 4·4 potential.

Martin Luther King (Michael Luther King) was born on January 15, 1929.

The brilliant leader of the civil rights movement had a 5 Expression and a 5 Soul Urge. King worked as meaningfully as any American in this century to demonstrate the possibilities of using freedom constructively. This Nobel Prize winner is an *extremely rare* example of a powerful use of positive potential without any trace of the negative expression of the 5·5. When the doubled energy is properly harnessed, there is, as in King's example, a virtually limitless reservoir of positive power.

Montgomery Clift was born on October 17, 1920.

The superb actor had a 6 Expression and a 6 Soul Urge. His sensitive and brilliant performances in films (the positive expression of his 3 Life Path as well as the creativity of the 6 energy) made him a top box-office attraction. His difficulties in expressing friendship and love as well as his irresponsible personal habits, negative expressions of the 6·6 potential, contributed to his unhappy life and early death.

General Douglas MacArthur was born on January 26, 1880.

The superb strategist had an 8 Life Path and an 8 Birthday. He was directly responsible for many of our brilliant victories in World War II and served as virtual dictator of Japan after the armistice. His superb intelligence and ability to perform in difficult situations contributed to his shining reputation. His obsession with himself—his rigid attitudes, his cool manner, his prideful ways—kept him from achieving the presidency, as he would have liked. MacArthur used the positive side of the 8·8, but never overcame the problems presented by the negative potential.

Richard Nixon (Richard Milhous Nixon) was born on January 9, 1913.

This President has a 9 Expression and a 9 Birthday. During his term in office, Nixon was insensitive to others' needs. He was self-centered, often inflexible. He brought on his own downfall because he could not overcome the negative 9·9 energy.

In the examples above, you can observe the wide spectrum of expression possible with the doubled core elements. The step-by-step delineation which follows presents the special way a reading is handled with this type of energy.

All readings have some negative components to them, just as all people have some problems to work on. In the reading for Hal Allen in Chapter 7, the basic energy expressed has a strong positive direction so that the inclusion of some negative comments does not detract from the basically constructive tone. This is typical of most readings. In the reading which follows, however, the doubled core elements create such a strong negative potential that a constructive tone can only be established if the reading clearly emphasizes the positive potential while still effectively stating the negative.

Relation to age
The doubled core element readings have a slightly different cast depending on the age of the subject. In my experience, in subjects between birth and age twenty, the negative energy is usually strongly expressed, the positive energy likely to be in disbalance. In the delineation, describe the negative potential as the probable present state, but emphasize the positive potential and the direction to its achievement as desirable and viable objectives.

Between the ages of twenty and forty, a subject will usually come to grips with the alternatives. More often than not, the obstacles will, to a large extent, be overcome. A delineation given during this time would give almost equal weight to the positive and negative potentials, but would stress the considerable advantages of solving the life problems.

After age forty, there is a strong possibility that the subject is proceeding primarily with his positive potential, perhaps with minor fall-backs to earlier stages. The reading would emphasize the positive direction he has achieved and maintained, would discuss the negative potential as primarily a thing of the past.

The following delineation covers those parts of the 22 steps of Chapter 7 which are affected by the doubled core elements. We are reading for a fictitious subject, and assuming that the reading is given somewhere near Hilde's thirtieth birthday.

We'll proceed as we did in Chapters 7 and 8. We'll first list each step, followed by a *general* explanation when necessary. We will then indicate, in italics, precisely where the information for Hilde's *specific* delineation is to be found, and then show that portion of her synthesis derived by following the instructions. The actual delineation will be shown indented.

STEP 1

DERIVE THE ELEMENTS OF THE CORE.

From the calculation instructions in Chapters 3 through 6:

> Hilde Agatha Parsons was born on July 21, 1950. Therefore, she has:
>
> > 7 Life Path
> > 7 Expression
> > 6 Soul Urge
> > 3 Birthday

Step-by-step partial core synthesis with doubled core elements

STEP 2

EXPRESS THE CENTRAL FOCUS OF THE LIFE PATH.

The central focus remains the same irrespective of the other core elements.

From CHART 2: THE LIFE PATH *copy the central focus of the 7 Life Path shown in the upper horizontal division.*

> Learn the peace of mind that comes with knowing yourself. You have a good mind and a fine intuition. You must study and contemplate, learn not to judge from appearances, but search for the hidden truths. Your life should be devoted to analyzing the world about you, learning to trust your intuition, developing until you reach the highest levels of wisdom. You must not emphasize material things in your life, but rather must become aware of the non-material forces. You must learn to spend time by yourself without feeling isolated. You must learn to wait for opportunities which work to your advantage rather than actively seeking opportunities. Amid the hurly-burly of the world, your development depends on your ability to retire into yourself to find faith and peace.

STEP 3

EXPRESS THE SUB-FOCUS OF THE BIRTHDAY.

This step is not related to the doubled core elements. Proceed as in Chapter 7.

STEP 4

EXPRESS THE HARMONY OR DISCORD OF THE LIFE PATH/BIRTHDAY ASPECT.

This step is not related to the doubled core elements. Proceed as in Chapter 7.

STEP 5

DETERMINE THE HARMONY OR DISCORD OF THE LIFE PATH/EXPRESSION AND THE LIFE PATH/SOUL URGE ASPECTS.

Although we have not yet delineated the Expression and the Soul Urge, we must, at this point, determine the aspects related to the Life Path because that harmony or discord will modify the Life Path Characteristics and negative expression expressed in Steps 6 and 7.

From CHART 6: THE ASPECTS:

7 Life Path/7 Expression is usually very discordant.

Extremely self-contained and inflexible. A "different" point of view that may appear to others as considerably eccentric. Difficult to get to know—purposely puts others off because she is more comfortable keeping her distance from others.
    or
Timid, shy, retiring. Very dependent on others and most resentful of that dependency. Efforts to stand alone often thwarted.

Possible approach to alleviate difficulties: she must work to express more freely. She has to learn to take advantage of opportunities by being more adaptable. She must also learn to express feelings in an honest manner, rather than hiding them.

7 Life Path/6 Soul Urge is usually discordant. The potential of the 6 for responsibility and concern for others conflicts with the introspective potential of the 7.

From CHART 3: THE EXPRESSION *read the 7 Expression and from* CHART 4: THE SOUL URGE *read the 6 Soul Urge to become familiar with the basic reading for these elements.*

Not only is the Life Path/Expression usually very discordant, but the Life Path/Soul Urge is usually discordant, too. That's a lot of negative energy to overcome! Remember that Hilde, at age thirty, is likely to have a lot of awareness of her problems and is likely to be in the process of transforming her energies to more positive directions. The delineation could provide an active boost to Hilde's desire for transformation.

STEP 6

EXPRESS THE CHARACTERISTICS OF THE LIFE PATH.

Modify the Life Path characteristics based on the aspects found in Step 5.

From CHART 2: THE LIFE PATH *list the characteristics of the 7 Life path from the second horizontal division. Study each trait to determine the effect of the predominant discord with the 7 Expression and the 6 Soul Urge. Modify the characteristic to express this effect.*

> You are likely to have a "different" point of view because you probably operate on a considerably different wavelength than others. This will probably prove an extremely powerful tool for you, because it will give you access to unique solutions and unique approaches to problems which just aren't available to other people.

> At your age, you may have discovered that you sometimes have trouble communicating these special insights. Others may have difficulty understanding you or may even look at some of your approaches as eccentric. I suspect you're working on improving your communication so that your messages can be delivered with maximum impact. If, at times, you feel confused about some of these unusual ideas, it may be helpful to meditate or talk to a close friend to clarify the areas of confusion.

The 7·7 emphasizes the problems of the "differentness." The first paragraph expresses the very positive potential, the second paragraph discusses the problem and the solutions to the problem. Because of Hilde's age, the second paragraph is phrased on the assumption that she is already working on helping herself.

The short paragraph in Chart 2 on the "differentness" characteristic has been considerably changed to account for the effect of the 7·7 potential.

> I expect that you started out in life as a person

who was difficult to know well. You may have appeared cool and aloof, possibly timid, shy and retiring. I know that the distance you expressed in your early years was probably a surface veneer you felt you needed for protection. You've probably worked on overcoming this need to stand apart, have probably learned how to express your feelings far more openly and honestly than before. Continue your work in this area. The more open your feelings, the less distance you'll feel with others and the easier it will be to further your interests.

Again, the Chart 2 paragraph has been substantially revised to account for the 7·7 energy. When the positive aspects of the 6 Soul Urge are described, special emphasis should be placed on Hilde's potential to be sympathetic, kind and generous and to give out much friendship, affection and love, as described in CHART 4: THE SOUL URGE. *You may even want to mention this positive potential in the paragraph above and reiterate it in the Soul Urge description.*

You're likely to be introspective, somewhat turned in on yourself. You probably often appear reserved and thoughtful. There's another part of you, however, that expresses much in the way of friendship and affection, even shares some of the deep emotions. I expect that more of the second energy is expressed now than in your younger years. Continue to bring out that loving potential.

Here, we specifically mention the 6 Soul Urge as a contrast to the reserved approach. But the introspective quality is stated clearly, too. Don't distort the delineation because of the difficulty of expressing the negative traits—rather, learn to express them in a constructive light.

You probably primarily depend on yourself. . . .

The delineation would continue with the characteristics from Chart 2, strongly modified by the discordant energies.

STEP 7

EXPRESS THE CHARACTERISTICS OF THE BIRTHDAY.

This step is not related to the doubled core elements. Proceed as in Chapter 7.

STEP 8

DISCUSS THE NEGATIVE EXPRESSION OF THE LIFE PATH.

For most individuals, like Hal Allen in Chapter 7, the negative expression is determined, to a strong extent, by the free will and the environment, although it's also related to the Life Path/Expression aspect and the Life Path/Soul Urge aspect. For Hilde, though, the doubled core elements will tend to produce a negative approach to the Life Path, particularly in her early years.

From CHART 2: THE LIFE PATH *read the negative expression of the 7 Life Path in the third horizontal division. Since the delineation is being given in Hilde's thirtieth year, treat the negative expression as something that has probably been at least partially transformed.*

> I've already mentioned your tendency to be introspective and self-centered. Sometimes, a person with your chart configuration emphasizes these characteristics to become a virtual recluse. If this did occur in your early years, I suspect you found that the lack of contact was uncomfortable and made it difficult to grow and develop.
>
> Your chart indicates a strong inner life. If you found this introverted path of little satisfaction, particularly as a child or young adult, you may have tried to ignore your inner resources, concentrated instead on the gratifications of the material world. You probably found that this approach didn't give the satisfactions you expected. If you want to grow, you have a far better chance if you move onto your own track and develop your strong potentials.

STEP 9

EXPRESS THE ABILITIES OF THE EXPRESSION.

The abilities remain the same irrespective of the other core elements.

From CHART 3: THE EXPRESSION *copy the abilities of the 7 Expression shown in the upper horizontal division.*

> You have a good mind and good intuition. You're

capable of analyzing, judging, discriminating. You like to search for wisdom or hidden truths. You often become an authority on subjects that interest you—technical, scientific, religious or occult. You have the potential to be an educator, philosopher, researcher.

You have an awareness of spiritual matters, although this may be a latent characteristic. You operate on a "different" wavelength which may give you unique approaches and solutions to problems.

Although Hilde possesses these potential abilities, it's probable that all aren't being used. The delineation should indicate these possibilities.

It's possible that you're not using or developing all of these capabilities at this time. Some of your talents may have been used in the earlier part of your life and some may still be latent. Be aware of your capabilities, so that you can make use of them at appropriate times.

STEP 10

EXPRESS THE HARMONY OR DISCORD OF THE LIFE PATH/EXPRESSION ASPECT.

From CHART 6: THE ASPECTS *we already know that the 7 Life Path/7 Expression is very discordant. Rather than stress this strong negativity in one place, portions of the aspect were included in Step 6 and additional portions will be included in Steps 13 and 14.*

STEP 11

EXPRESS THE EFFECTIVENESS OF THE LIFE PATH/EXPRESSION COMBINATION.

The subject has a 7 Life Path and a 7 Expression. 7 – 7 = 0 spaces. When there are no spaces between the combined elements, they are negatively directed and relatively ineffective. There is no paragraph in the Table of Effectiveness in Chapter 7 to cover this because it is already covered in the very discordant Life Path/Expression aspect. The material is incorporated as discussed in Step 10.

STEP 12

DETERMINE THE HARMONY OR DISCORD OF THE EX-PRESSION/LIFE PATH AND THE EXPRESSION/SOUL URGE ASPECTS.

The harmony or discord of the aspects related to the Expression will modify the Expression positive attitudes and negative attitudes expressed in Steps 13 and 14.

From CHART 6: THE ASPECTS:

The 7 Expression/7 Life Path is usually very discordant. See Step 5.

The 7 Expression/6 Soul Urge is similar to the 7 Life Path/6 Soul Urge discussed in Step 5 and is usually discordant. The potential of the 6 for responsibility and concern for others conflicts with the introspective potential of the 7.

All the energy is either discordant or very discordant.

STEP 13

EXPRESS THE POSITIVE ATTITUDES OF THE EXPRES-SION.

Modify the positive attitudes of the Expression based on the aspects found in Step 12.

From CHART 3: THE EXPRESSION *list the positive attitudes of the 7 Expression from the middle horizontal division. Study each trait to determine how it is affected by the strong discord with the 7 Life Path and the discord with the 6 Soul Urge.*

> You probably have strong perfectionist tendencies which help you complete your projects in superb style. When you carry this to extremes or pursue perfection with an air of inflexibility, you may undermine your accomplishments.

The perfectionist tendency is appreciated when used in a balanced manner. The inflexibility noted in the 7·7 negative potential is added.

> You have a very logical, rational approach, little affected by your emotions.

This trait is not modified by the aspects. Although the 6 Soul Urge is emotional, the strength of the 7·7 takes precedence.

> You are usually willing to work to understand

deep, difficult subjects, to search for hidden fundamentals.

This trait is not modified by the aspects.

Although you have the potential to be peaceful and poised, particularly in your mature years, your self-contained nature and your tendency to be shy and retiring may stand in the way of achieving this potential with ease.

The 7·7 discord takes its toll here.

STEP 14

EXPRESS THE NEGATIVE ATTITUDES OF THE EXPRESSION.

Modify the negative attitudes of the Expression based on the aspects found in Step 12.

From CHART 3: THE EXPRESSION *list the negative attitudes of the 7 Expression from the bottom horizontal division. Study each trait to see how it is affected by the strong discord with the 7 Life Path and the discord with the 6 Soul Urge.*

I hope you've learned to put more trust in others than you did when you were younger. Your self-containment is likely to make it an effort to get close, but your concern for others, if you can express it openly, may lead the way to better relations.

The self-containment, from the 7·7 aspect, and the conflict between concern and introspection, from the 7·6 aspect, are both expressed.

In your early years you displayed a lack of adaptability, at times an extreme inflexibility. These traits work against you. This is an area where change would be of much benefit.

The 7·7 again.

The introspection and self-centered characteristics described next in Chart 3 have already been covered in relation to the Life Path traits and are omitted here.

There's certainly a loving, responsible side to your nature, but in the past, it's sometimes been overpowered by your critical, unsympathetic or intolerant attitudes. These latter characteristics are a strong obstacle to better relations with others.

The 7·6 conflict is expressed with, of course, a lot of emphasis on the positive 6 energy.

You usually prefer to work alone. . . .

The delineation would continue with the rest of the negative attitudes of Chart 3, modified by the discordant energies.

STEPS 15 THROUGH 22

Since these steps are not related to the doubled core elements, proceed as in Chapter 7.

The Birthday is usually compared only with the Life Path to determine harmony or discord. If the doubled elements are the Birthday and the Life Path, this is still the only Birthday aspect described, but that aspect modifies both the Birthday *and* the Life Path characteristics.

Change the steps of the core synthesis as follows:

STEP 6.   Express the characteristics of the Life Path, modified by the Life Path/Expression, Life Path/Soul Urge and *Life Path/Birthday* aspects.

STEP 8.   Discuss the negative expression of the Life Path, modified by the Life Path/Expression, Life Path/ Soul Urge and *Life Path/Birthday* aspects.

Although we've thought of the Birthday as only ten percent of the core, the discordant energy of the doubled elements is so strong that the Life Path/Birthday aspect should be weighted about the same as the Life Path/Soul Urge aspect.

Special delineation: Birthday and Life Path of the same number

Let's suppose, instead, that the Birthday and the Expression are the doubled core elements. Change the steps of the core synthesis as follows:

STEP 7.   Express the characteristics of the Birthday modified by the Life Path/Birthday aspect and the *Expression/ Birthday* aspect.

STEP 12.   Determine the harmony or discord of the Expression/Life Path, Expression/Soul Urge and *Expression/Birthday* aspects.

STEP 13.   Express the positive attitudes of the Expression, modified by the *three* aspects in Step 12.

Special delineation: Birthday and Expression of the same number

STEP 14. Express the negative attitudes of the Expression, modified by the *three* aspects in Step 12.

Here, the Expression/Birthday aspect should be weighted about the same as the Expression/Soul Urge aspect.

Special delineation: Birthday and Soul Urge of the same number

If the Birthday and the Soul Urge are the doubled core elements, change the steps of the core synthesis as follows:

STEP 7.   Express the characteristics of the Birthday modified by the Life Path/Birthday aspect and the *Soul Urge/ Birthday* aspect.

STEP 20   Review the harmony or discord of the Life Path/Soul Urge, the Expression/Soul Urge and the *Soul Urge/ Birthday* aspects.

STEP 21.   Express the positive attitudes of the Soul Urge, modified by the *three* aspects in Step 20.

STEP 22.   Express the negative attitudes of the Soul Urge, modified by the *three* aspects in Step 20.

Weight the Soul Urge/Birthday aspect somewhat less than the Soul Urge/Expression aspect.

Special case: master numbers as doubled core elements

If the doubled element is a master number, the delineation would be a combination of the sample delineations in this chapter and in Chapter 8. The negative potentials of 22·22 and 4·4 would dominate a reading where two elements are expressing 22 energy and the negative potential of 11·11 and 2·2 would similarly form a large portion of a reading where two elements are expressing 11 energy. The multiple comparisons described in Chapter 8 would be used.

With 22·22, if the reading is for a person less than twenty years old, the 4 energy—particularly the negative 4 energy—would be the focus of attention. The 22 positive potential would be mentioned as a goal to be achieved, if possible, by the eventual overcoming of the negative 4 and negative 22 potentials.

If the subject is over twenty, the subject's free will determines whether the 4 energy or the 22 energy is uppermost, so both 22 and 4 would be given equal attention in the reading. No matter what the age, the nervous tension associated with 22·22 is likely to be a predominant factor.

An 11·11 reading would be similar, with the 2 energy expressing strongly to about age twenty. The 2 or the 11, dependent on the subject's free will, would express strongly after that. The 11·11 high tension is likely to be a strong character determinant at any age.

If the core has a 22 element and a 4 element, the 22 would, of course, contain 22 and 4 potential and the 4 negative energy (from 4·4) would be prominent. The 22 energy would be covered as in Chapter 8, the 4·4 energy as described in this chapter. There would be *no* 22·22 energy present. With an 11 element and a 2 element, the 11 would be read as in Chapter 8, the 2·2 as in this chapter, and there would be *no* 11·11 energy present.

Doubled core elements occur with more frequency than you might expect. Considerably rarer are the subjects with tripled core elements. The tripled numbers are treated similarly to the doubled but, as you can appreciate, there is usually predominantly negative energy at the beginning of life and very substantial obstacles to be overcome.

I expect that in the lives of public figures with tripled core elements (1) the transformation from negative to positive energy occurs out of public view, or (2) the contributions based on their positive potential are made in spite of the substantial problems of the negative potential. For example:

Special case: tripled core elements

Howard Hughes (Howard Robard Hughes), the eccentric industrialist, was born on December 24, 1905.
He had a 6 Life Path, 6 Expression, 6 Birthday (and a 9 Soul Urge)

John Foster Dulles, the former Secretary of State, was born on February 25, 1888.
He had a 7 Life Path, 7 Soul Urge, 7 Birthday (and a 5 Expression).

And just think of this:

Special case: quadrupled core elements

Gore Vidal, the author, was born on October 3, 1925.
He has a 3 Life Path, 3 Expression, 3 Soul Urge and 3 Birthday!!!

PART III:
CHARACTER
DELINEATION—
THE MODIFIERS

THE RELATION OF
THE MODIFIERS
TO THE CORE

A complete delineation consists of a synthesis of the core with the modifiers. If we think of the core as a tennis ball, and the modifiers as pins stuck into the ball, a delineation would look like this:

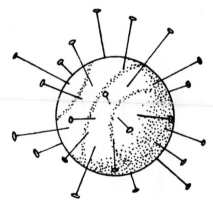

No matter how many pins you stick into the ball, the ball is clearly visible. NO MATTER HOW MANY MODIFIERS ARE ADDED TO THE CORE, THE CORE IS CLEARLY VISIBLE. The modifiers are important; they sharpen the focus, add color and nuance, identify additional potential strengths and potential obstacles. But, it is the *core's* focus which is sharpened; it is the *core* to which color and nuance are supplied; and it is the *core* to which additional potentials are added.

CHAPTER 10

USING THE MODIFIERS

A *MODIFIER* IS ANY ELEMENT USED IN A CHARAC-   Definitions
TER DELINEATION WHICH IS NOT ONE OF THE CORE
ELEMENTS. In each reading, there are usually between ten
and twenty-five modifiers.

A *MODIFIER NUMBER* IS THE NUMBER—1 THROUGH
9, 11 OR 22—CALCULATED FOR A PARTICULAR MODI-
FIER IN A SPECIFIC DELINEATION.

MODIFIER ENERGY (OR MODIFIER POTENTIAL) IS
THE ENERGY (OR POTENTIAL) ASSOCIATED WITH
THE MODIFIER NUMBER—the energy for individuation,
independence and attainment associated with the 1, the energy
devoted to relation and cooperation of the 2, etc.

From our tennis ball and pins analogy we can surmise that   How to
THE MODIFIERS ALWAYS MODIFY THE CORE, never   group the
the other way round. But what does that mean in doing a   energies by
reading?   modifier
Let's look at a core with a 3 Life Path, an 8 Expression, a 5   number
Soul Urge and a 4 Birthday. Connected to this core are eleven
modifiers. The eleven modifier numbers are 1,2,3,4,5,6,7,8,
9,11 and 22. In this simple case, with such diffused modifier
energy, the core will be clearly visible and the modifiers will be
secondary to the core elements.
Suppose, instead, we have the same core with these modifier
numbers: 4,4,4,4,4,4,5,5,5,5,5. We know from Part II that, in
the core, the Life Path has the most energy, the Expression has

somewhat less energy, the Soul Urge has less energy than the Expression and the Birthday has least energy of all. Adding the modifiers *changes the amount of energy* in the core elements, *but doesn't change the relative position* of the elements in regard to energy; the Life Path still has the most energy, the Birthday the least.

In the example under discussion, the core energies by themselves would be divided like this:

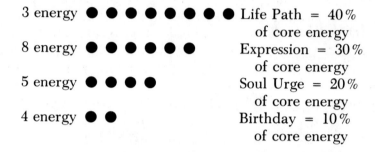

3 energy ● ● ● ● ● ● ● Life Path = 40%
                                          of core energy
8 energy ● ● ● ● ●   Expression = 30%
                                          of core energy
5 energy ● ● ●   Soul Urge = 20%
                                          of core energy
4 energy ● ●   Birthday = 10%
                                          of core energy

The modifier energies would be added with the understanding that the relative standing of the 3,8,5 and 4 energy stays unchanged. With the modifiers added, our diagram would look like this:

3 energy ● ● ● ● ● ● ●
8 energy ● ● ● ● ● ●
5 energy ● ● ● ● ○ ◖   added 5 energy
4 energy ● ● ○ ○ ○   added 4 energy

Even though there are six modifiers with a modifier number of 4, there is still more 5 energy than 4 energy expressed in the total. Even though there are five modifiers with a modifier number of 5 and *no* modifiers with a modifier number of 8, there is still more 8 energy than 5 energy expressed in the total.

In the delineation, the relative position of the core elements is expressed by:

1. How many pages (or how much time) is devoted to each element. In this example, the discussion of the 3 energy might occupy eight paragraphs, while the discussion of the 8 energy would be covered in six paragraphs.
2. The emphasis placed on each element. The paragraphs devoted to the 3 energy might start: "The strongest potential you have is. . . . " while the paragraphs devoted to the 4 energy might begin "In addition to the energies already described, you also have, in a more limited way, . . . "

By expressing the relative position of the core elements in the delineation, the core stays clearly visible and the modifiers are relegated to their significant, *but secondary*, role.

In a typical delineation, all the modifier numbers *don't* correspond with the numbers of the core elements. For instance, with that same core of 3 Life Path, 8 Expression, 5 Soul Urge and 4 Birthday, we might have the following modifiers: 1,1,1, 1,1,4,4,8,8,8,8. The 4 modifier energy would, of course, be added to the 4 Birthday energy and the 8 modifier energy to the 8 Expression energy.

There isn't any 1 energy in the core, but this energy, with its potential for independence and leadership, *is related*, I think you can see, to the 8 energy with potential for business, political or organizational leadership. We could group the energies, with the 1 modifier energy serving as a comfortable addition to the 8 core energy. The 1 modifier energy can then be expressed without limiting the visibility of the core. We would still, of course, preserve the relative positions of the core elements.

Our core-plus-modifier diagram would look like this:

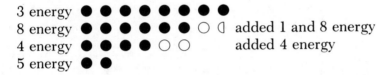

IF A MODIFIER NUMBER IS NOT THE SAME AS THE NUMBER OF A CORE ELEMENT, GROUP THE MODIFIER WITH THE CORE ELEMENT IT MOST CLOSELY RESEMBLES. If there isn't a 1 core element for instance, the 1 modifier number could be comfortably grouped with a core element of 8,4 or 5 energies. The 1 energy closely resembles 8 energy, has many qualities related to 4 energy, and some qualities related to 5 energy. If there was an 8 core element, the 1 modifier would best be related to it. If there wasn't an 8 core element, the 1 modifier could be grouped with a 4 core element. And, if there were neither an 8 nor a 4 core element, the 1 modifier would be grouped with a 5 core element. Let's express these relations in a simple table for easy reference:

Group	modifier with	core elements
1	1,8,4,5	
2	2,11,6	
3	3,6,9	
4	4,1,8	
5	5,3,1	
6	6,2,9,3	
7	7,1	
8	8,1,4,22	
9	9,6,3,2,11	
11	11,2,9,6	
22	22,4,8	

IF THERE ARE MODIFIERS THAT DO NOT CLOSELY
RESEMBLE ANY CORE ELEMENTS, GROUP THESE
MODIFIERS TOGETHER.

Given the same core with its 3 Life Path, 8 Expression, 5 Soul
Urge and 4 Birthday and the following modifiers—1,1,2,4,6,6,
7,8,8,8,11—the energies would be divided like this:

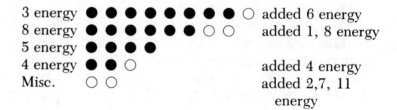

As you can see, the miscellaneous energies, those energies
that don't group with the core energies, form a separate group
with the least relative energy.

In the last example, we had 1,2,3,4,5,6,7,8, and 11 energy.
By grouping, we were dealing with five groups instead of nine
energies. In the reading, the 3 and 6 energies would be
delineated as one group. We're *not* saying that the 6 energy is
only used with the 3 energy. We *are* saying that it's easier to
describe a person's multitudinous characteristics coherently if
the similar 3 and 6 traits are spelled out together and the additional 3 and 6 traits are grouped in the same place. But, in life,
of course, the 6 energy can be used with any (or all) of the other
energies present.

Any energy, of course, may be used with any other energy.
Only the individual can know how he or she combines the different energies. Aside from keeping the core visible in the delineation, THE GROUPING OF ENERGIES ADDS TO THE
COHERENCE OF THE DELINEATION.

**Directing
modifiers**

Up to this point, we've assumed that *all* modifiers add
energy to the core energies. As a matter of fact, most modifiers
do just that. Sometimes, they add positive energy—enlarging
on the constructive possibilities described by the core potential.
Often, the modifiers add negative energy—introducing obstacles or handicaps which tend to block the constructive
potential.

There are a few modifiers which serve a different function.

DIRECTING MODIFIERS *DIRECT* THE ENERGIES DE-SCRIBED BY THE CORE AND OTHER MODIFIERS. In the reading, these directing modifiers (described in Chapters 19 and 20) are grouped together separately from both the core elements and the other modifiers.

In a typical delineation, then, we'll be dealing with four or five different energy groups plus the directing modifier group. A good system of organizing our information will be important to the success of the reading. I've found it helpful to use simple symbols to emphasize the core elements:

Calculation sheet

The Life Path is enclosed with 2 circles ◎

The Expression is enclosed with 1½ circles ◯

The Soul Urge is enclosed with 1 circle ◯

The Birthday is enclosed with ½ circle ∪

Figure 10-1 below is a calculation sheet for our old friend, Harlan William Allen, showing only the core elements we developed in Chapter 7.

Date of calculation ────────────● January 1981
Name by which person is now known ────────────● HAL ALLEN

The Life Path and Birthday calculation — { May 12, 1941
5 + 3 + 6 = 14 = ⑤

The Soul Urge calculation — { $\frac{2}{1 \quad 1}$ + $\frac{(19) \ 1}{9 \quad 91}$ + $\frac{6}{1 \quad 5}$ = ⑨

HARLAN   WILLIAM   ALLEN

The Expression calculation — { $\frac{8\ 1\ 9\ 3\ 1\ 5}{(27)\ 9}$ + $\frac{5\ 9\ 3\ 3\ 9\ 1\ 4}{(34)\ 7}$ + $\frac{1\ 3\ 3\ 5\ 5}{(17)\ 8}$ = 24 = ⑥

Figure 10-1
Calculation Sheet with Core Elements:
Hal Allen

By the time we've completed adding all the modifiers, our calculation sheet will be bulging with data. It'll look like Figure 10-2 on page 114.

January 1981
HAL ALLEN

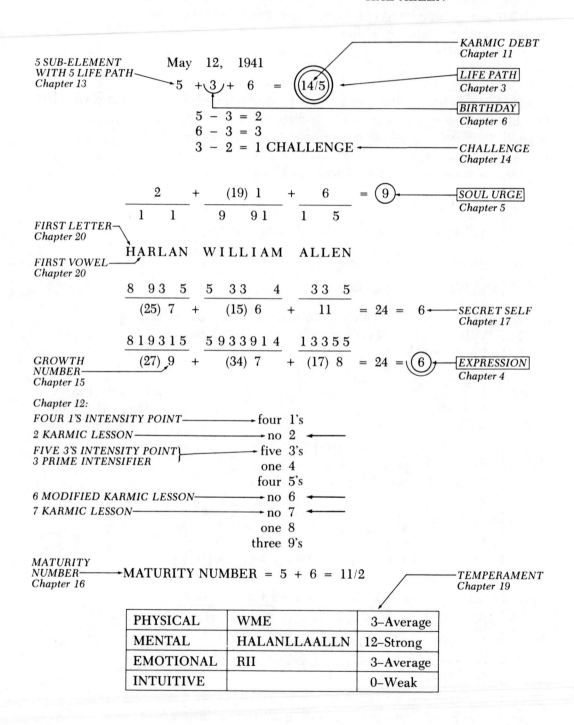

*5 SUB-ELEMENT
WITH 5 LIFE PATH*   May   12,   1941   KARMIC DEBT
Chapter 13   *Chapter 11*
                          5 + 3 + 6   =   (14/5)   LIFE PATH
                                                                              Chapter 3
                          5 − 3 = 2   BIRTHDAY
                          6 − 3 = 3   *Chapter 6*
                          3 − 2 = 1 CHALLENGE   CHALLENGE
                                                                              Chapter 14

                2   +   (19) 1   +   6   = (9)   SOUL URGE
              1   1   9   91   1   5   *Chapter 5*

FIRST LETTER
Chapter 20

FIRST VOWEL   HARLAN   WILLIAM   ALLEN
Chapter 20

              8   93   5   5   33   4   33   5
               (25) 7   +   (15) 6   +   11   = 24 =   6   SECRET SELF
                                                                              Chapter 17

              8 1 9 3 1 5   5 9 3 3 9 1 4   1 3 3 5 5
GROWTH   (27) 9   +   (34) 7   +   (17) 8   = 24 = (6)   EXPRESSION
NUMBER   *Chapter 4*
Chapter 15

Chapter 12:
FOUR 1'S INTENSITY POINT ────────────▶ four 1's
2 KARMIC LESSON ──────────────────▶ no   2 ◀────
FIVE 3'S INTENSITY POINT ─────────▶ five 3's
3 PRIME INTENSIFIER   one   4
                                         four 5's
6 MODIFIED KARMIC LESSON ──────────▶ no   6 ◀────
7 KARMIC LESSON ──────────────────▶ no   7 ◀────
                                         one   8
                                        three 9's

*MATURITY
NUMBER* ────────▶ MATURITY NUMBER = 5 + 6 = 11/2   TEMPERAMENT
Chapter 16   *Chapter 19*

PHYSICAL	WME	3–Average
MENTAL	HALANLLAALLN	12–Strong
EMOTIONAL	RII	3–Average
INTUITIVE		0–Weak

Figure 10-2
Complete Calculation Sheet:
Hal Allen

The organization sheet (Figure 10-3 below) is helpful in clarifying the energy groups.

Column A lists the different energies from 0 through 22. (Yes, there is one modifier, the Challenge, where the 0 sometimes occurs.)

Column C, the center column, is specially outlined. Here, we list all the energy which, depending on the person's will, can be used with positive *or* negative potential. This energy includes all the core elements and some of the modifiers.

Column B, the positive energy column, lists the modifiers with an *excess* of a specific energy, usually indicating a positive potential.

Organization sheet

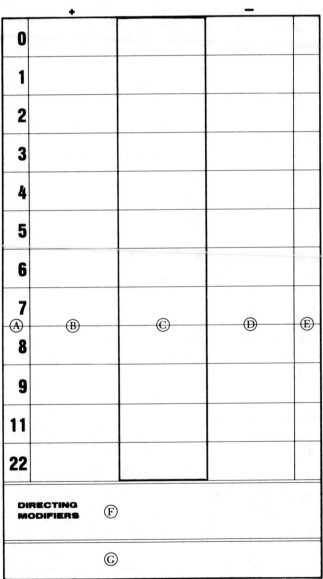

Figure 10-3
Organization Sheet

Column D, the negative energy column, lists the modifiers with a *lack* of a specific energy or an imbalance which produces a negative potential.

Column E lists the energy group with which each energy will be identified for the purposes of the delineation.

Row F lists the directing modifiers.

Row G lists miscellaneous information.

Hal Allen's organization sheet

If we start to fill out the organization sheet with the core elements describing Harlan William Allen (or Hal Allen for short), it will look like Figure 10-4 below.

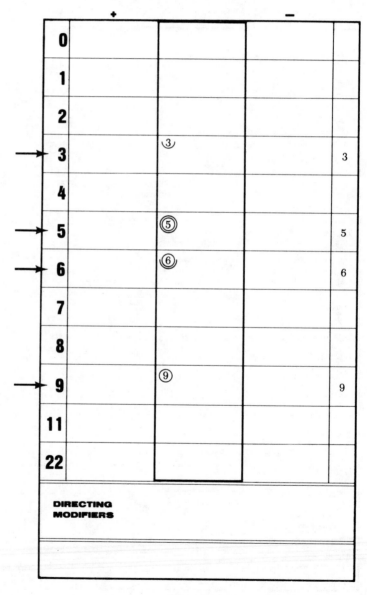

Figure 10-4
Organization Sheet with Core Elements

An arrow in the left-hand column emphasizes the core element energy groups.

In the right-hand column, each core element will, of course, be identified with the energy group with its own element number.

Let's add Hal's modifiers to the organization sheet (Figure 10-5 on page 118). Instead of naming the modifier, let's use a big black dot for each modifier.

In the right-hand column, we see that most of the energy is grouped with the core energy. Only the 7 energy, shown in parentheses, doesn't closely resemble any core energy. For Hal's delineation, the core and modifier energies would appear like this:

5 energy	●●●●●●●○○○○	added 5 and 1 energy
6 energy	●●●●●○○○	added 6 and 2 energy
9 energy	●●●●○○	added 9 and 11 energy
3 energy	●●○○○	added 3 energy
Misc. energy	○	added 7 energy

Just looking at Hal's organization sheet, even with dots substituted for the modifiers, we can begin to see how much data is supplied by the modifiers. Without knowing any more about them, we can start to understand how the modifiers color the core.

> Independence or attainment is likely to be important to Hal (*two 1 modifiers*). He is apt to show strong independent feelings (*positive 1 modifier*) tempered with difficulties with independence (*negative 1 modifier*). He's probably good at expression and is capable of expressing the joy of living (*two positive 3 modifiers*). Hal is likely to be a responsible person (*neutral 6 modifier added to 6 expression*) but may have more responsibility than he expects (*negative 6 modifier*).

Using only the keywords for some of the modifiers, we begin to have a much fuller picture of our fictitious Hal. (Read the above paragraph along with the summary of Hal's core on page 71.) In the next chapters, we'll introduce all the modifiers commonly used, define them, weight them and clarify the special energies they bring. We'll show how to integrate each of the modifiers into a reading. In Chapter 21, we'll add all of Hal's modifiers to his core to produce a complete delineation. By the end of Part III, you'll have all the information for basic character delineation.

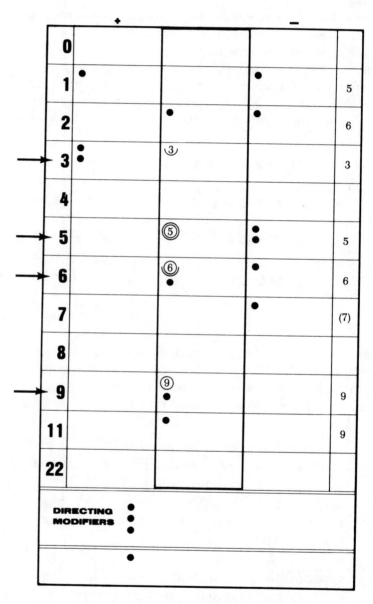

Figure 10-5
Organization Sheet with Black Dots for Modifiers

There's a full-size blank organization sheet (Figure 10-6 on page 119). You may want to make copies and use it in organizing the data for your own delineations.

	+		−	
0				
1				
2				
3				
4				
5				
6				
7				
8				
9				
11				
22				
DIRECTING MODIFIERS				

Figure 10-6
Organization Sheet

CHAPTER 11

SIGNIFICANT DIFFICULTIES: THE KARMIC DEBTS

A KARMIC DEBT IS A SIGNIFICANT DIFFICULTY ENCOUNTERED IN THIS LIFE AS PAYMENT FOR THE MISAPPLICATION OF ENERGIES IN A PAST LIFE. When present, a Karmic Debt is a very important modifier.

Definition

In calculating the Life Path, Expression, Soul Urge and Birthday, the elements are reduced to a single digit or master number. If the number "behind" the single digit is a karmic number, the subject has a Karmic Debt. The karmic numbers are 13, 14, 16 and 19.

Calculation

4 reduced from 13 represents a 4 element with a 13 Karmic Debt.
5 reduced from 14 represents a 5 element with a 14 Karmic Debt.
7 reduced from 16 represents a 7 element with a 16 Karmic Debt.
1 reduced from 19 represents a 1 element with a 19 Karmic Debt.

Look back at Hal Allen's Life Path calculation on page 113. As you can see, he has a 14 Karmic Debt along with the 5 Life Path.

The Karmic Debt occurs in the Birthday for those born on the 13th, 14th, 16th and 19th of any month.

CHART 7: THE KARMIC DEBT on page 306 describes the different Karmic Debts. The upper horizontal division describes the reason for the debt and the *general* characteristics expressed when a core element is a karmic number. The other horizontal

Chart 7: The Karmic Debt

divisions express the *specific* effect on the Life Path, Expression and Soul Urge. The *specific* effect on the Birthday is already included in the description of the Birthday in CHART 5: THE BIRTHDAY.

Commentary

I express the significance of the Karmic Debt by writing the element as 13/4, 14/5, 16/7 or 19/1. The strong characteristics of the Karmic Debt may be one of the forces dominating the life. The Debt, caused by misuse of some of a person's forces in a previous existence, can be paid up in this life only by overcoming the strong negative effects of the very same forces. A Karmic Debt (sometimes called a Testing Number, Warning Number or Hidden Number) weighs a person down with negative potential. He must struggle against his own integral nature to pay the debt and balance the account.

Energies, you recall, can be expressed on a broad continuum stretching from the extreme positive to the extreme negative. Without a Karmic Debt, a person is free to pick the position on the continuum where he chooses to express his energies. With the Debt, he is forced to *start* at the negative extreme. If he is willing to understand the Debt, accept the burden and exert the effort, he can move to a more positive expression of the energy. In that sense, the Karmic Debt might be thought of as a symbol of reconstruction or regeneration.

The Debt is usually apparent to the individual, although he will often feel victimized by fate rather than responsible for the special experiences he has to face. If the delineation establishes the Debt as an energy which *can* be transformed by effort and awareness, the reading will serve an important end.

With a Karmic Debt present, there is no way to determine *if* or *when* the individual will learn to overcome the substantial obstacles to his progress. Few people prevail over the impediments by young adulthood. Many people (possibly most people) are still struggling with the negative emphasis of the Karmic Debt up to the age of forty. Until the handicaps are controlled, it's difficult to reach anywhere near the full positive potential. With a Debt present, the positive potential can be thought of as a goal to be reached when the blockages are gone.

Ted, for instance, with a 19/1 Expression, is likely to be so concerned with his own needs or so dependent on others that he will have difficulty approaching his executive and administrative capabilities for achievement and financial reward. Only when the negative 19/1 is understood and overcome can the positive 1 potential develop.

The effect of the Karmic Debt is very strong when the Life

Path or Expression is involved, less powerful with the Soul Urge, and weaker still with the Birthday.

Many people, when given a reading, tend to concentrate on the negative aspects of the delineation. The Karmic Debt is probably the most negative information you are transmitting and must be handled with extreme sensitivity. Don't gloss over the Karmic Debt because it is difficult to express positively. Rather, work on your delineation technique so that your description of the Debt will contribute to an accurate portrayal of the individual's basic structure and be helpful to him in understanding his impediments and learning to overcome them.

Here's an example of the portion of a delineation expressing the Karmic Debt of Pierce, age 30, who has a 13/4 Expression. You'll see how the delineation expresses the Debt's powerful influence. There are five steps involved:

Sample portion of a delineation

STEP A

An explanation that the positive potential can be fully developed only when the obstacles are overcome.

> The configuration of your chart indicates that, while you have some strong positive potential which can be developed, you started out in life with some blockages which must be overcome before you can make the most of the positive energy. I can't tell whether you've already overcome the obstacles—some people manage early in life, others spend a good number of years struggling with the impediments.

STEP B

A description of the general effect of the Karmic Debt.

From CHART 7: THE KARMIC DEBT, *13/4 general description in the top row.*

> You can't move ahead constructively unless you've overcome your obstinacy and dogmatism. You may feel limited and restricted, but if you rationalize your situation, it's difficult to change to a more productive path. You must learn to accept the responsibility for the predicaments in which you find yourself.

In order to approach your positive potential, you must learn to work hard, often far harder than your share a good part of the time. You must apply yourself to the work at hand, be aware of the larger picture while still completing all the details. You have to learn to accept the stringent limitations produced by the inordinate work load. If you choose to be lazy, indifferent, negative, or involved with trivia, the problems are likely to be magnified.

STEP C

A description of the specific effect of the Debt on the involved core element. This step is omitted for the Birthday since the specific effect is already included in the Birthday characteristics.

From CHART 7: THE KARMIC DEBT. *13/4 Expression description in the third row.*

You tend to use your abilities doggedly in a rigid, one-track direction. The intensity of your drive may work to your advantage but the effect of this drive is likely to be negated unless you widen your vision.

STEP D

A description of the negative characteristics of the core element. In a typical delineation, the negative traits are expressed as pitfalls to be avoided. With a Karmic Debt present, the negative characteristics are the probable traits expressed until such time as the handicaps are overridden. Be sure to include approaches to alleviate the expressed difficulties.

From CHART 3: THE EXPRESSION. *The description of the negative characteristics of the 4 Expression are in the bottom row.*

You're likely to be frustrated by your feelings of limitation or restriction, though often of your own making or existing only in your imagination. You have to learn to see what limitations you yourself are bringing to a situation.

Your fixed approach works against you. You must learn to be more adaptable and flexible.

You're likely to have strong likes and dislikes. Until they're moderated, they'll be stumbling blocks.

> Your tendency to be bossy, dominant and excessively disciplinarian will probably irritate others. You have to learn to get on better with family and friends or be prepared for much struggle.
>
> You tend to concentrate on the details to the exclusion of the big picture. Unless you can see the forest instead of the trees, you're working against your best interests.

STEP E

If the subject accepts reincarnation, you may want to conclude by specifically mentioning the Karmic Debt.

From CHART 7: THE KARMIC DEBT. *13/4 general description in top row.*

> Your requirement of hard work and your tendency to rigidity are payments to balance a karmic debt developed from a lack of application to work in a previous life.

There's some repetition here, just like there was in the core synthesis. Don't worry about it. We're learning some basic principles. In Part IV, Volume 2, we'll polish up the delineation and dispense with the repetition.

The energies should be delineated so that the subject can help his development by (a) accepting certain consequences of the energy as a part of his life, and (b) learning to transform negative into positive potential.

You'll find that about half of your subjects will have a Karmic Debt. Ten percent or so of my readings have involved people with two Karmic Debts. There are even a few people with more than two, but they are rare.

If there's more than one Debt, it is handled in the same manner except that more than one element is modified. If there's a multiple Debt involving the same number (as with a 19/1 Expression and a 19/1 Soul Urge), the effect of the Karmic Debt permeates the core along with the negative vibrations of the doubled number. Make sure to express this difficult combination so that the forces can be used constructively.

The significance of the number of Karmic Debts

An example   There's no question that a person's life shows the significant effect of a Karmic Debt. It is clear, though, that a knowledge and acceptance of a Debt will add to the subject's constructive development.

Catherine, for example, is a woman in her late twenties with a 16/7 Life Path and a 16/7 Expression. SEVENTY PERCENT OF HER CORE ENERGY IS (a) KARMIC AS WELL AS (b) A REPEATED NUMBER. Her life, as she described it to me, had been a succession of broken romances and continued job changes. Much of her energy had been spent in efforts to maintain a long relation or a job she liked, but her efforts had proved in vain. A year before her reading, she had recognized that she was not fated to have an ongoing romance or a continuing position. Acceptance of this transient state of affairs had considerably improved her life. The impermanence continued, but now she enjoyed her pleasures when they occurred rather than being caught up in her fear of their loss. When I explained the nature of her Karmic Debt, she was pleased that she had already, on her own, understood the situation. My explanation served as a reminder of her basic structure and a reinforcement to her positive attitude.

Catherine, like anyone with a Karmic Debt to repay, found her life substantially affected, but she had used her own efforts, as anyone can if they so desire, to exchange the negativity for a growing life.

Hilde Agatha Parsons (page 93 in Chapter 9) has a 7 Life Path and a 7 Expression. You may want to compare the effects of the 7·7 energy in her reading with the effects noted here with Catherine's 16/7·16/7.

Hal Allen's organization sheet   At the end of each chapter dealing with modifiers, we'll examine the effect of each modifier on Hal Allen, our fictitious subject from Chapter 7. In Chapter 21, we'll combine all of Hal's modifiers with his core synthesis to produce a complete (if still too wordy) character delineation.

Hal has a 14/5 Karmic Debt associated with his Life Path, as mentioned at the beginning of the chapter. His Karmic Debt is placed in the 5 modifier row on the organization sheet—in the negative energy column (Figure 11-1 on page 127).

Hal Allen's delineation   In Hal Allen's complete delineation in Chapter 21, the 14/5 Karmic Debt strongly modifies the description of Hal's 5 Life Path.

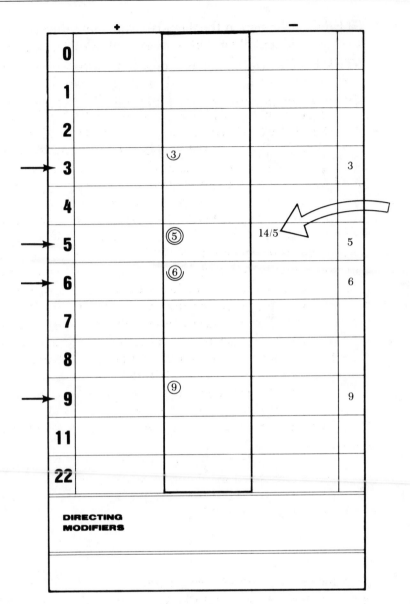

Figure 11-1
Organization Sheet with Karmic Debt added

Step 6, page 200, expresses the characteristics of the 5 Life Path. Here, the Karmic Debt adds:

STEP A. An explanation that the positive potential can be fully developed only when the obstacles are overcome. Some of the characteristics are revised because of the presence of the Debt.

Step 8, page 203, discusses the negative expression of the 5 Life Path. Here, the Karmic Debt adds:

STEP B. Changes in the negative expression due to the general effect of the Karmic Debt.

STEP C. Changes in the negative expression due to the specific effect of the Debt on the Life Path.

STEP D. Description of the negative characteristics as probable traits expressed until handicaps are overridden.

STEP E. Mention of the Karmic Debt in relation to reincarnation.

CHAPTER 12

STRONG POSITIVE AND NEGATIVE CHARACTERISTICS: THE INTENSITY TABLE
THE KARMIC LESSONS
THE INTENSITY POINTS
THE PRIME INTENSIFIER

THE INTENSITY TABLE IS A TABLE DERIVED FROM THE LETTERS IN THE NAME. IT INDICATES CHARACTERISTICS, IN ADDITION TO THE CORE CHARACTERISTICS, WHICH ARE OF ABOVE AVERAGE OR BELOW AVERAGE INTENSITY.

Definitions and calculations

When calculating the Expression, the number value of each letter is written below the letter. The Intensity Table (sometimes called the Inclusion Table) simply sums up how many 1's, 2's, 3's, etc. are present in the name.

We'll use Paul McCartney's birthname as an example:

```
JAMES    PAUL    M c CARTNEY
11451    7133    4 33192557
```

Total the quantity of each number and you have his Intensity Table:

five	1's		no	6 ⟵———
one	2		two	7's
four	3's		no	8 ⟵———
two	4's		one	9
three	5's			

For McCartney, the lack of 6 and 8 is emphasized by arrows placed to the right of the table.

When a number is lacking, that lack indicates the presence of a Karmic Lesson. A KARMIC LESSON IS A MODIFIER INDICATING POTENTIAL WEAKNESSES, DIFFICULTIES OR OBSTACLES BECAUSE THE MODIFIER ENERGY HAS NOT BEEN EXPERIENCED IN PAST LIVES. A Karmic Lesson is much less insistent than a Karmic Debt, but is still an important modifier.

In an average Intensity Table, the numbers would appear in these quantities:

Average Quantity	Number
three	1
one	2
one, two	3
one	4
three, four, five	5
one, two	6
zero, one	7
one	8
three	9

Whenever the quantity of a number exceeds or falls below the average, an Intensity Point is established. AN INTENSITY POINT IS A MODIFIER INDICATING CHARACTERISTICS OF ABOVE AVERAGE OR BELOW AVERAGE INTENSITY. It's an important modifier.

Comparing McCartney's table to the average table, McCartney has the following Intensity Points (Modifier numbers which have been established as Karmic Lessons are not duplicated as Intensity Points):

five	1's	exceed the average
four	3's	exceed the average
two	4's	exceed the average
two	7's	exceed the average
one	9	falls below the average

THE PRIME INTENSIFIER, THE INTENSITY POINT APPEARING IN THE LARGEST QUANTITY, INDICATES STRONG AND OBVIOUS CHARACTERISTICS. It's an important modifier.

There's an exception to be noted here. The 5 often appears in great profusion in the Intensity Table—remember that even five 5's is just an average quantity. Use the 5 as a Prime Intensifier only if (a) there are more 5's than any other number, *and* (b) there are six or more 5's.

In Paul McCartney's Intensity Table, there are only three 5's. There are five 1's, and the 1 is his Prime Intensifier.

In many charts, two or more numbers appear in the greatest quantity. If two numbers appear in greatest quantity, there are two Prime Intensifiers. (Again, the 5 would be a Prime Intensifier here only if there were six or more 5's.) If more than two numbers appear in greatest quantity, the energy is too diffused and there is *no* Prime Intensifier.

The Intensity Table often yields many modifiers. In Paul McCartney's example, we find eight modifiers:

> Karmic Lessons—6, 8
> Intensity Points—five 1's, four 3's, two 4's,
>   two 7's, one 9
> Prime Intensifier—1

Chart 8: The Intensity Table

CHART 8: THE INTENSITY TABLE on page 312 describes the modifiers derived from the Intensity Table. The average quantity of 1's, 2's, etc. is shown in the third row. Above the average, in the second row, are descriptions of Intensity Points where the quantity exceeds the average. As you can see, there are usually two descriptions for each modifier number. One description, somewhat above average quantity, usually indicates strong positive traits associated with the particular modifier energy, along with some negative characteristics requiring work. The second description, with an even greater than average quantity, indicates the very strong positive traits along with very strong negative traits brought about by the excess of modifier energy.

The top row describes the characteristics of the Prime Intensifier. The traits have already been noted in the row below, but the Prime Intensifier indicates that these particular qualities are likely to form a very strong and obvious part of the personality.

Just as the rows above the average quantity describe an excess of modifier energy, the rows below describe a lack of energy. In the fourth row, are descriptions of the Intensity Points where the quantity is less than average.

These Intensity Points always describe weaknesses or difficulties.

The bottom two rows discuss the Karmic Lessons. If there is a lack of a number in a name and that number *is not* one of the core elements, the description of the Karmic Lesson will be found in the bottom row. If there is a lack of a number in a name and that number *is* one of the core elements, this Modified Karmic Lesson is described in the second row from the bottom. Both a Karmic Lesson and a Modified Karmic Lesson indicate a significant coloration of the core, but the intensity of the lesson is somewhat mitigated with the Modified Karmic Lesson because of the energy available in the core.

Commentary: Intensity Points

If there's an average quantity of a number, the traits connected with that number are balanced, at least from the point of view of the Intensity Table. You'll find many names where the quantity is never far from the average. In this common case, there is a relatively subtle emphasis on the characteristics described by the Intensity Points. The more significant traits are the ones where the quantity of the number *diverges sharply* from the average.

An over-excess of 5, 7, or 8 will tend to give added impetus primarily to the positive traits associated with the modifier energies. Too many 3's or 4's will produce stress on both positive and negative traits. But too many 1's, 2's, 6's or 9's will overemphasize the negative side of the energies.

Imagine a person with six 3's, far more than the average one or two. It's true that there may be strong artistic talents expressed, but there may also be a tendency to be self-centered and selfish, scattering energies or acting in an immoderate manner (from the 3 page, second row, of Chart 8). If the core already indicates a potential for self-centeredness with strong 1, 4 or 8 energy, this Intensity Point will add to the stress on this characteristic. If, on the other hand, the core, with strong 2, 6, or 9 energy, indicates a giving, loving person, we would expect the addition of the six 3's to describe a giving, loving person who is, at times, unexpectedly selfish or extravagant.

The strength of the divergence is also significant when there's a smaller quantity than average. 5 is usually present in a larger quantity than other numbers. 9 is often found in above average quantity. And 1 is generally present in average or slightly below average quantity (two or three). When 1, 5 or 9 is present in less than average quantity, a significant disbalance is being described. If there's only one 1 or one 5 or one 9, the delineation will be strongly affected.

The average quantity is *not* proportional to the number of letters in the name. Six 3's or seven 1's are just as significant in a very long as in a very short name. If we find

one 1 or five or more 1's
four or more 2's
four or more 3's

four or more 4's
one 5 or seven or more 5's
four or more 6's
three or more 7's
three or more 8's
one 9 or five or more 9's

we can be sure that those Intensity Points will sharply alter the core description.

Commentary: Prime Intensifier

The significance of the Prime Intensifier is similarly related to the divergence from the average. If the Prime Intensifier is, for example, four 1's (one above average), the person will find it important to follow his own bent and make sure his needs are met (from the 1 page, top row, of Chart 8), but the emphasis on this characteristic is not likely to be particularly intense. But, suppose the person has *seven* 1's. You can be sure that *this* person will work long and hard at meeting his personal needs. If the core indicates the possibility of strong, self-centered energies (1,4, or 8 stressed), you can be sure that the person will appear as a dominating, even bullying sort. If, on the other hand, the core describes a more giving person (2,6 or 9 emphasized), the individual is likely to have less personal needs, but will, nevertheless, be sure to get *those* needs met. There's likely to be a core of iron that becomes most obvious at times when those limited needs are not being satisfied. If there's a conflict of core energies—such as 6 energy toward responsibility conflicting with 5 energy toward freedom—the person's discontent and frustration at meeting his confusing needs will be most apparent.

Commentary: Karmic Lessons

The Karmic Lesson represents energy to which a person has not been exposed in previous lifetimes. Whether the potential was purposely avoided or whether circumstances prevented the particular potential from surfacing is not clear, but the lack of exposure to the energy will make a strong mark on the subject in this lifetime.

Presence of a Karmic Lesson indicates the presence of certain types of situations and the necessity to use specific energies to deal with these situations. If there's a Karmic Lesson, there is no question that the situations will play an important part in the life. But the determination of whether the subject has the required energies or must develop them poses a more difficult question. Examination of the core and the other modifiers, often, *but not always*, provides some clues.

For example, Irene with a 4 Karmic Lesson is likely to face situations where an awareness of practicality, organization, hard work and concern with detail is required. (See the 4 page, bottom row, of Chart 8.) You can be sure that Irene is often going to be involved in experiences where she must work slowly, surely, consistently; must start at the foundation and build with care, with concern for the details and patience to see the experiences through to completion.

If Irene's core and other modifiers primarily emphasize freedom and versatility, she will start out in life feeling restricted by situations demanding patient and careful attention to detail. The experiences will require energies which she is unable to give and her development will be impeded as she struggles to develop the requisite energies. When Irene has learned her lesson and developed the required energies, the same or similar situations are still likely to be important in her life. Her learned ability to handle the situations, however, will not make them appear as obstacles. Rather, these experiences will now further her ability to grow and develop.

If Irene has a 4 Karmic Lesson, and the core and modifiers indicate additional energies devoted to care, patience, hard work as well as approximately equal energies devoted to freedom and versatility, it isn't possible to state whether the lesson poses an obstacle or not. You can only indicate the presence of the related situations, but you can't determine whether Irene will use the energies to advantage.

If Irene has a 4 Karmic Lesson, but also has core and modifier energies emphasizing care, patience and hard work, she will be born with the ability to handle the situations that will develop in that area, and her development will not be impeded.

Commentary: Modified Karmic Lessons

When the number of the Karmic Lesson also appears as a core element, we have a Modified Karmic Lesson. The experiences related to the Karmic Lesson will be present, but there will also be strong core energy available to deal with the experiences. The presence of a Modified Karmic Lesson with positive core potential indicates the innate ability to handle the situations which arise. Only if the core energy is expressing negatively (because of master numbers, doubled elements or Karmic Debts) will the situations prove an obstacle.

Organization sheet

The modifiers derived from the Intensity Table appear as follows on the organization sheet (Figure 12-1):

The Karmic Lesson(s) appear in the negative potential column.

The Modified Karmic Lesson(s) appear in the negative potential column.

The above-average Intensity Point(s) appear in the positive potential column.

The below-average Intensity Point(s) appear in the negative potential column.

The Prime Intensifier(s) appear in the positive potential column.

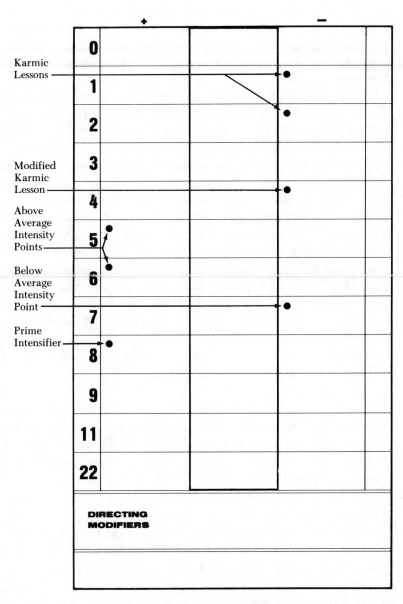

Figure 12-1
*Organization Sheet with Intensity Table Modifiers shown
as Black Dots*

Expressing the Intensity Table modifiers in delineation

The modifiers discussed in this chapter are important, but they rarely stand out in a reading. Usually, the effect of these modifiers is blended with the effect of other modifiers to subtly color the basic picture presented by the core. There are two common instances where the effect of the modifiers *is* strongly expressed:

a. When the Karmic Lesson indicates a situation which is distinctly conflicted with the other energies in the chart.
b. When an above average Intensity Point diverges greatly from the average.

Special cases

Occasionally, you'll meet an individual with *no* Karmic Lessons. This "old soul" has been reincarnated many times and has been exposed to all the lessons often enough to have some awareness of all of them. Don't expect this person to have little difficulty in life. Rather, expect that this person, particularly on reaching maturity, is likely to present a well-balanced personality and a depth of understanding.

Note this lack of Karmic Lessons at the bottom of the organization sheet (Figure 12-2 on page 137). Be sure to emphasize this extremely positive characteristic in the delineation.

The old souls are rare—probably some five percent of the populace. Most people have one or two Karmic Lessons. Three Karmic Lessons aren't even that far out of the ordinary. But if you find a subject with *four or more* Karmic Lessons, you are dealing with an individual who has not been exposed to about half of the energies that are available. A significant part of this individual's life will be used in coming to grips with these myriad lessons. Even if the person has some strong positive core or modifier energies which help with some of the lessons, he is still likely to feel considerably blocked.

When there are four or more Karmic Lessons, note this at the bottom of the organization sheet (Figure 12-3 on page 138) and express the resultant negative coloration in as constructive a manner as possible.

Only rarely will you find a 1, 5 or 9 Karmic Lesson. The energies denoted by the 1, 5 or 9 are quite common, and the lack of that energy provides a very significant coloration—just a little weaker than a Karmic Debt. The subject with this lack has an obstacle to overcome that is likely to be one of the important parameters in the character development.

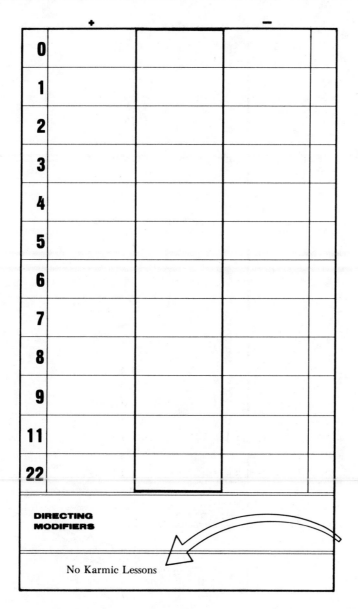

Figure 12-2
Organization Sheet with No Karmic Lessons

Almost as rare as old souls are individuals who have at least **Rarity** one 7 in their name. Perhaps ten percent of people will *not* **of the 7** have a 7 Karmic Lesson, indicating that this ten percent is more spiritually evolved than those lacking the 7. In our material- istic society, the qualities missing because of the lack of the 7 tend to be thought of as of little consequence, certainly of less consequence than the lack of any other number. If there is a 7 Karmic Lesson and no 7 core element or other 7 modifier, you may want to ignore the 7 Karmic Lesson altogether in the delineation. That isn't true of any other number.

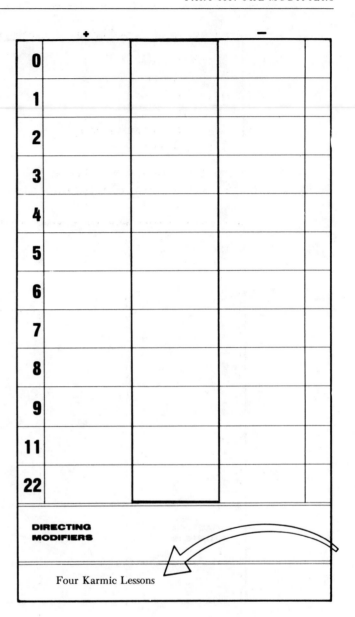

Figure 12-3
Organization Sheet with Four Karmic Lessons

Hal Allen's calculation   We'll calculate the Intensity Table for Hal Allen:

H A R L A N   W I L L I A M   A L L E N
8 1 9 3 1 5   5 9 3 3 9 1 4   1 3 3 5 5

four	1's		
no	2 ←	no	6 ←
five	3's	no	7 ←
one	4	one	8
four	5's	three	9's

From the Intensity Table, we find six modifiers:

Hal Allen's organization sheet and delineation

four 1's Intensity Point
    2 Karmic Lesson
five 3's Intensity Point
    3 Prime Intensifier
    6 Modified Karmic Lesson
    7 Karmic Lesson

For Hal, the organization sheet (Figure 12-4) suddenly is bulging with data. I don't think of Hal's Intensity Table as par-

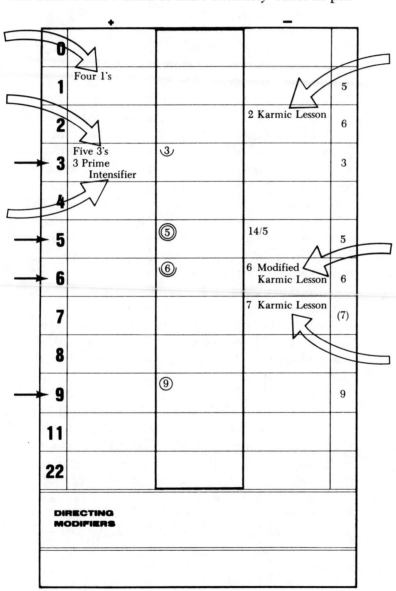

Figure 12-4
Organization Sheet with Intensity Table Modifiers

ticularly disbalanced, but there are enough divergences from the average to add a substantial number of modifiers. In many delineations, a better balanced Intensity Table might add only two or three modifiers rather than the six added here.

Hal's added modifiers are not of equal importance. Let's discuss the added modifier energies in relation to the related core energies shown in the right-hand column. (This column, you'll remember, lists the energy group with which each energy is identified for the purposes of this delineation, as determined by the table on page 111.)

With the 5 Life Path energy, we include the delineation of the 1 Intensity Point. Four 1's is only one above average, but this is one of the cases where the above-average energy has a strong *negative* cast. Since the Life Path energy is the most potent energy, we are adding an important coloration. The Life Path energy, devoted to learning freedom and expressing versatility (Chart 2, 5 Life Path) has already been strongly colored by difficulties in learning to use freedom constructively (Chart 7, 14/5 Karmic Debt) and now it is qualified by the tendency to act in a self-centered and dominating way (Chart 8, four 1's Intensity Point). The fun that often is associated with a 5 Life Path seems quite different now that some colorations are added. Hal can overcome the obstacles and go on to the ultimate delight of using the positive potential of the 5 energy, but, unless he has some offsetting energies (which, as we proceed with the modifiers, we'll find he doesn't), he probably has a way to go to overcome the problem areas. (See Step 8, page 203 of Hal's delineation.)

With the 6 Expression energy, we include the delineation of the 2 Karmic Lesson and the 6 Modified Karmic Lesson. We are adding two Karmic Lessons to the second most potent energy—obviously an important added coloration. Because of his 6 Expression, Hal tends to be responsible, helpful, loving and generous (Chart 8, 6 Expression). We can now expect that he will be called on to carry a far heavier share of responsibility than average (Chart 8, 6 Modified Karmic Lesson), but he can certainly accomplish this with the 6 Expression energy. In addition, Hal is likely to find himself in situations where sensitivity, consideration for others, and awareness of detail are required (Chart 8, 2 Karmic Lesson). With both 6 and 9 core energies, I would expect Hal to be capable of handling these types of situations. (See Step 13, page 208, for the description of both lessons.)

(The Life Path modifiers have added a strong negative cast to the Life Path energy, but the Expression modifiers have only indicated that Hal will get many opportunities to use the abilities he undoubtedly possesses. You might want to contemplate the divergence of the Life Path energy and the Expression energy. How is Hal going to handle that?)

With the 9 Soul Urge energy, we have, as yet, no modifiers. We cannot add any coloration to the core description.

With the 3 Birthday energy, we include the delineation of the five 3's Intensity Point and the 3 Prime Intensifier. The 3 Birthday energy is the least potent of the core energies, but five 3's represent a major divergence from the average of one or two. These modifiers, at first glance, seem to represent an important coloration of only a small part of Hal's total energy.

Let's look at that more closely. From Chart 5, 12 Birthday, we know that Hal is sensitive and emotional with creative ability. These same potentials are displayed in the 6 Expression energy as well as the 9 Soul Urge energy. Three of the four core elements verify Harlan's creative potential. This potential is not a *small* part of his total energy, but rather an *extremely significant* portion of that energy.

Now, add the data from the modifiers. We see strong artistic talent, excellent imagination, strong capability with words (Chart 8, five 3's Intensity Point) and these qualities are likely to be most obvious (Chart 8, Prime Intensifier 3). The major divergence from average of the Intensity Point produces an *important* coloration of some of Hal's *major* potential. (See Step 3, page 199 for the effect of the two 3 modifiers. Note how strongly the characteristics are emphasized.)

The 7 Karmic Lesson does not group with any of the core energies and would be treated as a miscellaneous energy. (Because it's a miscellaneous energy in this delineation, the 7 in the right-hand column of the organization sheet is shown in parentheses). With our current data (and even when we've looked at all the modifiers) this 7 Karmic Lesson is the only expression of 7 energy. Since the 7 Karmic Lesson need be discussed only when other 7 energy is available, we can ignore it in this delineation.

CHAPTER 13

BEGINNING OBSTACLES: THE SUB-ELEMENTS OF THE CORE

If a person was born on March 13, 1952, the Life Path calculation would, of course, look like this:

Definition

$$\text{March} \quad 13, \quad 1952$$
$$3 \quad + 4 + \quad 8 \quad = 15 = \boxed{6}$$

The 6 Life Path is the core element.

THE 3, 4, AND 8 ARE SUB-ELEMENTS. The sub-elements sometimes introduce an important modifier.

Let's study a fictitious individual born on

Example

$$\text{July} \quad 4, \quad 1950$$
$$7 + 4 + \quad 6 \quad = 17 = \boxed{8}$$

with the name of:

$$\frac{1}{1} \quad + \quad \frac{7}{1\ 6} \quad + \quad \frac{(20)\ 2}{9\quad 6\quad 5} \quad = 10 = \boxed{1}$$

CARL   HAROLD   CHRISTOPHER

$$\frac{3\,1\,9\,3}{(16)\ 7} + \frac{8\,1\,9\,6\,3\,4}{(31)\ 4} + \frac{3\,8\,9\,9\,1\,2\,6\,7\,8\,5\,9}{(67)\ (13)\ 4} = 15 = \boxed{6}$$

Carl's chart was constructed to illustrate two groupings of sub-elements forming two important modifiers.

Sub-element and core element with same number

IF A SUB-ELEMENT IS THE SAME NUMBER AS THE CORE ELEMENT, THE SUBJECT WILL PROBABLY *START OUT IN LIFE* EXPRESSING ONE (OR BOTH) NEGATIVE EXTREMES OF THE POTENTIAL INSTEAD OF THE POSITIVE POTENTIAL:

1. USING THE ENERGY SO EXCLUSIVELY THAT IT BECOMES PART OF A DISBALANCED APPROACH. POSITIVE POTENTIAL *MAY* BE EXPRESSED AT THE SAME TIME.

2. ALMOST COMPLETELY IGNORING THE POTENTIAL.

This is, of course, similar to the doubled core elements we discussed in Chapter 9. But consider this:

> If the Birthday (ten percent) and the Soul Urge (twenty percent) have the same number, thirty percent of the core energy is doubled.

> If the Life Path (forty percent) and the Expression (thirty percent) have the same number, seventy percent of the core energy is doubled.

With a doubled core element, thirty to seventy percent of the core energy is affected.

Here we're dealing with only *one* element, so the effect tends to be less potent.

> If the Soul Urge is involved, twenty percent of the core energy is doubled.

> If the Expression is involved, thirty percent of the core energy is doubled.

> If the Life Path is involved, forty percent of the core energy is doubled.

> (The Birthday isn't included here since it has no sub-elements.)

With an element and a sub-element doubled, twenty to forty percent of the core energy is affected. Although this is usually less than the doubled core element, you can see that, at times, it may be extremely significant.

In Chapter 9, dealing with doubled core elements, two elements were involved and a substantial part of the delineation was revised to show the negative impact. Here, we're dealing with only one element and less potent energy. Revise the portion of the delineation dealing with that element *alone*.

In Carl's chart at the beginning of the chapter, there is a 1 sub-element along with the 1 Soul Urge. Carl will probably start out in life expressing one (or both) negative extremes of the 1·1 energy.

From CHART 6: THE ASPECTS, we find that 1·1 is usually very discordant, with:

> Overemphasis on self and own needs. Little concern for others
>
> or
>
> Timid, afraid to stand on own two feet. Afraid of standing up for self.

In Carl's example, the negative 1·1 energy affects the description of the various parts of the Soul Urge *alone:*

> Step 15. Motives of the Soul Urge.
> Step 21. Positive attitudes of the Soul Urge.
> Step 22. Negative attitudes of the Soul Urge.

The description in each of these steps will be modified by the 1·1 description from Chart 6. The delineation would indicate that the positive potential can be well-expressed only when the obstacles—the negative potential— have been overcome. Like the repeated core elements, progress on the obstacles is usually significant between ages twenty and forty. If, as in this case, Carl is in his thirties, the delineation would be written assuming he's made some progress against the obstacles. If Carl was under twenty, the delineation would be written assuming that he's in the middle of the struggle to overcome these obstacles.

By using the 1·1 only as a modifier of the *specifically affected element* (and *not* when the element is in aspect with another element), the modifier effect is delineated in proper proportion to its effect on the individual's potential.

The delineation is similar if two, three (or four) sub-elements have the same number as the core element.

IF TWO SUB-ELEMENTS HAVE THE SAME NUMBER, THE SUBJECT WILL PROBABLY *START OUT IN LIFE* EXPRESSING ONE (OR BOTH) NEGATIVE EXTREMES OF THE POTENTIAL:

Two sub-elements with same number

1. USING THE ENERGY SO EXCLUSIVELY THAT IT BECOMES PART OF A DISBALANCED APPROACH.

2. ALMOST COMPLETELY IGNORING THE POTENTIAL.

This grouping is considerably less potent than the first one. Again, progress is usually made on the impediments between ages twenty and forty.

In the delineation, the negative extremes would be described by the doubled number aspect (CHART 6: THE ASPECTS). (For the purposes of this modifier, the Birthday is considered a sub-element of the Life Path.)

In Carl's example, there are two 4 sub-elements as part of his 6 Expression. The delineation of this 4·4 modifier might read as follows:

> You probably started out in life feeling limited or tied down, although the restrictions you felt may have been of your own making or have sprung from your imagination. The limitations are likely to have been aggravated by your rigid attitudes, your stubbornness, your obsession with system and order or your concentration on details to the exclusion of the larger picture (*4·4 aspect from* CHART 6: THE ASPECTS).
>
> You may, at that time in your life, also have run into problems because of your tendency, at times, to be disorganized and irresponsible (*4·4 aspect from* CHART 6: THE ASPECTS).
>
> I suspect that, now that you're over thirty, you may have changed at least some of this early behavior so that the limitations you once felt are apt to be considerably reduced.

The delineation is similar if three (or four) sub-elements have the same number.

Hal Allen's organization sheet and delineation

What about Hal Allen?

May 12, 1941
 5   3   6   = (14/5)

——2—— + ——(19) 1—— + ——6—— = (9)
 1   1   9   9 1   1   5

HARLAN   WILLIAM   ALLEN
8 1 9 3 1 5   5 9 1 1 9 1 4   1 3 3 5 5
——(27) 9—— + ——(34) 7—— + ——(17) 8—— = 24 = (6)

Hal has a 5 sub-element behind his 5 Life Path. It's shown in the negative energy column on his organization sheet (Figure

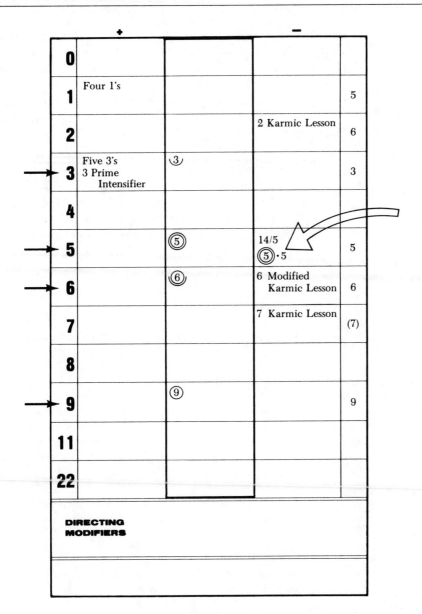

Figure 13-1
Organization Sheet with Doubled Elements·Sub-Elements

13-1 above). The description of the 5·5 negative potential reiterates, to an extent, some of the traits associated with his 14/5 Karmic Debt. Since the Karmic Debt has already been so strongly expressed in the delineation, there's no reason to repeat the material.

CHAPTER 14

ANOTHER
BEGINNING OBSTACLE:
THE CHALLENGE

THE CHALLENGE IS AN OBSTACLE ENCOUNTERED IN THE EARLY YEARS OF LIFE, AT LEAST, DUE TO THE EMPHASIS PLACED ON THE NEGATIVE EXTREME OF THE POTENTIAL. The Challenge is an important modifier.

Definition

The calculation of the Challenge is the only modifier calculation involving subtraction. Always, of course, subtract the smaller number from the larger. Before subtracting, reduce a master number to a single digit.
For example:

Calculation

April	16,	1958
4	7	5

$7 - 4 = 3$ Subtract the month digit and the day digit.

$7 - 5 = 2$ Subtract the day digit and the year digit.

$3 - 2 = 1$ Challenge   Subtract the two remaining numbers to determine the Challenge.

November	22,	1975
11	22	22
2	4	4

Reduce the master numbers to single digits.

$$4 - 2 = 2$$

Subtract the month digit and the day digit.

$$4 - 4 = 0$$

Subtract the day digit and the year digit.

$$2 - 0 = 2 \text{ Challenge}$$

Subtract the two remaining numbers to determine the Challenge.

Chart 9: The Challenge/ The Growth Number

The Challenges are described in the top row of CHART 9: THE CHALLENGE/THE GROWTH NUMBER on page 326. There are no Challenges for 9, 11 or 22, but there is a 0 (zero) Challenge. This is the only place in numerology in which the zero is found.

Commentary

The 1 and 2 Challenges are most frequent, the 0 and 3 somewhat less frequent, the 4 and 5 considerably less frequent. Very occasionally, you'll find a 6, 7 or 8 Challenge, but they're considerably more difficult than the others. The 7 Challenge, in particular, may have a substantial impact and needs much work to be overcome.

And *overcome* is the right verb to apply to *all* the Challenges—or more correctly, converting the negative emphasis of the early years to positive potential.

The Challenge represents experiences which are likely to occur frequently in the life. In the beginning years, just about everyone approaches these situations negatively. By using the willpower, an individual can learn how to deal with the same forces in a constructive manner. The situations recur—but instead of representing obstacles, the situations provide potential for positive growth and development.

Let's look at Lloyd, for instance. Like many of us, he has a 2 Challenge. As a child, Lloyd was timid and shy. His family, especially, could see that he had deep feelings, but they were rarely expressed. As he moved into his teen years, Lloyd was close with only a handful of friends. He was sensitive to criticism, occasionally to the point of tears. It was often easier for him to forego a social occasion than to deal with others who, in fact or in his imagination, were unaware of his sensitivity. Sometimes, when he felt ignored—and with his timidity, he was often overlooked—the hurt would be extreme.

A perceptive high school teacher recognized Lloyd's writing talents and encouraged him to develop this special ability. Lloyd became one of the editors of the school literary magazine and, in his senior year, won a city-wide award for his poetry. Lloyd's peers began to observe his sensitivities and his ability to use them to enlighten others. Receiving praise (instead of the criticism he so feared) allowed Lloyd to expand his writing talents to express the deep feelings he had so long repressed. The shy, reclusive child was becoming a confident and sensitive young man.

Lloyd had enough willpower (along with some fortuitous circumstances) to change the negative emphasis of his Challenge to a positive expression—with dramatic results. With the Challenge, it's never clear at what age this shift will occur. Most people begin to express constructively in their early teens, others continue to emphasize the negative extreme into their adult years.

You may find that the Challenge—with its two poles—may be one of the more enlightening pieces of information in the delineation. Most people will know exactly what you mean when you describe the negative potential, but the possibilities of the positive energy, available with *only* an effort of the will, may never have crossed their minds. Since the Challenge situations tend to recur throughout the life—Lloyd, as an example, will always find his sensitivity playing a vital role in his well-being or distress—the advantage of the conversion to the positive is obvious.

Special cases

If the Challenge number is the same as any of the core elements, that element tends to be affected by the negative Challenge emphasis. This emphasis is substantially lighter and easier to overcome than the negativity of a repeated core element or a Karmic Debt, but the Challenge's negativity may be more apparent in the life.

If the Challenge number is the same as a repeated core element or Karmic Debt, the Challenge adds its own burden to the already significant negativity.

If the Challenge number is the same as a negative Intensity Point or a Karmic Lesson, the life is likely to emphasize the negative aspect of that continuum, particularly in the early years.

Expression in delineation

The paragraphs describing the Challenge would be included along with the descriptions of other modifiers with that same modifier number. Since there's no way to determine when the positive conversion takes place, the reading must express both positive and negative as if either one is currently effective.

Hal Allen's organization sheet and delineation

Hal has a 1 Challenge which is placed in the negative energy column on his organization sheet (Figure 14-1 below). Step 8 of Hal's delineation, page 203, includes the effect of the Challenge and deals with Hal's probable domination by others in his early years. Study this step carefully to see how several modifiers are blended.

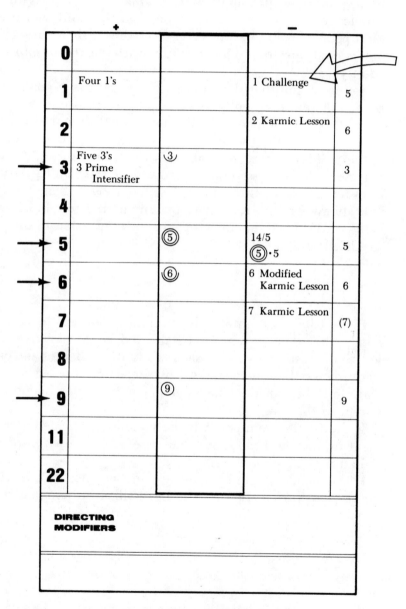

Figure 14-1
Organization Sheet with Challenge

CHAPTER 15

A GUIDE TO GROWTH: THE GROWTH NUMBER

THE GROWTH NUMBER DESCRIBES THE ENERGY WHICH WILL ILLUMINATE THE ESSENCE OF THE EXPERIENCES AND HELP EXPAND A PERSON'S DEVELOPMENT.

Definition

Commentary

If we think of a strong Intensity Point as a potent supplier of energy, the Growth Number, by contrast, is a poor energy supplier, supplying perhaps ten or twenty percent of the Intensity Point potential. The Growth Number is an important modifier, though, because its energy, *along with similar energy*, points the way to growth and development.

If the Growth Number is matched by a core element or positive modifier (or by similar positive potential) and is not in conflict with other energy, the individual is likely to grow and develop. If, for example, there's a 1 Growth Number along with a 1 Expression and no energy tending to stifle independence or promote dominant traits, then the individual is likely to use the 1 energy to expand his experiences.

If the Growth Number is matched by a core element or positive modifier (or by similar positive potential) but is in conflict with other energy, the subject's use of his free will will determine whether he grows and develops. As an example, if there's a 5 Growth Number along with a 5 Life Path and a 13/4 Expression, the individual will have to determine whether he uses the positive potential and grows, or whether he succumbs to the negative energy.

If the Growth Number is not matched by a core element or positive modifier (or by similar positive potential), the individual, particularly in the early years, may show little development.

Calculation   The Growth Number is the sum of the letters of the first name, reduced to a single digit or master number. For instance:

$$
\begin{array}{l}
\text{ANNETTE} \\
1\ 5\ 5\ 5\ 2\ 2\ 5 \quad = 25 \\
\qquad\qquad\qquad = 2 + 5 = \quad 7 \ \underline{\underline{\text{Growth\qquad Number}}}
\end{array}
$$

$$
\begin{array}{l}
\text{ADR I AN} \\
1\ 4\ 9\ 9\ 1\ 5 \quad = 29 \\
\qquad\qquad\quad = 2 + 9 = 11 \ \underline{\underline{\text{Growth\qquad Number}}}
\end{array}
$$

Chart 9: The Challenge/ The Growth Number   The Growth Numbers are described in the bottom row in CHART 9: THE CHALLENGE/THE GROWTH NUMBER on page 326.

Examples   Suppose we look at Janet with a 5 Growth Number and the following core:

4 Life Path
8 Expression
1 Soul Urge
7 Birthday

and modifiers similar to the core elements. Janet is likely to be hard-pressed to grow and develop comfortably. The rigidity of the 4 and 8 energies as well as the inward-turning 7 potential will hardly work toward the versatility, adaptability and excitement defined by the 5 Growth Number. Only a small portion of the 1 energy, the motivation to create and originate, tends in the 5 direction. The delineation should stress the importance of that part of Janet's Soul Urge potential in illuminating the depth of her experience. The reading should also explain how the other energies will tend to block the experiences.

Lillie, on the other hand, has that same 5 Growth Number, but her core has:

3 Life Path
5 Expression
22 Soul Urge
2 Birthday

and modifiers similar to the core elements. The 5 Expression, of course, gives Lillie the ability to express the very energy the Growth Number is defining. And the 3 and 22 energy also have an expansive potential. With this core, Lillie has a good chance for development.

The Growth Number and the Life Path

Don't misunderstand the relative importance of the Growth Number and the Life Path. Although the Growth Number describes the energy which helps expand a person's development, *the development itself is along the Life Path.*

In Janet's example, the energy related to her 5 Growth Number will light the way along her 4 Life Path. Her ability to be versatile and adaptable will help her with the hard work and service she's likely to encounter. In Lillie's example, the 5 Growth Number delight in change and variety will help expand Lillie's ability to express the joy of living—her 3 Life Path lesson.

Special case

Did you notice, in reading the descriptions of the Growth Numbers on Chart 9, that 1 through 9 define energies with reasonable possibilities? And that 11 and 22 are significantly more difficult? Only rarely will an individual have the potential to expand his life as defined by the master numbers. Unless there's some strong 11 core or modifier energy to match the 11 Growth Number, you can be certain that growth along the 11 path will present some difficulty. Similarly, some strong 22 core or modifier energy would be needed for development with a 22 Growth Number.

As in other master number cases, the lower level of these energies may provide a more acceptable alternative. If 11 core or modifier energy is available, give the subject the choice of both the 11 *and* 2 Growth Number paths. If 11 energy isn't available, the 2 Growth Number alone should be described. Similarly, use the 22 *and* 4 Growth Number paths if 22 potential is available—only the 4 Growth Number if the 22 potential is not.

Hal Allen's organization sheet and delineation

The Growth Number is placed in the center column of the organization sheet. Hal Allen, with a 9 Growth Number, would now have an organization sheet as shown in Figure 15-1 on page 156.

Since Hal has a 6 Expression and a 9 Soul Urge, we'd certainly expect some positive energy to expand his experiences in accordance with the 9 Growth Number description. See Step 15, page 211 of Hal's delineation, where his Growth Number is described.

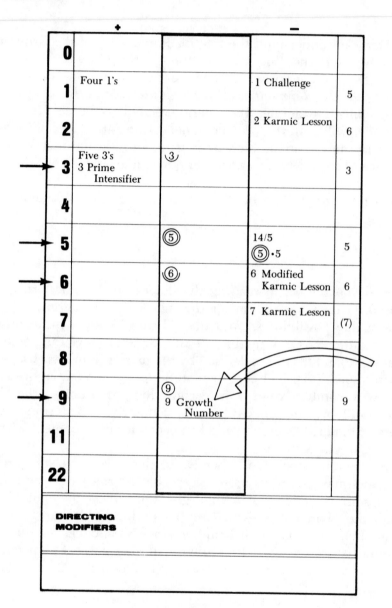

	+		−	
0				
1	Four 1's		1 Challenge	5
2			2 Karmic Lesson	6
3	Five 3's 3 Prime Intensifier	③		3
4				
5		⑤	14/5 ⑤·5	5
6		⑥	6 Modified Karmic Lesson	6
7			7 Karmic Lesson	(7)
8				
9		⑨ 9 Growth Number		9
11				
22				
DIRECTING MODIFIERS				

Figure 15-1
Organization Sheet with Growth Number

CHAPTER 16

A LATER LESSON
TO BE LEARNED:
THE MATURITY NUMBER

THE MATURITY NUMBER DESCRIBES A SUB-LESSON INTRODUCED AT MATURITY. If you think of the Life Path, or main lesson, as a highway, the Maturity Number represents a widening of the highway during the mature years. The Maturity Number (or Power Number or Reality Number) is often an important modifier.

Definition

The Maturity Number is the sum of the Life Path plus the Expression, reduced to a single digit or master number.

Evan has a Life Path of 7 and an Expression of 8.

$$7 + 8 = 15$$
$$= 1 + 5 = \underline{6 \text{ Maturity Number}}$$

Richard has a Life Path of 2 and an Expression of 9.

$$2 + 9 = \underline{11/2 \text{ Maturity Number}}$$

Calculation

CHART 10: THE MATURITY NUMBER on page 340 describes the different Maturity Numbers. The first and second rows delineate two different readings, depending on whether the sub-lesson that's introduced is brand new or is related to

Chart 10: The Maturity Number

energies introduced at birth. (The bottom row will be discussed later under Special Cases.)

First row

The first row describes an individual with a Maturity Number that matches a core element, an Intensity Point or a Karmic Lesson. Here, there's usually less strain than in the second row descriptions where there is no matching energy. Robert, for instance, has a Maturity Number with the same number as the Life Path. I think you can see that, at maturity, all that's happening is that Robert's Life Path lesson is being brought up for reevaluation. All the Life Path traits have probably been used, at least to some degree, in the years leading up to maturity. These characteristics were probably used to make progress in the lesson outlined by the Life Path and, of course, they're available for continued use during the maturity reassessment. In this example, then, Robert would basically be checking his progress along the Life Path at maturity and making some adjustments, when necessary, to better assimilate the lesson he's been working on all his life.

Let's suppose that the Maturity Number, instead of being the same as the Life Path, is the same as the Expression, Soul Urge or Birthday. Or that there's an above-average Intensity Point with the same modifier number. Here, a new sub-lesson is being introduced by the Maturity Number, but the basic energy to work on the new sub-lesson has been operating since birth. That's certainly comfortable energy to have available. It's been developing all these years and now it can be put to work in the service of the new sub-lesson. In this case, as in Robert's example in the last paragraph, the individual is essentially checking his growth and making some adjustments—but he certainly isn't being jolted by a completely new direction.

If the Maturity Number has the same modifier number as a negative Intensity Point or Karmic Lesson, the individual has been working, prior to maturity, to overcome the obstacles presented. The introduction of the sub-lesson at maturity re-emphasizes the progress (or lack of progress) made with this energy.

Second row

Suppose that the Maturity Number is *not* similar to any of the core elements and *doesn't* have a matching Intensity Point or Karmic Lesson. Sometime in mid-life, the individual will become aware of a new sub-lesson to be learned, a sub-lesson which doesn't match any of the strong energies he's been developing from birth. It's true that the sub-lesson brings some new energies with it—the energies usually associated with the modifier number. But these energies, compared to the birth energies, are weakly expressed, and, being new to the individual, would take some assimilation before they are fully operational. This example, covered in the second row in Chart 10, describes a Maturity Number that is an important modifier indeed.

Here's Octavia, for instance, with an 11 Life Path, 6 Expression, 9 Soul Urge and 5 Birthday. Octavia has a great deal of helping, loving energy (from 6 and 9) and a lot of idealistic and spiritual energy (from the 11). She may well find her way as a counselor, a teacher, a social worker, a numerologist or astrologer—there are many possibilities here to make use of the positive potential. At maturity, Octavia would become aware of her 8 Maturity Number (11 + 6 = 17   1 + 7 = 8). Here at mid-life, our helping, loving, idealistic, spiritual Octavia feels a need or desire to learn the satisfactions of the material world and the power which comes with its mastery. Her path through life probably doesn't feel like it widened gradually—it's more like an abrupt U-turn.

Along with these material desires, Octavia is likely to feel the stirrings of some new energy—in her case, some new 8 energy. If we look at the characteristics of the 8 Life Path (second row of CHART 2: THE LIFE PATH) we'll have a good picture of that new energy. Octavia is likely, at maturity, to feel somewhat more ambitious and self-confident than in her early years, a bit more efficient and energetic, too. She's becoming, possibly through painful past experience, somewhat more realistic and practical than is usual with an 11 Life Path. And she's starting to be a bit more stubborn and rigid than she used to be, not a bad trait for a person with the 6·9 tendency to be a doormat. As you can imagine, this new energy feels considerably weaker than the energy she's used all her life. Octavia is going to have to move slowly, develop the energy and assimilate it.

The Maturity Number sometimes manifests itself as the slow development of some newfound understanding, sometimes as a dramatic awareness sparked by an unforeseen crisis. Development of the Maturity Number potential usually gives the individual better control of the life along with a sense of deeper fulfillment.

Octavia may have done her good works, yet somehow, in the back of her mind, always felt that her direction was largely dictated by the social work agencies and schools which employed her. Her mature awareness of the material world will allow her to develop better control of her life. More money and higher status means she can, to a greater extent, pick and choose the precise work *she* wants to accomplish. This, in turn, is likely to lead to more satisfaction. For Octavia, the Maturity Number marks an important guidepost to a new direction—with probable difficulties and significant ultimate benefits.

The age for applying the Maturity Number

The Maturity Number is the only modifier that doesn't start operating at birth. It starts operating at maturity—but just when does a person reach maturity? This is far more a philosophical or psychological question than a numerology question. In my experience, a person's maturity seems directly related to that person's commitment to growth. I've known a few individuals who showed conspicuous signs of maturity at thirty-five or so, but I expect, for the majority of people, maturity is likely to set in somewhere between forty and fifty. And some people, by design (or is it lack of design?) don't seem to develop maturity no matter how long they live.

For numerology purposes, I wouldn't even mention the Maturity Number in a delineation unless the subject is at least in the thirties. From forty on, I would delineate the sub-lesson in detail, particularly in those cases, like Octavia's, where new energies are also introduced.

Special case: Karmic Debt

If there's a Karmic Debt behind the Maturity Number—13 behind the 4, 14 behind the 5, 16 behind the 7, 19 behind the 1—the individual is apt to find obstacles in the sub-lesson path. If we're dealing with a Maturity Number which doesn't introduce new energy, the impediments are probably negative developments of existing energies which are painfully highlighted at the mid-life reevaluation. If we're dealing with the introduction of new energy, the blockages are likely to appear as an integral part of the new sub-lesson. Sometimes, one of the obstructions itself can signal the onset of the sub-lesson.

The obstacles are described in the bottom row of Chart 10. They provide vital information for the delineation.

Special case: master numbers

If the Maturity Number is a master number, the individual has the choice of operating on the very difficult higher level or the considerably easier lower level of that energy.

If there's no previous strong master number energy, it's extremely difficult (it may feel impossible) to start working with this high-level potential so late in life. In a delineation, emphasize the lower level sub-lesson and briefly mention the higher sub-lesson in passing. Don't go further with the higher level unless the subject indicates a particular interest in it.

If there *is* previous strong master number energy, it is, of course, considerably easier to work with the higher level sub-lesson, particularly if the individual has already developed some of his master number potential. In a reading, mention both sub-lessons with equal emphasis and let the individual make his own choice.

Special case: repeated core element

When there are repeated core elements, we're dealing with a person likely to be struggling with negative potential—during the early years, at the very least. We know, from Chapter 9, that the negative potential is likely to be converted to positive sometime between twenty and forty. Now, if there's a matching Maturity Number, we can expect the effect of its potential to be felt sometime after thirty-five, quite possibly before the negative energy is fully converted.

In this complex situation, the Maturity Number is likely to introduce a sub-lesson which isn't new, but which is incompletely assimilated. In the delineation, the sub-lesson would be described as a reevaluation of an existing lesson. We would indicate that the energies introduced at maturity are likely to give positive impetus to previous negatively directed potential.

Blaine, with a 1 Life Path, a 1 Soul Urge—*and* a 1 Maturity Number—is, at age thirty-five, likely to either overemphasize himself and his own needs or be timid and afraid to stand up for himself (1·1, CHART 6: THE ASPECTS). At maturity, he's likely to reevaluate his progress toward independence, find that he's either dominating or dependent (First row, 1 Maturity Number, Chart 10). Blaine may now begin to gain the awareness and use of his inner strength, his leadership capability, his potential for accomplishment (1 characteristics, CHART 2: THE LIFE PATH). The Maturity Number will tend to help him toward the independence which may have proved elusive up to maturity.

Expression in delineation

Here's Stephen, age forty-three, with a 3 Maturity Number and a 3 Soul Urge. The description of the effect of Stephen's Maturity Number would, of course, be an example of the case where no new energy is introduced.

In Step 15 of a delineation (from Chapter 7) the Soul Urge motives are described. You may remember that the motives remain the same irrespective of the other core elements.

Stephen's 3 Soul Urge motives (Top row, CHART 4: THE SOUL URGE) might read as follows:

> You are likely to want to express your delight in life, your sense of joie de vivre. You probably want an active social life with many close friends and diverse activities. You're apt to want to express artistic talents, particularly your talent with words, by speaking, writing, acting or singing. You want your home and work environment to reflect the beauty you enjoy creating.

From the first row of the 3 Maturity Number, CHART 10: THE MATURITY NUMBER, we can add the following:

> Now that you're in your early forties, I expect you're going to run into some experiences that may make you want to reevaluate how well you've satisfied some of the desires just mentioned. When you're with others, for instance, are you comfortable giving of yourself openly, warmly, spontaneously? Do you know how to thoroughly enjoy yourself at social gatherings? And have you learned to fully express the artistic and creative side of your personality?
>
> You may find, at this time in your life, that you want to change some of your attitudes and actions in order to give freer rein to your self-expression.

Hal Allen's organization sheet and delineation

Hal Allen's Maturity Number introduces the complexity of dealing with a master number. With a 5 Life Path and a 6 Expression, Hal would have an 11/2 Maturity Number. There's no other 11 energy in his chart, so it would be difficult for him to assimilate the new 11 sub-lesson at mid-life. His delineation stresses the 2 sub-lesson (while only mentioning the new 11 sub-lesson). And, since he has a 2 Karmic Lesson and similar 6 and 9 energy, we're not working with new energy here.

Hal's organization sheet (Figure 16-1 on page 163) shows the 11 Maturity Number in the 11 row. The 2 Maturity Number which is being emphasized is shown in the 2 row. Both are in the center column.

See Step 13, page 208, for a description of Hal's 2 Maturity Number and Step 21, page 213, for a mention of Hal's 11 Maturity Number.

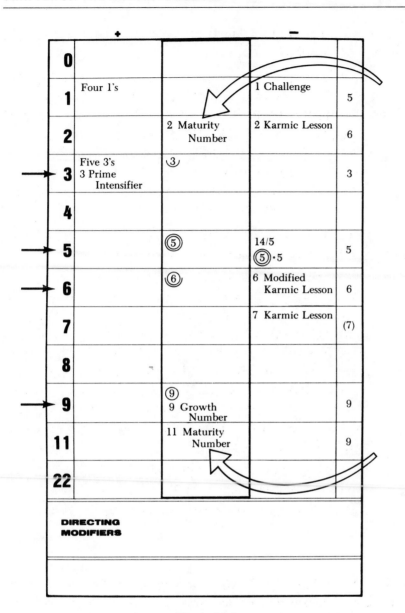

Figure 16-1
Organization Sheet with Maturity Number

CHAPTER 17

AN INNER DREAM:
THE SECRET SELF

THE SECRET SELF DESCRIBES A DREAM OF DESIRES CHERISHED DEEP IN THE RECESSES OF THE MIND. The Secret Self (or Quiescent Self or Quiet Self or Latent Self) is a modifier of lesser importance.

Definition

The Secret Self adds a special energy even though it's rarely connected to the realities of an individual's life. It usually doesn't have any relation to a person's opportunities, abilities or apparent desires. It's *always* a pleasurable fantasy, usually a fantasy of achievements which the individual makes little effort to actually accomplish. The contrast between the fantasy and the life is often fascinating and perplexing, though most people readily acknowledge their love of the fantasy as well as their lack of interest in making it a reality. Though only a disconnected dream, the Secret Self adds a dimension to the individual, a dimension different than that added by any other modifier.

The Secret Self is derived by finding the sum of the number values of all the consonants in each name, reducing this sum to a single digit or master number, then adding the sums of all the names together and reducing that total to a single digit or master number. For instance:

Calculation

ABRAHAM   LINCOLN
29 8 4   3 53 35
(23) 5   +   (19) 1   = 6 Secret Self

FRANKLIN   DELANO   ROOSEVELT
6 9   5 2 3   5   4   3   5   9   1   4   3 2
       (30) 3   +   (12) 3   +   (19) 1   = 7 Secret Self

HARRY   S.   TRUMAN
8   9 9   1   2 9   4   5
      (26) 8   + 1 +   (20) 2   = 11 Secret Self

Commentary   The Secret Self is simply a dream with the keywords or essence of the Secret Self number as the ultimate development of the dream. Lincoln, for instance, with his 6 Secret Self, probably looked forward, in his mind's eye, to the beauty of home, family and friends; Roosevelt, in his private fantasy, is likely to have delighted in being an all-wise mystic (7 Secret Self); Truman, in secret, is apt to have contemplated a life dedicated to a spiritual mission (11 Secret Self). These three men of action cherished such very different dreams. Can you see how this modifier gives you such a special insight?

There are only a few instances where the Secret Self has any chance of being related to reality.

If the Secret Self and the Life Path are the same number, the desire of the Secret Self matches the opportunities of the Life Path. Here, the individual may work to obtain the pleasure of harmonizing the dream with the real world.

If the Secret Self and the Soul Urge are the same number, the fantasy desire of the Secret Self matches the apparent desire described by the Soul Urge. The fantasy becomes a realistic desire here with the possibility of fulfillment dependent on the rest of the core and the modifiers.

Expression in delineation   The Secret Self, if included at all, is mentioned in the delineation along with other modifiers of the same or similar number. If the Secret Self doesn't match the Life Path or the Soul Urge, it can be omitted or included with a minimum description. (I usually include it because it fascinates *me*, and because it often adds a dramatic contrast.) If the Secret Self matches the Life Path or the Soul Urge, the deep satisfaction obtainable with the possibility of fulfillment should be discussed along with a full description of the dream.

The Secret Self is placed in the central column of the organization sheet (Figure 17-1 below).

Hal Allen's organization sheet and delineation

HARLAN   WILLIAM   ALLEN

$$8\ \ 93\ 5 \quad 5\ \ 33 \quad 4 \quad 33\ 5$$

$$(25)\ 7 \ + \quad (15)\ 6 \quad + \quad 11 \quad = 24$$

$$= \underline{6\ \text{Secret Self}}$$

Turn to Step 13, page 209, for a description of Hal's Secret Self. Since his 6 Secret Self doesn't match either his 5 Life Path or his 9 Soul Urge, the description is minimized.

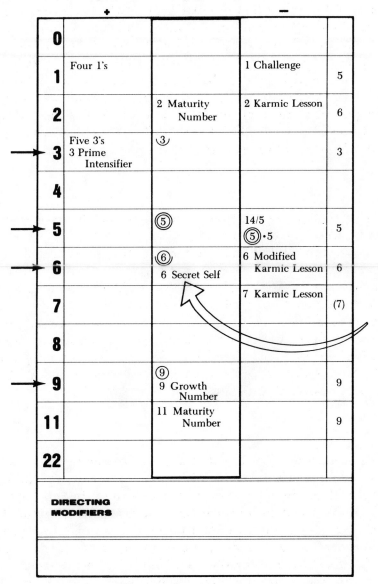

Figure 17-1
Organization Sheet with Secret Self

CHAPTER 18

NUANCES:
GROUPS,
NUMBERS BEHIND
THE CORE ELEMENTS

WHEN 40% OR MORE OF THE ELEMENTS AND SUB-ELEMENTS BELONG TO A GROUP, THE GROUP ENERGY IS AN IMPORTANT MODIFIER.

Groups

You may remember that, in Chapter 2, we discussed the fact that some of the energies naturally work together. Here are the most common groups:

1,4,8	:	business, system and order, self-centeredness.
2,6,9	:	helping, caring
3,6,9	:	artistic, creative
7,11,22	:	nervous tension
11,22	:	special potential

If some of the elements are part of the group, the elements' description alone will indicate the group energy. Sometimes, though, you'll find groups primarily of sub-elements. Unless their energy is described, this important effect would not be noted.

Carl, on page 143 of Chapter 13, has a lot of numbers from the first group.

His Life Path is 8.
His Soul Urge is 1.
His Birthday is 4.
One Soul Urge sub-element is 1.
Two Expression sub-elements are 4.

Of the twelve elements and sub-elements, six belong to the 1,4,8 group, indicating that Carl would probably express a strong leaning toward business, system and order as well as displaying a tendency to be self-centered. Since three of his elements are in this group, it's not necessary to describe the group energy in a separate paragraph in the reading.

Numbers behind the core elements

My birthname is Matthew Oliver Goodwin.

The calculation for my Expression would, of course, look like this:

$$\begin{array}{ccccc}
\text{MATTHEW} & & \text{OLIVER} & & \text{GOODWIN} \\
\underline{4\ 1\ 2\ 2\ 8\ 5\ 5} & & \underline{6\ 3\ 9\ 4\ 5\ 9} & & \underline{7\ 6\ 6\ 4\ 5\ 9\ 5} \\
(27)\ 9 & + & (36)\ 9 & + & (42)\ 6 \qquad = 24 = \boxed{6}
\end{array}$$

THE 24 IS THE NUMBER "BEHIND" THE 6. IT ADDS A TRACE OF COLORATION TO THE DESCRIPTION OF THE CORE ELEMENT. It is a modifier of lesser importance.

The purest form, say, of the 6 Expression would occur when there is *no* number behind the Expression, just the sub-elements. For instance:

$$\begin{array}{ccccc}
\text{HENRIETTA} & & \text{JEAN} & & \text{HUME} \\
\underline{8\ 5\ 5\ 9\ 9\ 5\ 2\ 2\ 1} & & \underline{1\ 5\ 1\ 5} & & \underline{8\ 3\ 4\ 5} \\
(46)\ (10)\ 1 & + & (12)\ 3 & + & (20)\ 2 \qquad = \boxed{6}
\end{array}$$

This pure form, of course, represents an individual who is responsible, helpful, loving and sympathetic.

We have, from Chapter 13:

$$\begin{array}{ccccc}
\text{CARL} & & \text{HAROLD} & & \text{CHRISTOPHER} \\
\underline{3\ 1\ 9\ 3} & & \underline{8\ 1\ 9\ 6\ 3\ 4} & & \underline{3\ 8\ 9\ 9\ 1\ 2\ 6\ 7\ 8\ 5\ 9} \\
(16)\ 7 & + & (31)\ 4 & + & (67)\ (13)\ 4 \qquad = 15 = \boxed{6}
\end{array}$$

Now Carl has a 15 behind the 6. We would expect Carl to emphasize his own needs a bit more than Henrietta (from the self-centered 1 and 5 traits) and tend to be a bit looser and freer in his committments (from the restlessness of the 5).

My name, above, with the 24 behind the 6, would mean that I tend to be very responsible, helpful, loving and sympathetic (the 2 adds energy similar to the 6 energy), along with a trace of stubbornness or rigidity (a 4 trait).

And finally:

WALLACE WELLS MANDEL

$$\frac{5\ 1\ 3\ 3\ 1\ 3\ 5}{(21)\ 3} + \frac{5\ 5\ 3\ 3\ 1}{(17)\ 8} + \frac{4\ 1\ 5\ 4\ 5\ 3}{22} = 33 = \textcircled{6}$$

With that 33 behind the 6, Wallace would tend to show optimism and enthusiasm (3 characteristics) along with his loving, responsible nature. The 33 doesn't express as a negative doubled 3 but, rather, as the positive side of the 3—emphasized.

These are, admittedly, rather subtle nuances. Include them in the delineation when it feels comfortable.

Hal Allen has:

> 6 Expression
> 9 Soul Urge
> 3 Birthday
> 6 sub-element in the Life Path
> 9 sub-element in the Expression
> 6 sub-element in the Soul Urge

Hal Allen's organization sheet and delineation

Six of his twelve elements and sub-elements belong to the 3,6,9 group. This should be noted in the bottom row of his organization sheet (Figure 18-1 on page 172).

Since Hal's strong artistic and creative potential is described by his core elements, it's not necessary to devote any additional space in the delineation to the group energy.

A description of the numbers behind Hal's elements—the 14 behind his 5 Life Path and the 24 behind his 6 Expression—are not included in the delineation, either. The 1 energy is already described with Hal's four 1's Intensity Point and 1 Challenge. The 2 energy is discussed relative to Hal's 2 Maturity Number and 2 Karmic Lesson. The 4 energy is not specifically mentioned in Hal's delineation. His opposing 5 energy is so strong that this subtle 4 potential would be of little consequence.

You'll find that there are only occasional instances where either the group energy or the numbers behind the elements need mentioning.

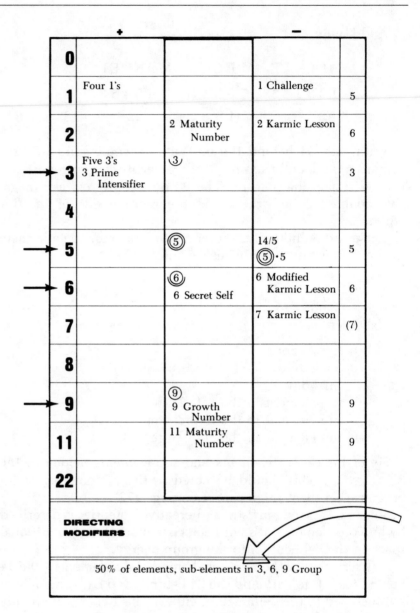

	+		−	
0				
1	Four 1's		1 Challenge	5
2		2 Maturity Number	2 Karmic Lesson	6
3	Five 3's 3 Prime Intensifier	③		3
4				
5		⑤	14/5 ⑤·5	5
6		⑥ 6 Secret Self	6 Modified Karmic Lesson	6
7			7 Karmic Lesson	(7)
8				
9		⑨ 9 Growth Number		9
11		11 Maturity Number		9
22				

DIRECTING MODIFIERS

50% of elements, sub-elements in 3, 6, 9 Group

Figure 18-1
Organization Sheet with Group shown

CHAPTER 19

THE BASIC VIEWPOINT:
THE TEMPERAMENT

THE TEMPERAMENT DESCRIBES THE DISPOSITION **Definition**
OR BASIC VIEWPOINT DETERMINED BY THE RELA-
TIVE PROPORTION OF PHYSICAL, MENTAL, EMO-
TIONAL AND INTUITIVE COMPONENTS. Remember, in
Chapter 10 (page 112), we introduced the idea of directing
modifiers, modifiers that direct the energies of core elements
and other modifiers? The Temperament is the first of the direc-
ting modifiers that we're going to discuss.

The Temperament (or Planes of Temperament or Planes of
Expression or Plane of Consciousness) is a very important
modifier. The disposition or balance of qualities brought to our
activities is often a significant determinant of the work we do
or the friends we make. The core, of course, represents the very
essence of a person, but the person's Temperament—his basic
viewpoint—may be important in attracting friends, mates or
business associates.

The Temperament is composed of four components, each **The**
representing a different area of consciousness: **Components**

> The Physical Component
> is represented by the body,
> deals with the senses.
> The Physical viewpoint is concerned with tangible
> form, material matters, practical affairs, physical
> adventures.

The Mental component
is represented by the mind,
deals with thinking, reasoning, logic, facts.
The Mental viewpoint is concerned with mental activities, business enterprises, political affairs.

The Emotional component
is represented by the emotions,
deals with the feelings.
The Emotional viewpoint is concerned with feelings, affection, artistic endeavors, creativity, imagination.

The Intuitive component
is represented by the spirit,
deals with inner awarenesses.
The Intuitive viewpoint is concerned with sensitivity to non-material experience—spiritual, religious, psychic, metaphysical—and ultimate wisdom.

Calculating the components

Each letter of the alphabet belongs to one component group as shown in this table:

	A	B	C	D	E	F	G	H	I	J	K	L	M	N	O	P	Q	R	S	T	U	V	W	X	Y	Z	Totals
Physical				D	E								M										W				4
Mental	A						G	H		J		L		N		P											7
Emotional		B							I						O			R	S	T				X		Z	8
Intuitive			C			F					K						Q				U	V			Y		7

Calculate the Temperament by placing each letter of the name in its appropriate place in the Temperament table. For instance, Woodrow Wilson's birth name was:

THOMAS WOODROW WILSON		Totals
Physical	MWDWW	5
Mental	HALN	4
Emotional	TOSOOROISO	10
Intuitive		0

Summarize the Temperament table information on one line:

5 Physical, 4 Mental, 10 Emotional, 0 Intuitive

The strong components significantly affect the disposition. The weak components also significantly affect the disposition—negatively, because of their lacks. The average components allow the energy related to their area of consciousness to develop, although the energy is not likely to be emphasized as much as the energy related to the strong components.

Calculating the components' strengths

The strong components are:

> The component with the largest number, and
> Any other component with a number equal to at least 60% of the largest number.

The weak components are:

> Any component with a number less than 25% of the largest number.

The average components are:

> Any component with a number less than 60% of the largest number and 25% or more of the largest number.

In Woodrow Wilson's example:

> 10 Emotional is the largest number. This is a strong component.
> > 60% of 10 = .60 x 10 = 6
> > 25% of 10 = .25 x 10 = 2.5
>
> 5 Physical is less than 6 and more than 2.5. This is an average component.
> 4 Mental is less than 6 and more than 2.5. This is an average component.
> 0 Intuitive is less than 2.5. This is a weak component.

Summarizing Wilson's relative component strengths:

10 Emotional	5 Physical	4 Mental	0 Intuitive
Strong	Average	Average	Weak

What's the effect of the relative component strengths? Here's a brief rundown:

Component Descriptions

PHYSICAL COMPONENT

WEAK

Viewpoint or disposition:
> Material matters are not of particular interest.
> Practicality has little to do with judgments.

Often characterized or expressed by:
> Avoidance of hard work and situations requiring concentration.
> Lack of physical discipline.

STRONG

Viewpoint or disposition:
> Concerned with material matters.
> Extremely practical. Solid common sense view.
> Concerned with economical use of resources.
> Turns ideas into material reality.
> Prefers system and order.

Often characterized or expressed by:
> Physical endurance.
> Practical nature.
> Capability of extreme concentration.
> Determination.
> Strong opinions, forceful.

MENTAL COMPONENT

WEAK

Viewpoint or disposition:
> Mental matters are not of particular interest.
> (This component gives *no* indication of subject's intelligence.)
> Lack of concern with reason, logic, facts.

Often characterized or expressed by:
> Little explanation of motivations.
> Disinterest in leadership.
> Lack of will power.
> Lack of mental discipline.

STRONG

Viewpoint or disposition:
> Concern with reason, logic, facts.
> Reason is likely to be one of prime motivators.
> Concern with leadership.

Often characterized or expressed by:
> Desire to reach logical conclusion.
> Logical deductions used as motivating force.
> Activity in large business, politics.
> Determination.
> Intellectual orientation.

EMOTIONAL COMPONENT

WEAK

Viewpoint or disposition:
> Feelings—his own or others—are not of any particular interest.
> Likely to have difficulty accepting his own emotional nature.
> Views life with little sentiment and imagination.

Often characterized or expressed by:
> Limited expression of feelings.
> Lack of creative imagination.
> Unsentimental approach.

STRONG

Viewpoint or disposition:
> Extremely emotional point of view.
> Little concern with facts.
> Very sympathetic.
> Very sentimental.
> Much imagination.

Often characterized or expressed by:
> Direct and open expressions of friendship, affection, love.
> Artistic and creative endeavors.
> Nervous nature.

TOO STRONG (More than twice closest component, or more than all other components combined.)

Often characterized or expressed by:
> Lack of clarity or confusion introduced by a too emotional viewpoint.
> Overwhelmed by imagination.
> Extremely nervous nature.

INTUITIVE COMPONENT

WEAK

Viewpoint and disposition:
> Intuitive awarenesses, spiritual, psychic and metaphysical matters are of little interest.
> Distrusts inner voice.

Often characterized or expressed by:
> Little concern with inner development.

STRONG

Viewpoint and disposition:

> Deep intuitive awarenesses. Concerned with wisdom, fundamentals.
>
> Listens to inner voice for guidance.
>
> Understands humanistic goals. Awareness of brotherhood of man.
>
> Concerned with spiritual, philosophic, inventive matters.

Often characterized or expressed by:

> Actions based on understanding, wisdom.
>
> Tolerant and compassionate approach.
>
> Unusual thinking or behavior, likely to attract attention.

TOO STRONG (5 or more)

> Extremely unusual thinking or behavior, likely to attract attention, possibly negative attention.
>
> Possibility of delicate health.

Using the component descriptions

Translating Woodrow Wilson's components into a beginning description of his Temperament:

> Wilson is likely to have an extremely emotional point of view, a disposition displaying much imagination and creativity (*from his strong Emotional component*). His too emotional level is apt to add confusion, aggravated by his extremely nervous nature. (*His Emotional component is greater than the other components combined.*) He probably shows little intuitive awareness (*from his weak Intuitive component*).

Temperament as modifier

Being a directing modifier, the Temperament is different than the other modifiers we've studied so far. The other modifiers describe additions to or subtractions from the core's inherent energy. The Temperament doesn't describe an addition or subtraction of energy, *but a disposition toward the use of the energy.* If you visualize the core and modifiers sending out a flow of energy, the Temperament would act like a filter, allowing only a portion of the energy to flow through.

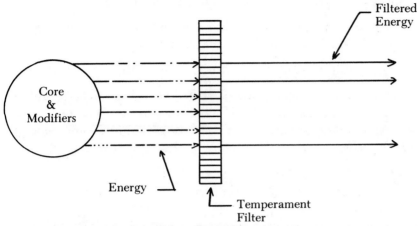

Figure 19-1
Temperament as direction modifier

In other words, the individual's Temperament or disposition toward his basic energy potential determines the portion of the energy potential he is likely to use and the kind of use he can make of that portion. (In the examples that follow, we're going to deal, for simplicity's sake, with only the core energies. But, in a delineation, both the core and modifier energies would be involved.)

Here's Olivia with the following core:

6 Life Path with much emotional energy potential

5 Expression with much physical and mental energy potential

7 Soul Urge with much intuitive and mental energy potential

8 Birthday with much mental energy potential

Olivia, in this simplified look at her energy, has a substantial amount of all four kinds of potential. What kind of a Temperament filter would let all that energy through? A Temperament filter that had a good balance of its components—that is, four strong components. (If there were only one or two strong components and the rest were average components, it's likely that all the energy could get through the filter, but it would be easier for the strong components to get through and they would tend to dominate the Temperament.) It could be summarized something like this:

5 Physical   4 Mental   5 Emotional   3 Intuitive

For Olivia, the Temperament is just about a transparent filter, allowing all the energies to pass through for maximum impact. Olivia, with her broad spectrum of energy, has all facets of her inherent potential available.

Suppose Olivia's Temperament looked like this:

      8 Physical   7 Mental   6 Emotional   5 Intuitive

or like this:

      3 Physical   3 Mental   4 Emotional   3 Intuitive

The description of both of these Temperaments would be similar to the description of Olivia's original Temperament. The digits themselves are, in this case, less important than the *PROPORTIONAL RELATION* of the digits to each other.

What if Olivia, with the same core, has an extremely disbalanced Temperament, one that looks like this:

      2 Physical   8 Mental   3 Emotional   1 Intuitive

With this Temperament, Olivia would display little interest in material matters (weak Physical component), feelings (weak Emotional component) and spiritual, psychic and metaphysical matters (weak Intuitive component). She would, on the other hand, display an extremely intellectual point of view and be apt to show considerable interest in business or political affairs (strong Mental component).

This disbalanced Temperament could be represented by a filter which would predominantly pass the mental energies. Of the core potential, the 8 Birthday is primarily mental and the 5 Expression and 7 Soul Urge have significant mental potential. A good deal of these energies are likely to be operable in Olivia's life—only the primarily emotional 6 Life Path will tend to be blocked by this Temperament filter.

Organization sheet

The Temperament, along with the First Letter and the First Vowel discussed in the next chapter, are the only directing modifiers. These three modifiers are grouped in the next to last row of the organization sheet labeled *DIRECTING MODIFIERS* rather than being grouped by modifier numbers.

How to use the Temperament in a delineation

In the delineation, the Temperament is summarized in a few separate paragraphs rather than being included in the body of the reading with the other modifiers.

The Temperament, like the core and other modifiers, describes the probable conditions at birth. The individual's free will determines if the Temperament will be modified during the life. For most people, there appears to be relatively little modification. If the Temperament, then, indicates a strong bias, it is likely that some of the energies won't ever be explored or expressed. Occasionally, if the individual has a strong energy bias muffled by the Temperament, he may choose to modify the Temperament to allow these energies to surface. By including all the energies in the body of the delineation and confining the Temperament description to a few separate paragraphs, we are describing all the potential energies but expecting that only those energies that "pass the filter" will be expressed. The way is left open for a modification of the Temperament with consequent expression of the additional energies.

A friend of mine will serve as a good example. Daniel has very strong *intuitive* energies in his core, but a Temperament with a strong *Physical* component and a weak Intuitive component. His early years were devoted to the construction business, with no interest in anything that he could not see demonstrated or scientifically proved. In his later years, he has become fascinated with the occult world, although still maintaining his construction interests. He approaches the occult world, an expression of his *intuitive* energies, with heavy emphasis on the system and order he can find, a manifestation of his strong *Physical* component. Daniel is now making better use of his intuitive energies with his Physical component than in his early years. In time, he may choose to enlarge the scope of his Temperament filter, increase the power of his Intuitive component to further accommodate his interest in the occult.

We'll look at Emily, with the following core:

> 8 Life Path
> 4 Expression
> 6 Soul Urge
> 1 Birthday

Temperament delineation example

and the following Temperament:

> 7 Physical   8 Mental   3 Emotional   1 Intuitive

Emily has strong Physical and Mental components, an average Emotional component and a weak Intuitive component.

From the component descriptions on pages 175-178, we would expect the following:

> Strong Physical component: Extremely practical, common sense point of view expressed with concentration and determination.

Strong Mental component: Motivated by reason, concerned with leadership. Intellectual orientation may be expressed in large business or politics.

Weak Intuitive component: Little interest in spiritual, psychic and metaphysical matters.

The strong Mental and Physical components will allow the use of much of the 8, 4 and 1 core energies. The weak Intuitive component will, in Emily's case, have little effect because there is little intuitive energy inherent in the core.

The delineation paragraphs describing Emily's Temperament might read like this:

Emily has a reasonably well-balanced temperament: her concern with mental and material matters is likely to be emphasized, her concern with feelings is present but less strongly stressed. (*Since there is little intuitive energy or intuitive direction, it's not even mentioned.*)

Emily's strong concern with logic and reason (*strong Mental*) is likely to prove of importance in her business dealings (*8 Life Path*). Her executive ability (*8 Life Path, 1 Birthday*) may be enhanced by her concerns with leadership (*strong Mental*) as well as her will and determination (*strong Physical*). Her extremely practical and realistic nature (*strong Physical*) and her concern with the economical use of resources (*strong Physical*) would stand her in good stead in the business world (*8 Life Path*), although her strong opinions (*strong Physical*) might just emphasize her tendencies to rigidity or stubbornness (*8 Life Path, 4 Expression*). Her strong sense of system and order (*4 Expression, strong Physical*), her ability to turn ideas into material reality (*strong Physical*) and her intellectual orientation (*strong Mental*) will certainly help her to manage and regulate (*4 Expression*) her activities.

With her average Emotional component, Emily's emotional energies, primarily expressed in her 6 Soul Urge, will pass through the Temperament filter, but won't be as emphasized as her other core energies.

Hal's Temperament is calculated as follows:

Hal Allen's organization sheet and delineation

HARLAN WILLIAM ALLEN	Totals
Physical	WME	3
Mental	HALANLLAALLN	12
Emotional	RII	3
Intuitive		0

Mental component   = 12 _____ strong
Physical component   = 3 (less than sixty percent of 12, but just
                            twenty-five percent of 12)____average
Emotional component = 3 (less than sixty percent of 12, but just
                            twenty-five percent of 12)____average
Intuitive component   = 0 (less than twenty-five percent of
                            12) _____ weak

Hal's Temperament—strong Mental component, weak Intuitive component—is shown in the directing modifier row of the organization sheet (Figure 19-2 on page 184).

Turn to Step 24, page 214, and read the paragraphs describing Hal's Temperament.

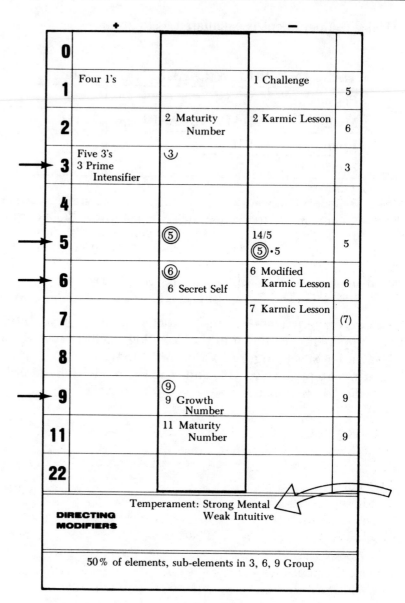

	+		−	
0				
1	Four 1's		1 Challenge	5
2		2 Maturity Number	2 Karmic Lesson	6
3	Five 3's 3 Prime Intensifier	③		3
4				
5		⑤	14/5 ⑤·5	5
6		⑥ 6 Secret Self	6 Modified Karmic Lesson	6
7			7 Karmic Lesson	(7)
8				
9		⑨ 9 Growth Number		9
11		11 Maturity Number		9
22				

Temperament: Strong Mental Weak Intuitive

DIRECTING MODIFIERS

50% of elements, sub-elements in 3, 6, 9 Group

Figure 19-2
Organization Sheet with Temperament

CHAPTER 20

THE APPROACH
TO EXPERIENCE:
THE FIRST LETTER
THE FIRST VOWEL

Definition

THE FIRST LETTER AND FIRST VOWEL OF THE NAME DESCRIBE THE NATURAL OR INNATE APPROACH, THE METHOD OF RESPONSE AND REACTION TO EXPERIENCE. The First Letter and First Vowel are directing modifiers.

These are important modifiers. Since the nature of a person's experience is structured by the core and since the approach to this experience is structured by the First Letter and First Vowel, the approach can have a LIMITING or STABILIZING or ENHANCING effect on a person's experience.

With an effort of the will, the approach can be shifted. It takes a significant force to change the approach so that, for instance, there is an enhancing effect rather than a limiting effect on a person's experience. You are, to a great extent, attached to the First Letter and First Vowel much as you're connected to the core.

Some numerologists define the First Letter (or Cornerstone) as the approach to material experience, the First Vowel as the approach to spiritual or non-material experience. In my experience, the approach to material *and* spiritual experience is an amalgam of the letter *and* vowel. The vowel predominates, supplying sixty percent of the direction while the letter supplies forty percent.

Chart 11: The First Letter

Turn to CHART 11: THE FIRST LETTER, page 354. Here you'll find descriptions of the portion of the approach symbolized by the consonants. The vowels are not included in this chart, but are found on CHART 12: THE FIRST VOWEL. W and Y are sometimes consonants and sometimes vowels. Chart 11 describes W and Y as consonants while Chart 12 describes these letters as vowels.

To the right of each letter on Chart 11 is a key phrase summarizing the characteristics described.

The traits described are often symbolized in the letter itself. For example:

> H, M rest solidly on two legs, denote awareness of the material world.
>
> (A, a vowel, rests on a similar base, soars upwards to symbolize originality and creativity.)
>
> B, D (and O, a vowel) are enclosed, self-protected, retiring.
>
> E, C are open-ended, spontaneous, adventurous.
>
> Y has two arms, two directions, a sense of uncertainty, vacillation.

As shown on Chart 11, the letters can be grouped according to modifier energies. For example, all letters with 1 modifier numbers—A,J,S—represent qualities of leadership while all letters with 7 modifier numbers—G,P,Y—represent qualities of thinking. The fourth horizontal row compares the letters directly above.

The letters can also be grouped horizontally. In the upper row, A through I (the first through the ninth letters), the energy is usually positively oriented—C is a spontaneous creator while D is a steady builder.

In the second row, J through R (the tenth through the eighteenth letters), the energy is considerably less pure. L represents the reasoning creator (as opposed to the spontaneous creator of C) and M is a controlled builder (compared to the steady builder of D). In the top row, the noun and adjective of the key phrase are supportive; in the second row, the adjective generally weakens the thrust of the noun.

And, in the third row, S through Z (the nineteenth through the twenty-sixth letters), the energy often feels misdirected. W represents an encounterer, but, unfortunately, a *limiting* encounterer (as compared to the E adventurous encounterer). Y represents an *uncertain* thinker. The noun and the adjective tend to be at odds with each other. The notable exception here, like the K exception in the second row, is the V inspirational master.

Think of the descriptions as only a beginning in your understanding of the individual letters. With the key phrases and descriptions as a base, compare the characteristics you observe in people and enlarge your awareness of the letters.

CHART 12: THE FIRST VOWEL, page 368, describes the portion of the approach symbolized by the vowels. As shown on the chart, the vowels must be viewed in terms of their pronunciation:

Chart 12: The First Vowel

> Long vowels—A in James, E in Eva, I in Ida—contain energy in the purest, most positive form.
>
> Short vowels—I in Lisa, O in Oliver, U in Ruth—have the same general characteristics as the long vowels, but they have considerably less power and are more muted in expression.
>
> Combined vowels are two vowels combined in the same syllable—AU in Aubrey, E in Eugene, AY in Raymond. The power and expression of the combined vowels are as muted as the short vowels.

Familiarize yourself with the approach represented by each vowel and the nuances reflecting the vowel's pronunciation.

A   stresses LEADERSHIP, individuality, creativity.
E   stresses ADVENTURE, activity, change.
I   stresses HUMANITARIANISM, creativity, deep emotions
O   stresses HARMONIZATION, responsibility, self-containment, concealed feelings.
U   stresses SENSITIVITY, intuition.
W   stresses VACILLATION.
Y   stresses THOUGHT, analysis, introspection, vacillation, intuition.

Commentary

With just a little memorization, you can begin to use the First Letter and First Vowel. For instance, the next time you meet a Mary, see if you can see the leadership, the individuality, the creativity associated with the A along with the controlled, practical and steadying effect of the M. The characteristics just mentioned describe the way Mary approaches experience—which, in terms of numerology, is the way Margaret and Maria and Mark and Matthew and Matilda also approach experience. The approach will appear somewhat differently in all the different Marys and Margarets, of course, depending on their cores and other modifiers. But, when you start to look, you'll be amazed (a) that the approach is usually very much apparent, and (b) that the approach is expressed in such a variety of ways because of the presence of the other numbers. I particularly enjoy this exercise because it doesn't involve any calculations. With a little practice, you can shake hands with a person, think about their first name, and, almost instantly, have some useful awarenesses.

This may be fun to practice, but you can't, of course, use the First Letter and First Vowel all by themselves and expect to acquire a deep understanding of another person. These are two *modifiers* and must always be viewed as *modifiers* of the core energies. Let's examine a few illustrations of the natural approach *modifying* the core.

Example: The core energies are *limited*

Muriel has a   6 Life Path
                     1 Expression
                     2 Soul Urge
                     7 Birthday

Muriel's energy is likely to be devoted to harmonizing and balancing situations (6), leading and promoting (1), giving love and affection (2), as well as expressing some creative urges (6).

Muriel's long First Vowel U describes, among other traits, a conservative streak and a sense of indecisiveness. Muriel's First Letter M indicates a controlled approach, self-discipline and a steady, thorough worker. Muriel's approach to her experiences is likely to reflect these characteristics. She'll tend to LIMIT her growth because of her approach. (It's true that the U will also stress sensitivity and idealism while the M will also stress organizational ability. The positive qualities of these traits will, of themselves, enhance the possibilities for growth, but the total effect of the MU leans toward the conservative and controlled—toward limiting development.)

Example: The core energies are *enhanced*

Clive has the same core as Muriel.

But Clive's long First Vowel I describes a very intense approach with much passion and sensitivity. And Clive's First Letter C stresses an exhilarating expression of the joy of living coupled with spontaneous creative inspiration. Since Clive's response to his experience will probably stress these traits, his approach will ENHANCE his development.

Don has a   5 Life Path
             3 Expression
             1 Soul Urge
             2 Birthday

Example: The core energies are *stabilized*

Don's energy is probably involved in making the most of the exciting opportunities he finds (5), expressing the joy of living (3), actively seeking situations where he can use his abilities (1).

Don's short First Vowel O indicates stress on responsibility, self containment, controlled emotions, an innate understanding of how to protect himself from life's storms. Don's First Letter D describes a self-disciplined, efficient, conservative approach. With a different core, Don's natural approach might stifle and restrict his growth, but, with his high-flying core energy, Don's approach is more likely to STABILIZE his development.

It's usually fairly simple to describe the natural approach to experience, but it's not always as easy, as in the above three examples, to pinpoint the limiting, stabilizing or enhancing tendencies. If the effect of the approach on a person's experience proves more complex than in our simple examples, describe which individual traits are limiting, which stabilizing and which enhancing. And it's fine if it feels a little ambiguous! Life—and character traits—more often than not, are full of complexities and ambiguities. A partially ambiguous reading is merely a reflection of the person's ambiguous structure!

Here are a few special cases:

Special cases

When the first letter *is* the First Vowel, as in *A*bigail, *E*verett or *Y*vette, the traits of the First Vowel provide the complete description of the natural approach.

When there are combined vowels, the traits usually ascribed to the First Vowel are actually a combination of the traits of the two vowels involved. The vowel which is more strongly pronounced would tend to be more strongly expressed in the approach.

For example, the combined vowels at the beginning of *Au*drey are also the first letters. The A is the stronger sound in the first syllable, so the A traits predominate over the U traits.

The combined A describes a sensitive leader, while the combined U describes a conservative receptor. I would expect any Audrey to have an innate approach stressing her leadership ability, her originality and her good mind (A characteristics), helped by her sensitivity and somewhat blunted by her indecisive ways (U characteristics).

When there are combined vowels and one of them is a W or Y, the W or Y traits are always weaker than the traits of the other vowel. If the vowel is W, it adds its approach along with a vacillating nature. If the vowel is Y, it adds a vacillating nature only.

For example, Boyd's natural approach is a combination of the traits of the combined vowels OY (sixty percent) with the First Letter B (forty percent). O describes a responsible, conservative, self-contained, sympathetic individual. Y adds indecision and restlessness. B's approach is shy, retiring, indecisive, very sensitive and very emotional.

Boyd's natural approach to experience would tend to be:

conservative	(from the O)
self-centered	(from the O)
sympathetic	(from the O)
very sensitive	(from the B)
very emotional	(from the B)
indecisive	(from the B and Y)

When the modifier number of the First Letter or First Vowel is the same as the number of a core element, there is a strong ENHANCING effect. The enhancing effect of the vowel is considerably stronger than the enhancing effect of the letter.

The I in *Michael* describes the approach of a humanitarian. If Michael has a Life Path of 9, he will tend to approach the opportunities of the 9—giving of himself for the deep satisfaction of giving—with innate understanding.

When the modifier number of the First Letter or First Vowel is the same as a doubled core element, there is a strong LIMITING effect. The limiting effect of the vowel is considerably stronger than the limiting effect of the letter.

The D in *Daniel* describes the approach of a steady builder. If Daniel's Expression and Soul Urge are both 4, he will tend (according to the 4·4 aspect in CHART 6: THE ASPECTS) to feel:

Limited, tied down, frustrated, or
Disorganized, unaccountable.

With his innate approach partially described by the self-disciplined, rigid, self-contained approach of the D, you can be sure he'll feel limited, tied down and frustrated rather than disorganized and unaccountable. You can also be sure that his innate approach will emphasize the similar qualities in his Expression and Soul Urge. His rational approach will tend to limit his development.

How to use the First Letter and First Vowel in a delineation

In a delineation, the expression of the First Letter and First Vowel is best described in a separate paragraph or two discussing the characteristics of the natural approach to experience as well as the tendency to limit, stabilize or enhance the core energies.

Betty has a   1 Life Path
             4 Expression
             8 Soul Urge
             6 Birthday

Betty's energy is likely to be devoted to achieving independence (1), assuming leadership (1), carrying responsibility (4), organizing (4), using her executive abilities (8), being a good friend (6).

The paragraphs in her delineation expressing the First Letter and First Vowel might read as follows:

> Betty is likely to approach her life experiences with a feeling of adventure (E), a desire for excitement and variety (E). She tends to adapt herself well (E). She uses her good mind (E), her good perceptions and judgments of people, motivations and events (E) as well as her capability with details (B). She knows how to foster harmony in groups in which she's involved (B). These characteristics will tend to enhance her role as a leader and executive.
>
> Betty's extreme sensitivity sometimes makes it difficult to work with others who are less sensitive (B). Her tendency to be shy, retiring and self-contained (B) often keeps her more comfortable in a subordinate role (B). Although she starts many projects, she tends to abandon some of them or set them aside for a later time (E). These traits are likely to limit her strong capability for leadership and organization.

Here, we discuss both enhancing *and* limiting traits. Note that more space is devoted to the predominant E traits than to the B characteristics.

Hal Allen's organization sheet and delineation

Hal's First Letter and First Vowel, along with his Temperament, are placed in the row reserved for directing modifiers on the organization sheet (Figure 20-1 below). These three are the only modifiers *not* grouped by modifier numbers.

Turn to Step 25, page 216, and read the paragraphs of Hal's delineation which discuss his natural approach to experience.

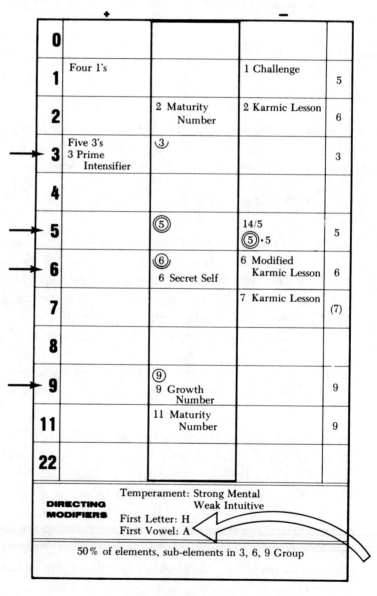

Figure 20-1
Organization Sheet with First Letter and First Vowel

CHAPTER 21

SYNTHESIS OF THE CORE AND MODIFIERS

We've now examined all the modifiers, one by one, and become reasonably acquainted with their relative importance, their modifying powers and their peculiarities. The modifiers have been carefully separated in order to make the distinctions among them as clear as possible. At last, we're ready to combine the modifiers with the core elements to arrive at a complete synthesis.

The delineation that follows starts with the slightly fuzzy black-and-white reproduction of Harlan William Allen that we produced in Chapter 7 when we synthesized the core elements. By adding the modifiers, we'll convert the blurred black-and-white photo into a full-color focused portrait. Harlan (or Hal) will, of course, have the same characteristics in the portrait that he did in the reproduction, but the clearer focus and the added color will bring out considerably more detail.

Hal Allen's calculation sheet

Hal's delineation, like all others, starts with the calculations. Here's Hal's calculation sheet (Figure 21-1 on page 194), complete with all the modifiers.

Hal Allen's organization sheet

Based on the idea of grouping comparable energies to add to the coherence of the delineation, here's Hal's organization sheet (Figure 21-2 on page 196), showing the modifiers along with the core elements. The right-hand column indicates the modifier number with which each energy is to be grouped.

January 1981
HAL ALLEN

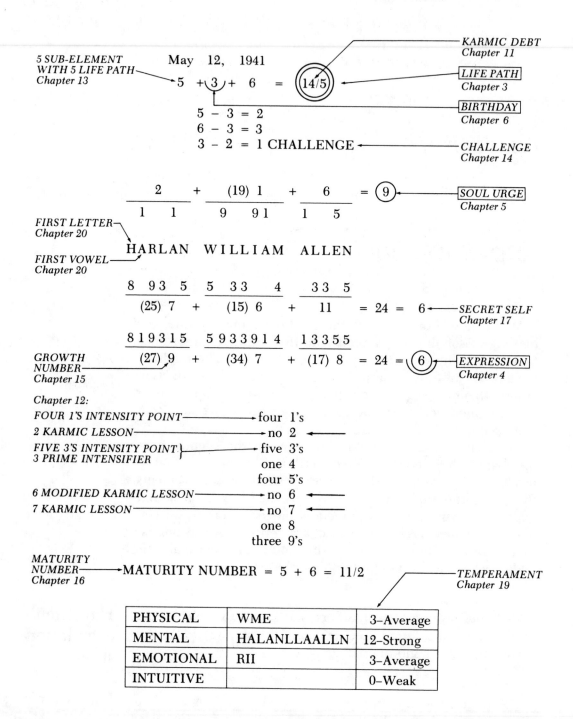

Figure 21-1
Calculation Sheet:
Hal Allen

Here are Hal's energy groups shown diagramatically just as they were back in Chapter 10:

5 energy ●●●●●●●○○○○ added 5 and 1 energy

6 energy ●●●●●○○○ added 6 and 2 energy

9 energy ●●●●○○ added 9 and 11 energy

3 energy ●●○○○ added 3 energy

Misc.
energy ○ added 7 energy

In Chapter 10, we didn't have any information about the specific modifiers. Now that we do, we can convert the energy group diagram into an outline for Hal's delineation, using the actual modifiers listed on his organization sheet. (And, at the end of the outline, we'll add the directing modifiers, which, though discussed in Chapter 10, were not included in the diagram.)

5 ENERGY AND RELATED ENERGY

Core:	5 Life Path
Modifiers:	14/5 Karmic Debt
	5 Life Path/5 sub-Life Path
	Four 1's Intensity Point
	1 Challenge

6 ENERGY AND RELATED ENERGY

Core:	6 Expression
Modifiers:	6 Secret Self
	6 Modified Karmic Lesson
	3,6,9 group: fifty percent of elements and sub-elements
	2 Maturity Number
	2 Karmic Lesson

9 ENERGY AND RELATED ENERGY

Core:	9 Soul Urge
Modifiers:	9 Growth Number
	11 Maturity Number

3 ENERGY

Core:	3 Birthday
Modifiers:	Five 3's Intensity Point
	3 Prime Intensifier

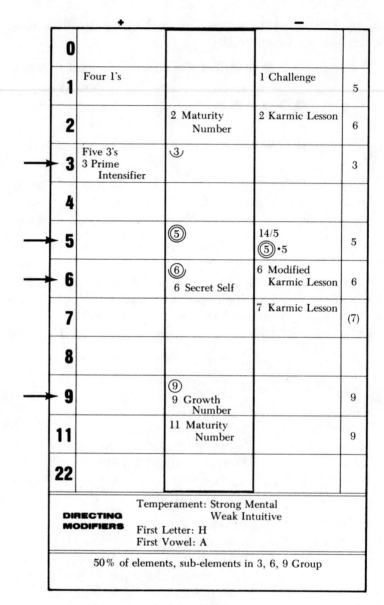

	+		**—**	
0				
1	Four 1's		1 Challenge	5
2		2 Maturity Number	2 Karmic Lesson	6
3	Five 3's 3 Prime Intensifier	③		3
4				
5		⑤	14/5 ⑤•5	5
6		⑥ 6 Secret Self	6 Modified Karmic Lesson	6
7			7 Karmic Lesson	(7)
8				
9		⑨ 9 Growth Number		9
11		11 Maturity Number		9
22				
DIRECTING MODIFIERS	Temperament: Strong Mental Weak Intuitive First Letter: H First Vowel: A			
	50% of elements, sub-elements in 3, 6, 9 Group			

Figure 21-2
Completed Organization Sheet:
Hal Allen

MISCELLANEOUS MODIFIERS

Modifiers: 7 Karmic Lesson

DIRECTING MODIFIERS

Temperament: Strong Mental,
                    weak Intuitive

First Letter: H
First Vowel: A

We want to be sure that the core is preserved in the reading. To do this, we'll use the 22 steps of the core synthesis of Chapter 7 as a base. We'll insert the modifiers in the relevant places based on the outline we've just developed.

Let's look, for instance, at the 5 and 6 energy in the outline. The heart of the 5 energy is, of course, the 5 Life Path which is described in Steps 2 through 8. The description of the four modifiers connected with the 5 Life Path will be inserted in the most appropriate place in those steps. The 6 Expression, covered in Steps 9 through 14, will have its five corresponding modifiers inserted in the most appropriate place in those steps or, in one instance which we'll note, omitted as repetitious. When we've completed the 22 steps, we'll add an additional step to describe the miscellaneous energy and two additional steps to describe the directing modifiers.

We now have a plan of action!

Hal Allen's complete step-by-step delineation

Below, then, is Hal Allen's complete synthesis. We'll list each step, just as we did in Chapter 7, then provide explanations, in italics, of the many modifications to the original core synthesis required by the addition of the modifiers.

The actual delineation will be shown indented. The delineation contains all the paragraphs from the original core synthesis *plus* additional paragraphs describing the modifiers.

A paragraph taken intact from Hal's core synthesis looks like this:

> Although you may well be involved in domestic activities, you may feel the pressures of the responsibilities conflicting. . . .

A paragraph from Hal's core synthesis which is now deleted looks like this:

> ~~There's a chance that you'll be so exhilarated with the opportunities before you, that you'll flit from thing to thing with. . . .~~

A new paragraph, not originally included in the core synthesis, looks like this:

> You will unlock your experiences when you give of yourself for the pleasure of giving—giving money, time, friendship, affection, love. . . . .

NUMEROLOGY DELINEATION
FOR
HARLAN WILLIAM ALLEN
BORN MAY 12, 1941

STEP 1

DERIVE THE ELEMENTS OF THE CORE.

The calculations for core and *modifiers replaces this original step in the core synthesis. The calculations are shown on the calculation sheet on page 194.*

STEP 2

EXPRESS THE CENTRAL FOCUS OF THE 5 LIFE PATH.

The central focus remains fixed, irrespective of all modifiers.

The original paragraph is unchanged.

> The central focus of your life is learning the exhilaration of the *constructive* use of freedom. Life is full of exciting opportunities for you—there can be much variety, change, unusual happenings, unusual people, unforeseen adventure. You will find that you are capable at almost any task, that you are talented in a number of directions. The world is your oyster—there are exciting things to do at every turn—and that undoubtedly is the difficulty. You must learn how to pick and choose; how to seek experiences which will be of benefit, how to discard those things that are not working, how to profit from every experience. You must learn not to waste your time or scatter your forces, not to get lost in purely physical delights—food, sex, drink or drugs. It can be sheer delight to be a rolling stone, but the frustration of moving from place to place, from person to person, from opportunity to opportunity may eventually overwhelm the delight.

STEP 3

EXPRESS THE SUB-FOCUS OF THE 3 BIRTHDAY.

> While you're learning how to use freedom, learn the joy of expressing yourself. Give of yourself, openly, warmly, with delight. ~~Learn, too, to express~~

> ~~yourself, using your good imagination, your ar-~~
> ~~tistic abilities, but especially, your ability with~~
> ~~words.~~

Note that a portion of the original paragraph above has been deleted since similar material is covered in the added paragraph below. We're trying to minimize the repetition throughout.

*Add the five 3's Intensity Point (*CHART 8: THE INTENSITY TABLE*) and the 3 Prime Intensifier (*CHART 8: THE INTENSITY TABLE*) here.*

These predominantly positive modifiers are added here to the positive energy of the 3 Birthday. These modifiers could have been included in Step 7: Characteristics of the Birthday. They're included here instead because I wanted to start the reading on a strong positive note. There's going to be a lot of negative energy expressed in this delineation—the 14/5 Karmic Debt in particular. If you begin the reading very positively, the subject is likely to be more receptive when the going gets rough.

> Learn, too, to express your superior talents in music, art or writing, reinforced by your excellent creative imagination. In particular, you're likely to have a strong capability with words—your verbal and written self-expression may be one of the areas where you really shine. Your creative talent, imagination and verbal abilities are probably a-mong your most obvious strong traits.
>
> If you scatter your energies or act immoderately (and you do have these tendencies), you'll be working against your own best interests.

The description of the 3,6,9 group is omitted from the delineation because it covers the same material as these 3 modifiers.

STEP 4

EXPRESS THE HARMONY OR DISCORD OF THE 5 LIFE PATH/3 BIRTHDAY ASPECT.

The paragraph is deleted. It's essentially repeating a portion of Step 3.

~~Your ability to give of yourself in social situations as well as with creative expression—most likely with words—will help in working toward an awareness of the constructive use of freedom.~~

STEP 5

DETERMINE THE HARMONY OR DISCORD OF THE 5 LIFE PATH/6 EXPRESSION AND THE 5 LIFE PATH/9 SOUL URGE ASPECTS.

There's no description included here.

STEP 6

EXPRESS THE CHARACTERISTICS OF THE 5 LIFE PATH.

The 14/5 Karmic Debt (CHART 7: THE KARMIC DEBT) describes obstacles to be overcome. The existence of the Karmic Debt is explained in the paragraph below.

The major negative effects of the Debt are described in Step 8.

> The configuration of your chart indicates that you started out in life with some blockages which must be overcome before you can make the most of your strong positive potential. I can't tell whether you've already overcome the obstacles—some people manage it early in life, others spend a good number of years struggling with the impediments.

Since the Karmic Debt blocks the early growth of the potentials, the first two original paragraphs are deleted and replaced by new paragraphs reflecting the ultimate *development of the potential rather than the* immediate *use of the energy at birth.*

Remember that Harlan is in his forties at the time of the reading and has probably overcome some of the Karmic Debt obstructions. There's no way to read at precisely what age the various obstacles have been or will be constructively managed.

> ~~You are probably versatile and active and can do almost anything with superior talent. Although you are interested in the new, different or progressive, you usually proceed here with awareness of your responsibilities and concern for others.~~

Here are some of the strong positive potentials you may be using now or can ultimately develop:

You'll be able to show your versatility and do almost anything with superior talent. Your interest in the new, different or progressive will be balanced with your awareness of your responsibilities and concern for others.

~~You are apt to be clever, with an inborn ability to accomplish what you want. You may be a quick thinker with a good ability to analyze, although that ability isn't always used to further your best interests.~~

You can learn to use your cleverness along with your inborn ability to accomplish what you want. You'll be able to use your quick thinking and good ability to analyze to further your best interests.

Delete the paragraph below and don't replace it with a new paragraph. The restlessness, etc. are considerably aggravated by the Karmic Debt, but the potentially erratic nature is fully covered in Step 8.

~~Although you sometimes have feelings of restlessness, impatience and the desire to try something new, these feelings are tempered by your desire for balance in your life and those around you as well as your concern for giving to others.~~

The original paragraph below is deleted and replaced by a paragraph reflecting the erratic nature emphasized by the Karmic Debt.

~~Although you love change and enjoy travel and adventure, you are also capable of routine tasks demanded by your sense of responsibility. At times, these traits may produce feelings of conflict.~~

Early in life, your ability to perform the routine tasks demanded by your sense of responsibility is likely to conflict with your free spirit. You'll have to learn how to deal more comfortably with this work.

The last three original paragraphs of this step describe traits which are likely to shine despite the handicap of the Debt, but the Debt is likely to create some problems so that the full brilliance of the described characteristics is somewhat restricted. The three replacement paragraphs clarify this state of affairs.

~~You are probably a delightful companion and can inspire and delight with your enthusiasm. You may occasionally have to temper your sudden impulses to change direction.~~

I'd expect that people's view of you as a delightful companion, bubbling over with new plans and enthusiasm, is one of your strongest potentials. You probably have to learn, though, to temper your sudden impulses to change direction.

~~You are enthusiastic. You tackle each new experience with renewed enthusiasm.~~

Your enthusiasm, too, is a strong potential, but you probably have to work to curb the excessively whimsical, inconsistent or unpredictable outbursts of your spirit.

~~You tend to express eternal youth. The excitement of life keeps you young.~~

You tend to express eternal youth. Although the excitement of life keeps you young, you may have to learn to distinguish between youthfulness and childishness.

STEP 7

EXPRESS THE CHARACTERISTICS OF THE 12 BIRTHDAY.

Omit the phrase covering creative talent since this is well-described in Step 3.

Omit the last sentence. The scattering is considerably aggravated by the 14/5 Karmic Debt. The potentially erratic nature is fully explored in Step 8.

You are probably good with words. ~~You work well using your original strongly creative approach.~~

You usually express the joy of living. People are likely to see you as cheerful, friendly and sociable, a good conversationalist, full of energy. You have a good mind. You're likely to be affectionate, loving and sensitive. Your strong feelings may cause occasional rapid ups and downs and you may tend to repress these feelings in business. ~~You usually have many interests, so you're likely to scatter your energy~~.

STEP 8

DISCUSS THE NEGATIVE EXPRESSION OF THE 5 LIFE PATH.

This step describes the negative effect of the major negative modifier—the 14/5 Karmic Debt.

As if that wasn't bad enough, we have three additional negative modifiers in this step:

a. The 5 Life Path/5 sub-element aspect, discussed just below.
b. The four 1's Intensity Point, discussed at the end of the step.
c. The 1 Challenge, also discussed at the end of the step.

These four negative modifiers are all grouped with the 5 energy, and this step is where all their negative potential is described. This is undoubtedly the most negative portion of the entire delineation. The impediments should be expressed as constructively as possible so as not to overwhelm the subject. Always indicate some positive action that will help alleviate the difficulties.

The 5 Life Path/5 sub-element aspect (CHART 6: THE ASPECTS) describes two possible negative directions: (1) freedom used carelessly, or (2) fear of freedom. The first possibility, similar to part of the 14/5 Karmic Debt, is discussed later in this step. The second possibility occurs infrequently, but should be mentioned.

The original first paragraph of this step describes this fear of freedom and the added paragraph comments on its rarity.

When you are hesitant about using your freedom, it may seem easier to retreat into a safe and stable situation. When you do this, the changes and uncertainty will still be there, but you'll probably have difficulty dealing with them.

There's not too much chance that you'll be afraid of freedom and retreat like this. If you do, though, you certainly won't be learning how to overcome the obstructions.

The original paragraph below is deleted . . .

~~There's a chance that you'll be so exhilarated with the opportunties before you, that you'll jump from thing to thing with maddening speed, lost in over-indulgence or erratic behavior. This is apt to bring much frustration.~~

*. . . and replaced with four paragraphs describing the negative effect of the 14/5 Karmic Debt (*CHART 7: THE KARMIC DEBT*). Note that the problems covered in the first two paragraphs are the same problems that result from the 5·5 aspect.*

You're likely, particularly in your early years, to go from activity to activity with maddening speed, changing direction at the drop of a hat. At the least, your actions will tend toward the erratic. You can't move ahead constructively until you've learned to tone down this side of your nature. Jumping around, with little sense of accomplishment or accountability, works against you.

Your tendency to overindulgence in eating, sensuality, liquor or drugs also gets in the way of forward progress. Learn to curb your appetite for excessive physical stimulation.

You must learn the important lesson of change: to begin to nurture an interest or relation, to experience it in full bloom, to detach from it when it is completed. This is likely to be a difficult lesson. Instead of appreciating the beauties which enter (and leave) your life, you may be beset with disappointment at losses which are either beyond your control or caused by your lack of awareness.

You can approach your positive potential when

you overcome these obstacles and, also, learn to profit from your experience instead of repeating mistakes. Until you shift to a positive direction, you are likely to meet delays or losses.

The original paragraph below is deleted . . .

~~These negative expressions are unproductive. They should be avoided in order to proceed constructively with your development.~~

. . . and replaced with this paragraph explaining why the subject faces so many handicaps.

Your problems with freedom and overindulgence are payments in this life to balance a Karmic Debt developed from a misuse of freedom in a previous life.

These new paragraphs below complete Step 8. They cover a combined description of the four 1's Intensity Point (CHART 8: THE INTENSITY TABLE) and the 1 Challenge (CHART 9: THE CHALLENGE/THE GROWTH NUMBER).

There are some problem areas not related to the Karmic Debt.

A part of you tends to be self-centered with strong interests that must be satisfied. This self-centered part tends to control and dominate, but the domination usually offends others.

In your early years, you may have felt dominated by people with strong influence, probably parents or others on whom you were dependent. You may have felt that your desires weren't being met, your needs opposed. To feel less restricted, you may have tried to please everyone, but you're not likely to have found much satisfaction in that endeavor. You probably ended up displeased yourself as well as confused and resentful.

Using the courage of your convictions in taking care of your own needs should have helped. You probably have to remain watchful to protect yourself from domination, but dominating others is certainly not the answer.

You can exhibit much courage and independent feelings, often in the face of great difficulties, but your potential to use your original ideas and leadership abilities for positive ends may be stifled by your self-centered lack of awareness.

Step 8 is undoubtedly the most complex part of the delineation. Be sure you understand the derivation of all the material.

With the completion of Step 8, we've completed the portion of the reading devoted to the 5 Life Path and its related energies. Now, we move on to the 6 Expression and its related potential.

There are five modifiers related to the 6 Expression. The 3,6,9 group description can be omitted since the description would only repeat information already covered in Step 3. The remaining modifiers are either neutral or add difficulties along with the energy to resolve the problems—a far cry from the deep negativity of Step 8.

STEP 9

EXPRESS THE ABILITIES OF THE 6 EXPRESSION.

Add a new portion at the beginning of the original paragraph as a transition from the 5 Life Path to the 6 Expression description.

Along with the part of you that's a free spirit, there's another completely different side of you —the ~~you are probably a~~ responsible, helpful and conscientious person. You have the ability to rectify and balance inharmonious situations and you would be available to give help and comfort to those in need. You would work well where the care of the old, young or sick are involved. You probably show concern for the betterment of the community. ~~You are apt to possess creative and artistic talents.~~

Delete the last sentence above. It's similar to Step 3. The next original paragraph remains unchanged.

It's possible that you're not using or developing all of these capabilities at this time. Some of your talents may have been used in the earlier part of your life and some may still be latent. Be aware of your capabilities, so that you can make use of them at appropriate times.

STEP 10

EXPRESS THE HARMONY OR DISCORD OF THE 5 LIFE PATH/6 EXPRESSION ASPECT.

The original paragraphs remain unchanged.

You are probably exhilarated by all the exciting opportunities and adventures so often present in your life. It may be difficult, at times, to give up this excitement to satisfy your responsibilities. There may even be times when you want to shirk these responsibilities or give them up altogether to enjoy the excitement of freedom.

Ignoring your responsibilities will probably not be very satisfying for you. You have to find some way to satisfy the adventurous side of your nature and, at the same time, enjoy the pleasures you receive when you express the responsible, conscientious side. You may find that an out-of-the-ordinary job may be helpful in balancing the quiet stability you may desire in a close family. Or, you might plan exciting trips or follow some unusual avocations to offset the solid, respectable job which gives you satisfaction.

STEP 11

EXPRESS THE EFFECTIVENESS OF THE 5 LIFE PATH/6 EXPRESSION COMBINATION.

The original paragraph remains unchanged.

You have the potential to take advantage of the opportunities presented with relative ease, to make the most of the experiences which come your way. Your natural abilities will probably find ample field for expression. The environment will allow your talents to be displayed and appreciated. As your capabilities find the opportunities

to expand to meet their potential, your development will progress in a manner which may bring
you much satisfaction.

STEP 12

DETERMINE THE HARMONY OR DISCORD OF THE 6
EXPRESSION/5 LIFE PATH AND THE 6 EXPRESSION/9
SOUL URGE ASPECTS.

There's no description included here.

STEP 13

EXPRESS THE POSITIVE ATTITUDES OF THE 6 EX-
PRESSION.

*The four modifiers related to the 6 Expression are all included
in this step. Their effect is to significantly increase Hal's capabilities beyond what was apparent in the description of the core
alone.*

The first original paragraph remains . . .

When you are involved closely with people, you
are probably most loving, friendly and appreciative of others, as well as very sympathetic, kind,
generous and understanding. There may be times,
though, when you prefer not to be involved at all.

*. . . enhanced by some of the characteristics described by the 2
Karmic Lesson (CHART 8: THE INTENSITY TABLE) . . .*

You're likely to find yourself in situations where
a sensitive nature, along with a diplomatic manner
are imperative for positive development. You were
probably born with an innate ability to express
these traits.

*. . . and with Hal's sensitivity highlighted, because of the 2
Maturity Number (CHART 10: THE MATURITY NUMBER).*

Now that you're in your forties, you may want to
reevaluate the satisfactions you've derived from
your sensitivity. Have you developed so that your
strong sensitivity can be comfortably used? Have
you learned how to say and do what you need
without feeling your sensitivity compromised? Do

<u>shyness or uncertainty block you from a full expression of your sensitivity?</u>

<u>At this time in your life, you may want to revise some of your attitudes and actions in order to better express your sensitivity and to better receive others' friendship and affection as a reward for that expression.</u>

The second original paragraph remains . . .

Although you may well be involved in domestic activities, you may feel the pressures of these responsibilities conflicting with your own need for individuality. The resolution of this conflict (or the lack of resolution) will determine how good a husband and parent you are.

*. . . enhanced by the characteristics described by the 6 Modified Karmic Lesson (*CHART 8: THE INTENSITY TABLE*).*

<u>You'll be capable of balancing, adjusting, harmonizing, serving others, and will show these traits strongly in marriage and parenting situations where these abilities are likely to be necessary to keep affairs running smoothly. You're likely to have much responsibility to carry, but you're willing and able to carry it. Family and friends will depend on you for support, and you'll be there when needed.</u>

This is a good place for a brief description of the 6 Secret Self.

<u>You probably have a dream of being part of a loving family—an adoring wife and children—in a beautiful home, with you as the guiding spirit.</u>

And here's the last original paragraph to complete Step 13.

You are probably extremely open and honest with others.

STEP 14

EXPRESS THE NEGATIVE ATTITUDES OF THE 6 EX-
PRESSION.

The original paragraphs remain unchanged.

> There is the possibility that you may be too exac-
> ting of yourself and willing to sacrifice yourself (or
> your family) for the welfare of others, but your
> strong individual needs will probably mitigate this
> attitude.

> At times, you may have substantial difficulty dis-
> tinguishing helping from interfering.

> Although you may express worry and anxiety, you
> are apt to try and cover these feelings and look at
> the bright side instead.

> The expression of your individual needs will prob-
> bably keep you from becoming a drudge because
> of excessive involvement with your respon-
> sibilities.

*With the completion of Step 14, we've completed the portion
of the reading devoted to the 6 Expression and its related
energies. Now, we move on to the 9 Soul Urge and its related
potential.*

*There are only two modifiers related to the 9 Soul Urge. The
9 Growth Number adds a strong note to Step 15. The 11 Maturity Number is mentioned in passing in Step 21.*

STEP 15

EXPRESS THE MOTIVES OF THE 9 SOUL URGE.

*The question here serves as a transition from the 6 Expression
to the 9 Soul Urge.*

> What are your deep inner motivations?

The original paragraph remains unchanged.

> Your inner nature wants to give of itself to
> others—usually in a humanitarian or philanthropic
> manner. You probably want to give much of
> friendship, affecton, love. You may want to give

your knowledge and experience. You may also want to share with others your artistic or creative talents. It's possible that these talents are of considerable magnitude.

The description of the 9 Growth Number (CHART 9: THE CHALLENGE/THE GROWTH NUMBER) *fits well here.*

You will help expand your development when you give of yourself for the pleasure of giving—giving money, time, friendship, affection, love, understanding, sympathy. You must give with little expectation of return or reward. Allow the needs of others to take precedence over your personal ambitions. This seemingly difficult direction can bring the deepest of satisfactions. You have a good deal of energy tending in this direction.

STEP 16

EXPRESS THE HARMONY OR DISCORD OF THE 5 LIFE PATH/9 SOUL URGE ASPECT.

The original paragraph remains unchanged, although it resembles Step 10. (In an advanced delineation, Steps 10 and 16 would be combined.)

Although your inner nature feels the need to give to others, you may often feel torn between this need and your stronger need to explore the exhilarating opportunities that present themselves for your personal development. You must learn to balance these opposing energies to avoid the frustration of missing an adventure or the sadness of not being available to those in need of your help.

STEP 17

EXPRESS THE EFFECTIVENESS OF THE 5 LIFE PATH/9 SOUL URGE COMBINATION.

The original paragraph remains unchanged.

Although you are able to recognize your opportunities, you find somewhat fewer possibilities than you would like to advance your inner devel-

opment. The experiences at hand, while not necessarily presenting opportunities to fulfill your inner
needs, are apt to act as a secondary motivating
force. Make the most of these experiences. Learn
to accept the natural pace of your development.

STEP 18

EXPRESS THE HARMONY OR DISCORD OF THE 6 EXPRESSION/9 SOUL URGE ASPECT.

The original paragraphs remain unchanged.

Your natural talent at being helpful and able to
balance inharmonious situations will be substantially aided by your inner need to give to others,
often without thought of yourself. You may be
much concerned with the betterment of the community and capable of assisting in that betterment.

You are apt to be strongly motivated to develop
your creative expressive talents.

STEP 19

EXPRESS THE EFFECTIVENESS OF THE 6 EXPRESSION/9 SOUL URGE COMBINATION.

The original paragraph remains unchanged.

Your motivation sometimes seems to outrun your
abilities. Although you have many ideas, your
natural talents don't necessarily help to advance
these ideas. Learn to be content with the realization that it will take more time than you would
prefer to fulfill your inner desires.

STEP 20

REVIEW THE HARMONY OR DISCORD OF THE 6 LIFE PATH/9 SOUL URGE AND 6 EXPRESSION/9 SOUL URGE ASPECTS.

There's no description included here.

STEP 21

EXPRESS THE POSITIVE ATTITUDES OF THE 9 SOUL URGE.

*Delete the first original paragraph since it's essentially repeat-
ing a part of Step 13.*

~~When you are concerned about others, you are very sympathetic, generous and kind. At these times, your sensitive nature expresses much love, compassion and tolerance. There may be times, though, when you prefer not to be involved at all.~~

Include this original paragraph.

You possess a deep, intuitive understanding of life, innate wisdom, good intuition and a broad point of view.

Add this brief paragraph to describe the 11 Maturity Number (CHART 10: THE MATURITY NUMBER). *As we mentioned in Chapter 16, there's only a small chance that the energy related to this Maturity Number will be activated.*

At this time in your life, you may begin to be a-ware of the spiritual world and the relation of that world to the material world.

Include this original paragraph.

You are capable, at times, of expressing high ideals and an inspirational approach. You are capable of being self-sacrificing, but this trait is apt to con-flict with your love of freedom.

Omit this paragraph. It's a repetition of part of Steps 15 and 16.

~~You can give freely without being concerned a-bout any return, although your desire to give may cause conflicts with your self-centered needs.~~

STEP 22

EXPRESS THE NEGATIVE ATTITUDES OF THE 9 SOUL URGE.

The original paragraphs remain unchanged.

You may be far too sensitive, extremely emotional with your emotions expressed very strongly.

You probably suffer from the conflict between your high spiritual aims and your need for freedom and personal expansion.

At times, you probably resent the necessity of giving. At times, when your giving conflicts with your own needs, you may not give, but you'll be dissatisfied anyway.

Sometimes you're disappointed in the lack of perfection in yourself and others.

Your tendency to be quite moody and critical at times is usually offset by your freedom-loving delight.

We've now completely described all the core elements and the related modifier energies. We'll add an additional step to describe modifier energies not related to the core elements.

STEP 23

DESCRIBE THE MISCELLANEOUS ENERGY.

Under Miscellaneous Energy in the delineation outline, we have only the 7 Karmic Lesson. You may remember from Chapter 12, that the 7 Karmic Lesson is present for most individuals but, unless accompanied by other 7 energy, doesn't need to be described. Therefore, in Hal's case, the Karmic Lesson description is omitted.

We'll add two additional steps to describe the directing modifiers.

STEP 24

DESCRIBE THE TEMPERAMENT.

Hal has a strong Mental component, average Physical and Emotional components and a weak Intuitive component.

The Temperament description is based on Chapter 19.

> You have a reasonably well-balanced temperament (*Strong Mental, average Physical and Emotional, weak Intuitive*), so most of your energy is likely to be used. The only parts that are not likely to be developed would be those portions having to do with spiritual, psychic or metaphysical matters (*weak Intuitive component*), and those make up only a small part of your basic potential. I would not

expect you to fully develop your understanding of life on a deep intuitive level (*9 Soul Urge, weak Intuitive component*), or to completely express an inspirational approach to your activities (*9 Soul Urge, weak Intuitive component*). In your mature years, there is the possibility of increasing your awareness of the spiritual world (*11 Maturity Number*), but I'd be surprised if you work on this very much (*weak Intuitive component*).

I'd expect a good deal of emphasis on mental matters—matters that deal with reason, logic and facts (*strong Mental component*). I'd expect you to come up with a lot of original intellectual ideas (*5 Life Path, strong Mental component*), and these may be instrumental in demonstrating your leadership abilities (*four 1's Intensity Point*). You're likely to use your strong verbal abilities (*five 3's Intensity Point, 3 Prime Intensifier*) to communicate your superior grasp of facts and reasons (*strong Mental component*), along with your feelings (*average Emotional component*).

Your ability to be helpful, to balance and harmonize situations (*6 Expression*) is probably expressed in a clear, reasoned way (*strong Mental component*). Your work with the old, young or sick (*6 Expression*) may involve organizing along with political or business activities (*strong Mental component*). You may show your humanitarian ways (*9 Soul Urge*) by expressing your sympathy and understanding (*average Emotional component*), or by physically caring for others (*average Physical component*), but I suspect that you may stress an intellectual orientation (*strong Mental component*) —by writing and speaking for causes in which you believe, for instance (*five 3's Intensity Point, 3 Prime Intensifier*).

You're good at taking care of the details (*2 Karmic Lesson*) and you're likely to handle them in a reasonable and logical manner (*strong Mental component*).

Your sensitivity (*6 Expression, 2 Maturity Number*) is likely to contribute to your ability to help others because of your fine grasp of the facts of a situation (*strong Mental component*).

STEP 25

DESCRIBE THE APPROACH TO EXPERIENCE.

*The description is based on the First Letter H (*CHART 11: THE FIRST LETTER*), and the First Vowel A (*CHART 12: THE FIRST LETTER*).*

The first paragraph lists traits which limit the experience. The last three paragraphs list characteristics which enhance the experience.

Those last paragraphs are important in concluding the delineation on a strong positive note.

You are likely to approach some of your life experiences with vacillating thoughts (*H*) and an inability to marshal your forces for maximum impact (*A*). This emphasis stresses your changeable nature (*14/5 Karmic Debt*) and tends to limit your experience.

I'd expect, though, that you approach much of your experience with a more positive direction (*more A and H traits are positive rather than negative*). I'd expect that you approach a good deal of experience as an executive or leader (*H*), using your good mind and creative mentality (*A*), tending to promote quietly in a progressive manner (*A*), with originality and innovation (*A*).

Your approach is likely to often stress your self-starting capability (*A*) and the high-level consciousness which allows you to meet situations with an extreme awareness of the material world along with the possibility of achieving material success — money, power, status (H).

In addition, your approach stresses your ability to work well with others (*H*) using your keen perception of people and events (*H*) as well as your sensitivity and idealism (*A*). All these positive emphases in your approach will tend to enhance your experience.

Use of modifiers, in Hal Allen's delineation

For this delineation, sixteen of the eighteen modifiers in the delineation outline on pages 195–6 were added to the core elements. (The description of the 3,6,9 group was omitted as explained in Step 3, and the 7 Karmic Lesson was omitted as explained in Step 23.) Approximately half of the original steps in the core synthesis were revised, some significantly, and three additional steps were added.

Do you remember the summary of the core synthesis in Chapter 7?

Core summary

Harlan William Allen, born May 12, 1941, is an active, versatile, freedom-loving person with much excitement and adventure in his life, enhanced by his expression of the joy of living. He has the capability of being responsible, loving and giving. He must learn to balance the somewhat self-centered exhilaration he finds in freedom with his inner need to give much to others in the way of friendship, love and affection. He has the potential for artistic or creative endeavor.

Core and modifier summary

A summary of the delineation with core *and* modifiers reads like this: (The additions to the original summary are underlined.)

Harlan William Allen, born May 12, 1941, has the potential to be an active, versatile freedom-loving person with much excitement and adventure in his life. He must first overcome his early tendencies to be erratic and overindulge in physical pleasures. He must also learn to profit from his mistakes and live comfortably with change. He can enhance his life by his expression of the joy of living.

He has the capability of being responsible and he'll have more responsibility than may seem a fair share. He's loving, giving, tactful, diplomatic and sensitive, but he does tend, at times, to be controlling and dominating. He'll unlock his experiences when he gives for the pleasure of giving with no expectation of reward or return.

Hal must learn to balance the somewhat self-centered exhilaration he finds in freedom with his inner need to give much to others in the way of friendship, love and affection. He probably has superior talents in writing—a strong capability with words—and he has the potential for considerable artistic and creative endeavor.

His basic viewpoint stresses a strong mental disposition. When he's approaching experiences positively, he emphasizes his leadership, creativity, awareness of the material world and ability to work well with others.

Commentary

Before proceeding to Part IV and advanced delineations in Volume 2, I think it would be advisable to concentrate on doing some readings as completely as we've done Hal Allen's—perhaps your own, some members of your family or a few close friends. Read for people you know well, so you can appreciate the correlation between the delineation and real life. For these readings, first synthesize the core as we did in Chapter 7—then add the modifiers as we did here.

I'll be the first to admit that there are a lot of fine points and a lot of details to think about and clarify. When we get to the advanced delineations, we'll learn how to arrive at a complete reading with a far easier flow than in this chapter. The easier flow, though, will, to a significant extent, be a product of an understanding of the individual modifiers and their relation to the completed delineation. If you take your time and build a solid foundation here, the advanced readings will be easier to handle and the whole field of numerology will, I expect, prove remarkably accessible.

THE
REFERENCE
CHARTS

THE REFERENCE CHARTS

CHART 1   **THE NUMBERS—BASICS**

The brief descriptions of all the numbers are similar to the descriptions in CHAPTER 2. See pages 12-14 of that chapter for a discussion of the relations among the numbers.

ODD NUMBERS

Concerned with the *individual* alone.
Related to relatively *abstract* concepts.
Involved with more *idealistic* endeavors.

EVEN NUMBERS

Concerned with the relation of the individual to the *group*.
Related to relatively *practical* concepts.
Involved with more *mundane* endeavors.

CHART **1**	**1**	INDIVIDUATION
NUMBERS—BASICS		INDEPENDENCE ATTAINMENT

ODD NUMBER

A person must distinguish himself from other people and acknowledge his own INDIVIDUATION. The individual has to develop the capability of standing on his own and going from dependence to INDEPENDENCE. Once independent, the person becomes aware of his potential for AT-TAINMENT as an individual—for creating and pioneering when working alone—to leading and managing as an individual working with others.

EVEN NUMBER

| CHART **1**

NUMBERS—BASICS | **2** RELATION
COOPERATION |

ODD NUMBER

EVEN NUMBER

Independence is important but has its limitations. There *are* other people all about, and another lesson involves being a meaningful part of a group—a small group like family or friends, a larger group like a business or community. The person must learn adaptability, service, consideration for others, i.e, the meaning of a RELATION with others, the idea of COOPERATION.

| CHART **1** | | **3** | EXPRESSION |
| NUMBERS—BASICS | | | JOY OF LIVING |

ODD NUMBER

A person must discover, both as an individual and as a group member, his capability of EXPRESSION: (1) artistic expression—writing, painting, sculpting, singing or any of the many other means of expressing inner thoughts and emotions, and (2) expression of feelings toward others—friendship, affection, love. The JOY OF LIVING can be expressed with optimism and enthusiasm. There can be a purity, even a naiveté here. (This is, perhaps, the most enjoyable lesson of all the numbers.)

EVEN NUMBER

CHART **1**		**4**	LIMITATION
			ORDER
NUMBERS—BASICS			SERVICE

ODD NUMBER

EVEN NUMBER

Life doesn't always present opportunities for singing and laughing. Life doesn't always appear expansive or yours for the taking. Often, it feels just the opposite. The individual must learn the difficult law of LIMI-TATION. Everyone has limitations—limitations presented by the environment, by the physical body, by the restrictions of the individual's viewpoints. Rather than struggle against these limits, it is necessary to learn to live with them, to accept them and to make a meaningful existence, not in spite of the limitations, but *because* of the limitations. It is a difficult lesson. The individual embarking on this course must learn system and organization, ORDER on a practical level. He must be prepared to be of SERVICE to others.

CHART 1	**5** CONSTRUCTIVE FREEDOM
NUMBERS—BASICS	

ODD NUMBER

There is a time for expansion, for dealing with change, unexpected happenings, adventure. This lesson usually gives a person an abundance of talents in every direction, the capability of accomplishing almost anything for which an opportunity is presented—and many opportunities *are* presented. With the freedom that this abundance of talent and opportunity brings, life can be exciting. But the lesson is more difficult: the individual must learn the CONSTRUCTIVE use of FREEDOM. The individual must not waste his many talents or misuse his ongoing opportunites; he must not get lost in solely physical desires—food, sex, alcohol, drugs. He must not scatter his potential and end up with frustration. He must make a meaningful existence by using freedom productively.

EVEN NUMBER

CHART **1** NUMBERS—BASICS	**6** BALANCE RESPONSIBILITY LOVE

ODD NUMBER

EVEN NUMBER

A person must learn to give the beauty of love and harmony, sympathy and understanding, protection and BALANCE. Along with the balancing, the lesson of RESPONSIBILITY can be a meaningful one. The individual may find himself responsible for more than what rightly seems his share. Others will recognize his strength, and he may be expected to help them if they are in need and cannot help themselves. He will probably be the one who holds the family together, who harmonizes and adjusts difficult situations. He may choose to limit himself to his family, his friends, possibly the close community. The friendship and LOVE the individual expresses to others will come back to him from those he helps. He can bask in the glory of a job well done and the quiet reward of friendship and love returned.

The individual's capability at harmony and balance may also be expressed creatively—there is the possibility of artistic achievement.

CHART 1

NUMBERS—BASICS

7 ANALYSIS
UNDERSTANDING

ODD NUMBER

There's a time for introspection, a time to subject all an individual knows to mental ANALYSIS, so that eventually a person possesses much of knowledge and UNDERSTANDING. Spiritual awareness is employed and emphasis on material matters avoided. Desire for material accumulation will probably lead the individual off the track, for this is a time for study and meditation, a time to know oneself—in the deepest way.

There will be much time spent alone—the person must learn to be alone and not feel isolated. Often, the individual will appear "different to others. His way of thinking or doing may be very much his own and may seem inexplicable to his fellow man. He must accept that he *is* on a different wavelength and find satisfaction in that. In a world where materialism rates so highly, the road for the counselor, the professor, the pure researcher may be a difficult one.

EVEN NUMBER

CHART 1
NUMBERS—BASICS

8 MATERIAL SATISFACTION

ODD NUMBER

EVEN NUMBER

The individual must learn to deal with the material things of life, the practical matters. He will find himself at home in the business world—with much capability as an efficient administrator or executive. He will learn how to handle money—how to accumulate it, how to spend it wisely. The individual will work for MATERIAL SATISFACTION. This may mean emphasis on money to buy the best in houses, cars, furnishings, trips. (Perhaps, if he can reach the highest level of this lesson, he will see that material freedom can mean relying very *little* on money or material matters. Few ever gain this insight.)

The individual will be very conscious of status in relation to material things and will work to satisfy his need for status to prove his superiority. He may appear single-minded, rigid or stubborn to others. Striving for power and high material goals may make him aware of the limitations of his ability or the restrictions of his circumstances.

CHART 1
NUMBERS—BASICS

9 SELFLESSNESS
HUMANITARIANISM

ODD NUMBER

There's a time to learn the satisfaction of giving to his fellow man. This is a difficult lesson. The satisfaction comes from the giving. There is little reward—the love and friendship are sometimes returned, the obligation often not repaid. The person must place all others before himself, must give for the sheer pleasure of giving, because he has learned the ultimate satisfaction of SELFLESSNESS and HUMANITARIANISM. The individual gives (1) by helping others or (2) by giving of himself in some form of creative expression.

EVEN NUMBER

CHART 1	
NUMBERS—BASICS	**11** ILLUMINATION

ODD NUMBER

The master numbers exist on a higher spiritual plane than the single digits. The first master number, the 11, must work to develop intuition, to tune into psychic forces not available to those with lower numbers. He must stand ready to be a channel with a message from above. In his life, he must inspire by his own example, living in the way revealed to him, spreading his ILLUMINATION for others to absorb and benefit. This number is as difficult as it is rewarding.

Often, particularly at an early age, the individual is aware of his special powers, yet unable to synthesize them for his own use or for the good of his fellow man. He is often a relatively impractical idealist, far more a dreamer than a doer. There is an undercurrent of nervous tension always present from the high power sources to which the individual is attuned. He has to learn to live with his special powers, to set himself aside from the world of material accumulation in order to better understand the powerful forces which can reveal a higher guidance.

EVEN NUMBER

CHART **1**
NUMBERS—BASICS

22 MASTER BUILDER

ODD NUMBER

EVEN NUMBER

The second master number, the 22, is potentially capable of combining the idealism of the first master number, the 11, with the ability to put these ideals into a concrete form. Enormous power is available to him to produce on a significant scale, for the benefit of humanity. When this potential can be realized, the individual becomes a MASTER BUILDER, capable of feats well beyond all others.

Few with this number can marshal their forces to reach anywhere near the ultimate potential. The individual is aware of the forces within him, aware also of the nervous tension that accompanies these forces. He spends his time grappling with powers that are difficult to comprehend and use. Often, he is seen by his fellow men as a person with enormous potential who has not, for some unexplained reason, been able to fully use his capabilities. The highest potential is also the most difficult to reach.

CHART **2**   **THE LIFE PATH**

CENTRAL FOCUS

      The Life Path is the major lesson to be learned in this life—the defined path which will provide the maximum in growth and development. This is the most important part of the core of a reading. See Chapter 3, page 23.

CHARACTERISTICS

      The outward manifestations of the Life Path. If the individual is expressing positively (and most people are), these characteristics should be readily apparent. If any of the characteristics are not expressed or even visible in a latent way, there is probably some negativity present.

NEGATIVE EXPRESSION

      The negative expression implies (1) the exaggeration of the lesson of the Life Path so that the extreme expressed is unproductive, or (2) the denial of the lesson of the Life Path in order to proceed in the opposite direction.

COMMENTARY

      Elaboration of some of the subtleties involved on the Life Path.

CHART **2**	**1**	INDIVIDUATION
THE LIFE PATH		INDEPENDENCE
		ATTAINMENT

CENTRAL FOCUS

The subject must learn the benefits of independence—a two-part learning process. First, the individual must learn to stand on his own two feet, learn not to lean on or depend on others. After the subject is indeed free of dependence, he can proceed to be a leader or creator. Once others sense the individual's independent capabilities, once he can accept and use his talents, there are likely to be substantial meaningful opportunities. Attainment of significant ends—material or otherwise—can follow.

CHARACTERISTICS

- Much inner strength.
- Leadership capability.
- Executive and administrative capability—always obvious although sometimes latent in application.
- Potential for accomplishment and financial reward—again obvious, although sometimes latent in application.
- Strong personal needs and desires. Feels it necessary to follow own convictions. Often surprised at others' resistance or the consequences of following own convictions.
- Self-centered. This may be extremely obvious, or may be hidden by a social veneer. The 1 will be very aware of the self-centeredness even if it's not outwardly apparent.
- The material needs may be large or small—but the 1 will spend the time necessary to satisfy these needs.

NEGATIVE EXPRESSION

A 1 still struggling with dependence may appear to be available at everyone's beck and call, with few needs of his own. No matter how giving the 1 appears, underneath the giving there will be much dissatisfaction with the dependent side. Often, though, the dissatisfaction may be well hidden.

Some 1's confuse independence and self-centeredness. They may be concerned with their own needs to the virtual exclusion of all else. This type of 1 may very well not know what is meant by self-centeredness or may even justify his self-centered position with a rational argument. In giving a reading to a 1 on whom there is no information, it is probably useful to clarify the difference between self-centeredness and independence.

Some 1's, lacking a sense of balance, may be so dominating and egotistical as to be their own worst enemies. Sometimes they burst with overconfidence, making them impatient with others' advice, unable to listen and benefit from others' opinions.

COMMENTARY

Some 1's spend most of their lives shaking off their dependent side. If this happens, they have little time left to reap the reward of being independent. 1's, particularly in the first stages of their life, often find themselves in situations where it is easy to be dependent and difficult to be independent. It is up to each 1 to struggle through to the second part of the lesson, where attainment can be achieved.

An aware 1 operating positively within the basic channel can be growing and experiencing much satisfaction throughout the life. There is much potential for accomplishment, achievement, creativity, and the potential *is* possible to reach (as compared, for instance, to the difficult-to-attain potential of the 11 or 22). The growing 1 can have a continuing feeling of satisfaction in his progress—and praise from others for his achievements. Often, he can receive good financial compensation, can satisfy his material needs, can reach a satisfying position of status.

CHART **2**
THE LIFE PATH

2 RELATION
COOPERATION

CENTRAL FOCUS

The subject must learn the satisfaction of contributing his capability as an organizer and facilitator in group situations. Here, although his contribution is seen, it will rarely receive full acknowledgement. He must learn that his use of quiet persuasion can accomplish as much as another's use of force. He must accept that his good ideas will often be better spread by others with more dynamism—that he can be the power behind the throne. If the subject can be comfortable with others getting credit for his ideas—that's part of the lesson, too.

The individual should develop his sensitivity and his skill at working with others to a high level. The world will be a better place because of his presence. He can glow quietly with the inner satisfaction of a job well done.

CHARACTERISTICS

- Sensitive to feelings of others.
- Cooperative. Capable of working patiently and carefully, doing much detail work if necessary. Rarely dominates a situation.
- Shows a great deal of consideration for others.

- A good friend. Expresses and receives friendship and love.
- Little concern with material needs or status. Usually can deny himself if others can thereby benefit.

NEGATIVE EXPRESSION

A 2 sometimes refuses to accept the role he is asked to play. He feels it's better to be an acknowledged leader than part of a group. His leading may be adequate, but is rarely dynamic. Sometimes, in a lead role, he will add confusion rather than harmony to a situation. He'll never understand why it happens that way, either. He's likely to blame others rather than himself.

Sometimes the 2, because of too much sensitivity, becomes shy and uncertain and contributes little as a group participant. He may protect his delicate ego by appearing apathetic or indifferent.

COMMENTARY

The key to growth and development for a 2 involves the control and balance of his sensitivity. He must find the path where he is not so sensitive that his feelings are constantly being hurt. His sensitivity to others must be so finely attuned that he can be a friend, lover or diplomat in the highest sense of these concepts.

It is too easy for the 2, trying his wings, to retreat with pain from situations where others are insensitive to him. He must learn how to deal with others' insensitivities without being overwhelmed.

A 2 operating in the right channel experiences a great deal of pleasure in life. He is the recipient of much love and affection from others.

CHART **2**
THE LIFE PATH

3 EXPRESSION
JOY OF LIVING

CENTRAL FOCUS

The subject must learn the joy of expressing himself. If he can be open, warm and full of delight, he is likely to be admired by others and desired as a pleasant companion. An easy lesson? In many ways the easiest and most delightful lesson: the experience of pure joy and the expression of that joy for others to share. It is the beginning of an appreciation of the beauty that can be in the world.

The individual should become aware of his spe-cial talents. He probably has a good imagination and artistic abilities to be developed. He can excel in creative work—painting, sculpting, music, perhaps. Most likely his creativity will be seen where verbal ability is important—in writing, acting or similar endeavors. He can express the beauty he experiences in his artistic work. His capability at creative self-expression is the highest level of attainment in this lesson.

CHARACTERISTICS

- Warm and friendly.
- Very social. A welcome addition to any social situation. Knows how to make others feel at home.
- Good conversationalist. A delight to listen to, and the ability to listen to others, too.

- Talent with words—speaking, writing, singing or acting as possible vocations or avocations.
- Creative imagination, often latent. The 3 recognizes the possibilities but may not be moved to develop the creativity.

NEGATIVE EXPRESSION

A 3 may be so delighted with the joy of living that his life becomes frivolous and superficial. He may scatter his abilities and express little sense of purpose.

When, on the other hand, he has difficulty developing his given capabilities, he may retreat into himself. He may feel uncomfortable in social situations, may prefer to hide his feelings rather than express them. He may appear moody or taciturn. If he is hurt by others, he may be critical or demeaning.

COMMENTARY

When a 3 is operating within the basic path, his approach to life is likely to be exceedingly positive, his disposition sunny. He seems to deal with problems with more ease than others. The 3's open disposition accepts the existence of problems, yet deals with them without being dragged to the depths of despair. Even while working through difficulties, the 3 will usually express warmth and friendliness. When he expresses his problems openly, he can often deal with them seriously but without rancor.

The 3 may mature later than others. His frivolity or moodiness may be difficult to shake. The frivolous 3 is often a delight, but is seen as a dilettante and treated as such. The moody 3 appears as an enigma because the cause of the moodiness is often not clear. The 3 is on a special lighter track, quite different from the other numbers. He may be able to get little help from others in learning to express his positive potential.

| CHART **2** THE LIFE PATH | **4** | LIMITATION ORDER SERVICE |

CENTRAL FOCUS

The subject must learn the advantage of order and system in accomplishing his work. He must also learn the rewards of service. He'll probably be involved in practical, down-to-earth work. Having determined where his duty lies, he must proceed with the hard work at hand, patiently and dependably.

The subject must learn to live with the law of limitation. He will be aware of limitations in his life—limitations of the environment, of his own physical body, of his individual viewpoint. Often, the subject may feel that circumstances limit him more than they limit others. He must learn how to live not *in spite of* the limitations, but *in harmony with* the limitations. He must learn to accept the restrictions rather than struggle with them. His life can then develop on a deep and beautiful path.

CHARACTERISTICS

- Practical.
- Capable of systematizing and managing. Can produce order where little existed.
- Willingness to work long and hard. Much patience with detail. Very conscientious. Often seems to do better with difficult problems than with simpler work. Often seems to make the work harder by his peculiar approach but, nevertheless, is capable of completing the work.
- Serious approach. Honest and sincere. Responsible.
- Strong likes and dislikes. Strong expression of what is right and wrong.
- Fixity of approach. This can range from the positive expression of great courage to the negative expression of extreme stubbornness. Others see the 4 as somewhat rigid, but the 4 can rarely see that quality in himself.

NEGATIVE EXPRESSION

The negative 4 can be overwhelmed by his feeling of limitation. He will feel tied down and frustrated. Often the limitations stem from his own stubborn, obstinate manner and his rigid approach, but he will be hard-pressed to see that he is causing his own problems. Sometimes, his concentration on details to the exclusion of the bigger picture limits his potential. His frustration sometimes expresses in bossiness and dominance.

Occasionally, the 4 will express his dissatisfaction with his Life Path by going in the opposite direction. He will be disorganized and irresponsible, with little sense of time and virtually no accountability to others. The chaos he creates around him will further upset him, but he will not be able to see himself as the cause.

COMMENTARY

This is a difficult lesson for many people. Few individuals want to learn to live with limitations. The usual reaction is to fight the restrictions rather than to accept them.

All 4's feel the sense of limitation. Only when they recognize the positive values inherent in limitation will their lives become growing and vital. The acceptance of limitation is the beginning of overcoming limitation as a negative part of the life. Limitation is also often in the eye of the beholder. What feels limiting to a 4 may not look limiting to an outside observer.

| CHART **2** THE LIFE PATH | **5** CONSTRUCTIVE FREEDOM |

CENTRAL FOCUS

The subject must learn the exhilaration of the *constructive* use of freedom. Life is full of exciting opportunities for this individual—there can be much variety, change, unusual happenings, unusual people, unforeseen adventure. The 5 will find that he's capable at almost any task, that he's talented in a number of directions. The world is his oyster—there are exciting things to do at every turn—and that, undoubtedly, is the difficulty. He must learn how to pick and choose; how to seek ex-periences which will be of benefit; how to discard those activities that aren't working; how to profit from every experience. He must learn not to waste his time or scatter his forces, not to get lost in purely physical delights—food, sex, drink, drugs. It can be sheer delight to be a rolling stone, but the frustration of moving from place to place, from person to person, from opportunity to opportunity may eventually overwhelm the delight.

CHARACTERISTICS

- Versatile and active. Can do almost anything. Can do many things with superior talent. Always involved with something new, different or progressive.
- Clever. An inborn ability to accomplish what he wants. Usually a quick thinker and a good ability to analyze. This ability isn't always used to further his best interests.
- Restless and impatient. May have difficulty sticking to a task. May give up an experience because of a desire to try something new, not because of completion of the first experience. Occasionally, becomes quite erratic.
- Loves change. Wants to travel, to see unusual places, unusual people, have exciting adventures. Usually has difficulty and is unhappy with routine tasks.
- Delightful companion. Can inspire and delight with his enthusiasm (as long as others are not put off by the sudden changes in direction.)
- Enthusiastic. Tackles each new experience with renewed enthusiasm.
- The eternal youth. The excitement of life keeps him forever young.

NEGATIVE EXPRESSION

A 5 can occasionally be overwhelmed by his opportunities. He can flit from thing to thing with maddening speed; he can change direction at the drop of a hat; he can get lost in overindulgence with little sense of the negative effects. The 5 can be so erratic that people around him get frustrated trying to keep up. Usually, the 5 is frustrated with himself, too, but the excitement of each new adventure keeps him going.

A very occasional 5 is hesitant about using his freedom. He will retreat into a safe (for him) type of situation—a nine to five job, a stable family unit. The changes and uncertainties that follow a 5 will still be there, but he will not express the facility to handle them. He will be frustrated with his safety, annoyed at the changes and uncertainty, but not willing to risk to learn about freedom.

COMMENTARY

Once on track, this can be a most delightful lesson. Getting on track is often difficult, usually takes up a good portion of the life. 5's often enjoy freedom with little understanding of the constructive use of freedom. With so much talent and versatility, with so many opportunities from which to choose, it's difficult to be concerned about con-structive vs. nonconstructive. Sometimes, many years will pass before the 5 will look back, realize how little has been accomplished with such an advantage in opportunities and abilities. When the rolling stone changes to a more positive expression of change, uncertainty and opportunity, the growth of the individual can be a joy to behold.

CHART 2
THE LIFE PATH

6 BALANCE
RESPONSIBILITY
LOVE

CENTRAL FOCUS

The subject must learn the deep pleasure of handling responsibility. He is born with the innate ability to give help and comfort whenever needed, to support those too weak to support themselves. Others will quickly recognize these capabilities and come to the 6 for help. He'll find himself responsible for far more than his fair share. He must accept the responsibility and learn to serve family, relatives and friends. He must be willing to give out much in the way of friendship and love, and will receive much friendship and love in return. The individual must always be there to help, sometimes even to his own disadvantage. He may have to learn to distinguish between helping and interfering.

The subject will usually seek the closeness of marriage, although he may have to work at the balance needed in marriage far more than he might expect. His ability to balance and harmonize may express in creative activities—art, music, writing—providing him with much pleasure.

CHARACTERISTICS

- Responsible. Always there to pick up the burden.
- Loving and appreciative. Always ready to help.
- Sympathetic and kind. Generous with all one's personal and material resources.
- Usually loves children. Makes excellent teacher.
- Capable of rectifying and balancing situations.

Probably the person in the family to whom others come when things are not in balance.
- One of the focuses of the life is usually family, relatives and friends.
- Rarely too concerned with material needs.
- Artistic.
- Emotional.

NEGATIVE EXPRESSION

There aren't many negative 6's around. Sometimes a person accepts and is overwhelmed by responsibility, and becomes a near-slave or doormat for others. This negative 6 will feel unhappy but will usually feel that this is his role in life.

Occasionally, the individual confuses responsibility for a situation with dominating a situation. Occasionally, too, the negative 6 is far too exacting (of himself and others), extremely critical and fussy at the same time.

The rare 6 who abdicates responsibility will feel tense and uneasy, always realizing he is not accepting the share that belongs to him. He may be laden with guilt and have difficulty continuing satisfactory relations with others.

COMMENTARY

The 6 usually accepts responsibility so readily that advantage may be taken of him without his ever being aware of it. At some period in his life, the 6 will probably get tired of the burden, may stop to clarify just how much responsibility he chooses to assume. When he examines his life situation, he will find that many do come to him because they are too weak to take care of themselves. He will find others, though, who lean on him out of force of habit—others who *are* capable of being responsible for themselves. He will do well to weed out those who need him from those who don't. Part of the lesson of responsibility is clarifying when and where the sense of responsibility is to be used.

6's are very exacting of themselves. Often, they're willing to sacrifice themselves (or their families) for the welfare of others. They may have to learn to temper their dreams of perfection. Sometimes, they have to learn to express their own individuality despite the heavy burden of responsibility they carry.

| CHART **2** THE LIFE PATH | **7** ANALYSIS UNDERSTANDING |

CENTRAL FOCUS

The subject must learn the peace of mind that comes with knowing himself. He has a good mind and a fine intuition. He must study and contemplate, learn not to judge from appearances. The individual's life should be devoted to analyzing the world about him, learning to trust his intuition, developing until he reaches the highest levels of wisdom. He must not emphasize material things in his life, but rather must become aware of the non-material forces. He must be able to spend time by himself without feeling isolated. The subject must learn to wait for opportunities which work to his advantage rather than actively seeking opportunities. Amid the hurly-burly of the world, his development depends on his ability to retire into himself to find faith and peace.

CHARACTERISTICS

- "Different". Operates on a different wavelength than others with access to unique solutions and approaches. He is often difficult for others to understand. Sometimes he has difficulty understanding himself.
- Difficult to get to know. Although he is often unaware of it, he often protects himself by giving out little about himself. He may appear aloof and cold, sometimes even hard. This is a surface veneer, but it is difficult to penetrate.
- Introspective. He is usually turned in on himself, often appears reserved and thoughtful.
- Depends on self primarily. Whether confident in his own abilities or not, he relies on himself. He seems afraid to trust others, doesn't ask to be trusted by others.
- Not too adaptable. He does things his own way, is not especially interested in other approaches. Since his view is often so different, it is difficult for him to see the advantages of others' ways of thinking and acting.

NEGATIVE EXPRESSION

The negative 7 sometimes becomes so introspective and self-centered as to be a virtual recluse. His lack of contact with others will make it difficult for him to grow and develop.

An occasional negative 7, finding the path too difficult, will try to ignore his own character and live in the material world without tuning in to his inner resources. He will find that little works for him, that he is beset with problems on all sides. Only if he can move onto *his* track, will life begin to have some meaning for him.

COMMENTARY

If the 7 can get in touch with the satisfaction of working as a teacher, counselor, researcher, or at any other job which calls on intuition, mind and spiritual awareness without stressing material benefits, he can find much in the way of satisfaction. Too often, the 7 struggles against the very experiences which will make his life work. The 7 may not like being by himself, he may want to enjoy good company and material pleasure. He must become aware of the excitements of the spiritual forces which can be used for his advantage. Once on track, his understandings and perceptions will provide ample, though "different", pleasures. The 7 can then progress toward ultimate wisdom and faith—the products of his growth and development.

CHART 2
THE LIFE PATH

8 MATERIAL SATISFACTION

CENTRAL FOCUS

The subject must learn the satisfactions of the material world and the power which comes with its mastery. He will be involved in practical, down-to-earth work. There will be little of dreams or visions. The individual will want to use his ambitions, his organizational ability, his efficient approach to carve a satisfying niche for himself. He will be concerned and involved with money,

learning of the power that comes with its proper manipulation. He'll be concerned with material things, desirous of obtaining the best and most comfortable for himself. He'll be concerned with status—his own status measured against the status of others. With growth and development, the subject will learn to achieve the power he desires.

CHARACTERISTICS

- Ambitious and self-confident.
- Efficient and energetic. Capable of organizing and administrating.
- Executive ability. Capable of taking charge and giving direction, even inspiring others.
- Dependable.
- Good at judging character. Aware of others and their relation to himself and his goals.
- Realistic and practical. Doesn't fool himself

with daydreams or fantasies.
- Tendency to rigidity or stubbornness. Because he is often strongly goal-oriented and so aware of reality, it is sometimes difficult for the 8 to see that there are other approaches beside his own. If he is aware of his rigidity (and most 8's are not), it will still take much work to overcome.

NEGATIVE EXPRESSION

The negative 8 may pursue his goals of money, status and power with such intensity and single-mindedness that, although he may achieve his ends, he will find little pleasure in the journey or the attainment. He may misuse power, become intolerant of others, be faced with much resentment and hostility.

Sometimes, the negative 8, although desirous of money and achievement, will be afraid to take the risks involved in asserting himself. He will feel limited and dissatisfied, but will have to achieve a higher level of self-confidence before he can comfortably make his presence known.

COMMENTARY

It is very easy for the 8 to lose his way. He may have difficulty seeing the forest instead of the trees. He may be so immersed in his attainment of money, material possessions, status and power, that he may not see that these are not ends in themselves—only the means to the ends. The goal, quite simply, is the *satisfaction* that can come with material freedom and power. All too often, this lesson is lost or confused.

If the material freedom, once achieved, does not provide pleasure, the 8 has not mastered the lesson. If the power, once achieved, is misused, the 8 is off the track. The 8 must learn, not only to achieve his goals, but to maintain a sense of proportion about those goals. Only when he is able to do this, will he be in a position to grow and develop.

CHART 2
THE LIFE PATH

9 SELFLESSNESS HUMANITARIANISM

CENTRAL FOCUS

The subject must learn the beauty of giving of himself for the deep satisfaction of giving—without thought of reward or return. A simple lesson in theory, a very difficult one in practice. The individual must practice selflessness, giving up ambitions and material possessions of his own for the common good. His innate love of his fellow man must be expressed with purity, from humanitarian interests alone. He must give love, help or understanding when needed, again with no thought of receiving anything in return. The difficulty on this path is, of course, the lack of return. The subject's pleasure comes in the giving. If he looks for more, if he has ulterior motives, the path will be difficult and there will be little reward or satisfaction.

The subject may give to others as a fine spouse, lover or friend, as a teacher or helper. He may give to others in terms of creative endeavor. He may, as a matter of fact, have much in the way of creative talent, but only in the purity of its expression will he find the way.

CHARACTERISTICS

- Much interest in others. Usually quite social. Sympathetic, tolerant and broadminded.
- Idealistic. Sometimes tempered with a more practical side, but idealistic nonetheless. Often disappointed at lack of perfection in the world.
- Romantic. Loves with depth and passion. Can be hurt by others whose response is not always as expected.
- Sensitive. Sees the world with much feeling and compassion.
- Creative ability. Often a great deal of imagination to go with talent. Sometimes, has difficulty finding outlet for expression.

NEGATIVE EXPRESSION

The negative 9 is fairly common. He has difficulty believing that selflessness and lack of personal ambition can be satisfying. He is often ambitious, desirous of much in the way of material rewards. He'll try to satisfy these needs, may even manage to attain some of the goals, but will find little of pleasure or satisfaction along the way. He may even end up embittered at the sorry results.

Sometimes, the negative 9 may be aware of the satisfaction of the humanitarian impulse, but will spend his time in dreaming or in going off in all directions at once. He will accomplish little and be dissatisfied.

COMMENTARY

9's can achieve as much as anybody in terms of status, recognition, receipt of love and friendship. But they receive the good things of life in a satisfying way primarily as they express their own selflessness and awareness of others. This can be a very difficult lesson. You have to head in what seems like the opposite direction to get where you're going. The 9 often rebels at the idea. It's difficult for him to conceive that he can be immensely satisfied as soon as he has given up the idea of needing personal satisfaction. He can find all the love and friendship he wants as soon as he stops looking for love and friendship for himself and gives out love and friendship to others instead. This is a very deep lesson, but the rewards to those who can follow this path are beyond description.

CHART **2**
THE LIFE PATH

11 ILLUMINATION

CENTRAL FOCUS

The subject must learn an awareness of the spiritual world and the relation of that world to the material world. With this master number, he has added perceptions, added awarenesses, different capabilities of understanding. These perceptions and capabilities take much effort to develop but, once developed, the individual is capable of far more ability and attainment than most others. The 11 must learn to trust and develop his own intuition to tune in to forces beyond. He would do well to involve himself with psychic or occult studies. He must recognize himself as a channel for awareness and inspire others with his purity. The subject will, with development and growth, become aware of the special knowledge that has been given to him. It is important that he spread this illumination for others' benefit.

CHARACTERISTICS

- Extremely capable at whatever work he chooses. Capable of rising to the top of his profession.
- Idealist. Has visions of a perfect world. Often makes himself unhappy with his need for perfection. Often disappointed by his own and others' imperfections.
- Impractical. Although he will usually function well, there will also be an impractical side brought about by his occasional difficulty in separating his fantasy from the reality. This impracticality may make it difficult for him to reach his goals.

- Dreamer. Often more dreamer than doer. Sometimes can dream of the accomplishment, but can't make it happen.
- Inspirational, although usually in a very quiet way. Others recognize some inner strength and awareness and can benefit from his lead.
- Nervous tension. The special awarenesses and capabilities are accompanied by tension. The tension is usually quite obvious, but is occasionally hidden beneath an applied veneer of strength.

NEGATIVE EXPRESSION

The negative 11 may use his special power for his own self-seeking ends. Although he may attain much, he will have missed the powerful lesson he should have learned. Despite his accomplishments, he will feel uneasy and dissatisfied.

An occasional negative 11 gets lost in his dreams, accomplishes little, and rationalizes his predicament to try to find satisfaction.

COMMENTARY

11 *is* special. He is capable of great accomplishments, although he will rarely reach anywhere near his potential. He may not even understand anything of discussions of the spiritual world. He may, instead, be operating on an intuitive level, so that his relation with any but the material world is not particularly clear to him.

11's special awarenesses are often difficult to handle. He can see the huge power potential that is present, but may be unable to focus the power to put it to practical use. The accompanying nervous tension can make him difficult to live with. He is so aware and sensitive that ordinary living may provoke all sorts of pressures which others never feel.

It usually takes an 11 a long time to get on the track. While he is searching for direction, he will be, quite probably, a difficult person to deal with. It is hard to sit on the powder keg of such power and be comfortable, and the discomfort is expressed by attacks of nerves or temper.

The 11 who is growing and developing is rare, but a beautiful person to behold. He is a person who has much to give to others.

CHART 2
THE LIFE PATH

22 MASTER BUILDER

CENTRAL FOCUS

The subject must learn the ultimate mastery of combining the highest of ideals with the enormous power to achieve the largest of material goals. With this master number, he has added perceptions, added awarenesses, different capabilities of understanding *plus* the ability to attain anything and everything in the way of material accomplishment. Although these ultimate powers are there, the subject must learn (and it's the most difficult of all the lessons) how to focus his large gifts into productive use. He must work for the benefit of mankind in order to achieve his own ultimate growth. He is capable of the largest of undertakings combining, perhaps, commercial or political forces of substantial magnitude. The potential is awesome—the individual's growth and development depend on his ability to come to grips with his power.

CHARACTERISTICS

- Extremely capable at whatever work he chooses. Capable of rising to the top of his profession. Even when the 22 is not accomplishing as he should, the latent capability is most obvious.
- Practical. An innate understanding of the forces involved in material problems.
- Unorthodox. His significant perceptions will provide him with avenues not available to others or often even not understandable to others. He is operating on a different wavelength than most of us—often his conduct is unorthodox, quite possibly he will appear eccentric.
- Charismatic. The glow of his inner fire will be visible to all. Even when he is not accomplishing all he should, others may well be drawn to the excitement of his activities.
- Nervous tension. The special awarenesses and capabilities are usually accompanied by an almost electric field of nervous tension. The tension can rarely be hidden.

NEGATIVE EXPRESSION

The negative 22 may turn his powers to his own selfish use. He may accomplish his goals, but he will learn little of the ultimate lesson. He will be aware of not using his talents wisely, but may feel incapable of heading in a more meaningful direction.

An occasional 22 is overwhelmed by his powers and retreats from them. He may accomplish little, feel frightened by the world around him, uncomfortable with his nervous tension.

COMMENTARY

You will look for a long time before you find a 22 accomplishing anything even vaguely close to his potential. Mostly, the 22 is in process, trying to handle the forces which feel too powerful to handle, trying to live with the tension which accompanies these forces. The latent power of the 22 will be obvious to all. People may shake their heads and wonder why he didn't do more with his potent energies. He will often be difficult to live with or deal with—he is *so* aware, *so* perceptive, *so* capable—and often *so* frustrated at not being able to put all the pieces together.

If and when the 22 harnesses his potential (and it is usually somewhat along in his mature life), he can be beautiful to behold. The vision of an individual, aware, superbly capable, dedicated to the service of humanity, attaining on the very highest levels—a superb vision, an ultimate dream worth the striving.

CHART 3   THE EXPRESSION

ABILITIES

The Expression is a person's potential natural abilities. See Chapter 4, page 31.

The natural capabilities and talents are significant in determining the type of work in which the subject will be most productive and content. If the subject is involved with work in which his productivity is poor and his satisfaction minimal, these innate abilities may be only occasionally or partially manifested.

POSITIVE ATTITUDES

The individual's attitudes when he puts his best foot forward will help him make progress along the Life Path.

NEGATIVE ATTITUDES

The exaggeration or denial of the positive attitudes produces negative attitudes, deterrents to progress along the Life Path. Awareness of these negative attitudes may be the first step in converting them to a more productive direction.

CHART 3

THE EXPRESSION

1 INDIVIDUATION
INDEPENDENCE
ATTAINMENT

ABILITIES

- Executive and administrative capabilities. Fine leader or promoter.
- Original and creative approach. (The creativity is not necessarily related to artistic endeavors; often, it's related to business matters.) Others will usually be needed to follow through and take care of the details after the direction has been initiated.
- Good mind and the ability to use it for advancement.
- Potential for achievement and financial reward. Can establish and/or run own business or have significant position in another's business.

POSITIVE ATTITUDES

- Prefers to proceed on own course. Usually prefers little input from others.
- Ambitious, determined.
- Positive, progressive.
- Self-confident.
- Self-reliant.
- Much will power, courage of the convictions.

NEGATIVE ATTITUDES

- Egotistical.
- Stubborn.
- Dominant, bossy.
- Too aggressive.
- Selfish, self-centered.
- Lazy, dependent.

| CHART **3** THE EXPRESSION | **2** RELATION COOPERATION |

ABILITIES

- Works well with others. Probably prefers partnerships to individual enterprises. (May have to learn that others may get credit for some of his ideas or accomplishments.)
- Sensitive to others' feelings. Diplomatic in handling complicated situations.
- Skillful at organizing and handling groups.
- Good facilitator. Contributes to group situations by use of persuasion rather than force.
- Capable of handling details well.
- Psychic abilities (often latent).

POSITIVE ATTITUDE

- Considerate, courteous.
- Cooperative.
- Adaptable.
- Modest. Can work comfortably without necessarily receiving full acknowledgement for contributions.
- Tactful, diplomatic. Innate desire for harmony.
- Friendly.

NEGATIVE ATTITUDES

- Over-sensitive. Too delicate ego is easily hurt.
- Shy, uncertain.
- Timid, fearful.
- Apathetic, indifferent.
- Lost in detail or careless with details.

CHART 3

THE EXPRESSION

3 EXPRESSION
JOY OF LIVING

ABILITIES

- Talent with words—writing, speaking, singing, acting, teaching are possible vocations or avocations.
- Can sell or entertain—knows how to present material with imagination.
- Artistic talents (often latent).
- Creative imagination (often latent).

POSITIVE ATTITUDES

- Expresses joy of living with optimism and enthusiasm.
- Friendly, affectionate, loving.
- Gracious, charming.
- Very social, good conversationalist.
- Cheerful, happy, merry.
- Loves a good time.
- Capable of providing inspiration for others.

NEGATIVE ATTITUDES

- Dilettante, scatters forces.
- Too easy going.
- Trivial, superficial.
- Critical, moody, too sensitive.
- Gossipy.

CHART **3** THE EXPRESSION	**4** LIMITATION ORDER SERVICE

ABILITIES

- Good organizer, manager. Can establish order and routine or maintain existing order or routine.
- Practical, down-to-earth approach.
- Strong capability to bring plans to a practical form.
- Can work long and hard. Conscientious and dependable.
- Patient with details, insists on accuracy.
- Works well in material mediums: as builder, engineer, craftsman, etc.
- Capable of writing or teaching, often on technical matters.

POSITIVE ATTITUDES

- Responsible. Fulfills obligations.
- Proceeds with job at hand despite seeming limitations or restrictions.
- Systematic, orderly.
- Serious, sincere.
- Honest, faithful.
- Helpful.
- Patient, persevering, determined.

NEGATIVE ATTITUDES

- Frustrated by feelings of limitation or restriction—often of own making or existing only in the imagination.
- Rigid, stubborn, dogmatic, fixed approach.
- Strong likes and dislikes.
- Bossy, dominant.
- Excessively disciplinarian.
- May concentrate on details to the exclusion of the larger picture.

CHART **3**	**5** CONSTRUCTIVE FREEDOM
THE EXPRESSION	

ABILITIES

- Talented and versatile. Capable of doing almost anything attempted, often extremely well.
- Good at presenting ideas. Understands how to approach others to get what is wanted.
- Good at selling. Innate ability to determine best way to succeed at particular sales situation.
- Enjoys and is successful working with people.
- Entertaining and amusing.
- Clever, analytical ability, often a quick thinker.

POSITIVE ATTITUDES

- Enthusiastic.
- Adaptable.
- Progressive.
- Loves change, likes to travel, see unusual places and people, investigate unusual ideas.
- Delightful companion.

NEGATIVE ATTITUDES

- Restless and impatient, may not stay with any project too long. Sometimes erratic.
- Scatters self and energy.
- Chafes at routine tasks or situations. Has difficulty with anything standard or rigid, such as regular office hours.
- Reacts strongly if he feels freedom of speech or action is being impaired.
- Often difficult to profit readily from experience.
- Often difficult to discard easily.
- May overindulge in eating, sensuality, drinking, drugs.
- Sometimes misses big picture because of excitement generated by new interest.

CHART **3**		**6**	BALANCE

CHART 3

THE EXPRESSION

6

BALANCE
RESPONSIBILITY
LOVE

ABILITIES

- Responsible.
- Helpful and conscientious. Capable of rectifying and balancing inharmonious situations.
- Gives help and comfort to those in need.
- Works well where care of old, young or sick is involved.
- Shows concern for betterment of community.
- Creative and artistic talents.

POSITIVE ATTITUDES

- Loving, friendly, appreciative of others.
- Sympathetic, kind.
- Generous, understanding.
- Often involved in domestic activities, usually good spouse and parent.
- Usually is open and honest with others.

NEGATIVE ATTITUDES

- Too exacting of self. Occasionally will sacrifice self (or family) for the welfare of others.
- Occasionally has difficulty distinguishing helping from interfering.
- May express worry and anxiety.
- May have difficulty expressing own individuality because of involvement with responsibilities. May, unknowingly, become a drudge.

CHART 3

THE EXPRESSION

7 ANALYSIS
UNDERSTANDING

ABILITIES

- Good mind, good intuition.
- Capable of analyzing, judging, discriminating.
- Searches for wisdom or hidden truths. Often becomes authority on subjects that interest him—technical, scientific, religious or occult.
- Potential to be educator, philosopher, researcher.
- Spiritual awareness (often latent). May be involved in psychic explorations.
- Operates on "different" wavelength which may give unique approaches and solutions to problems. (It also may make it difficult for others to know the person well.)

POSITIVE ATTITUDES

- Perfectionist. When carried to extremes, as it may well be, this tendency may interfere with work at hand.
- Very logical, rational approach. Approach shows little emotion. Too much emotion, if noted in other numbers, may cause difficulties.
- Willing to work to understand deep, difficult subjects, to search for hidden fundamentals.
- Potential to be peaceful and poised. Usually achieved only at maturity.

NEGATIVE ATTITUDES

- Little trust in others.
- Not very adaptable.
- Usually introspective, tends to be self-centered.
- Critical, unsympathetic, intolerant.
- Usually prefers to work alone. Must *learn* to be by himself and not feel isolated—may rebel at the idea of learning this.
- Difficulty with emotions—usually shows little of own emotions and may have difficulty understanding others' emotions.

CHART **3**	**8** MATERIAL SATISFACTION
THE EXPRESSION	

ABILITIES

- Organizational, managerial and administrative capabilities.
- Potential for achievement and financial reward. Can establish and/or run own business or have significant position in another's business.
- Efficient.
- Good judgment with money. Understands how to accumulate, handle and spend money.
- Good judgment of character.
- Uses a realistic, practical approach.
- Capable of handling large projects or interests. This capability may be latent or may be in the background because of characteristics of other numbers.

POSITIVE ATTITUDES

- Ambitious, usually in healthy way (unless overdone). Goal-oriented.
- Energetic.
- Self-confident.
- Dependable.
- Seeks material comfort. If overdone, this becomes a negative trait.

NEGATIVE ATTITUDES

- Rigid, stubborn.
- Overambitious, impatient with progress.
- Very exacting, both of self and others. Often intolerant.
- May strain after money, status or power to own detriment. May misuse power. May strain for material freedom so that even accomplishment of the freedom does not bring pleasure.
- Materialistic, to exclusion of other values.

| CHART **3** THE EXPRESSION | **9** SELFLESSNESS HUMANITARIANISM |

ABILITIES

- Humanistic interest and approach.
- Philanthropic, likes to help others.
- Sensitive to others' needs, much feeling and compassion.
- Works well with people.
- Potential for inspiring others—may be teacher, religious leader, counselor.
- Creative ability, imagination and artistic talent of the highest order (often latent).

POSITIVE ATTITUDES

- Much human understanding.
- Gives a lot to others, extreme of selflessness occasionally achieved.
- Personal ambition is usually in positive perspective.
- Interest in others—sympathetic, tolerant, broad-minded, compassionate, generous.
- Idealistic, disappointed at lack of perfection in the world.
- Romantic. Gives much friendship, affection, love. Can sometimes (in its highest expression) be content with minimal return.
- Aware of own feelings as well as others.

NEGATIVE ATTITUDES

- Selfish, self-centered.
- Unaware of real feelings.
- Insensitive to others' needs and feelings.
- Wants much friendship, affection, love. Sometimes has difficult (often aloof) attitude which makes it difficult for others to respond.
- Lack of involvement.

CHART **3**	**11** ILLUMINATION
THE EXPRESSION	

ABILITIES

- Inspirational, often inspires by his own example. Others usually can see his inner strength and awareness. Would be good spiritual adviser, philosopher, teacher, welfare worker.
- Very aware and sensitive with good intuition. Tie to spiritual world gives added depth to point of view.
- Often operating on psychic levels—may do well in psychic, mystic or occult studies.
- Good mind and analytical ability.
- Very capable at whatever work is chosen, but often has difficulty focusing ability to achieve ends.
- Usually works better outside the business world. If in the business world, his approach is often unusual.

POSITIVE ATTITUDES

- Idealistic approach. Often disappointed by own and others' imperfections. (Expresses ideals, even though they may prove impractical.)
- Deeply concerned with art, music, beauty.

NEGATIVE ATTITUDES

- Nervous tension almost always present.
- Often more dreamer than doer. Sometimes quite aimless.
- Too sensitive.
- Temperamental, temper.
- Impractical, sometimes has difficulty separating fantasy from reality.
- May impose ideas or standards on others in unfeeling way.
- Self-centered, inconsiderate.
- Wants to spread his illumination to others irrespective of others' desire or need.

| CHART **3** THE EXPRESSION | **22** MASTER BUILDER |

ABILITIES

- Extremely capable at whatever work is chosen.
- Capable of handling large scale undertakings. May accomplish significant undertakings in the material world.
- Capable of leading in new directions.
- Unorthodox approach to problems.
- Much unusual perception and awareness.

POSITIVE ATTITUDES

- Practical approach tempered by awareness of non-material forces.
- Idealistic.
- Inner strength visible to all. If developed, will attract others with charisma.
- May work for the good of all.

NEGATIVE ATTITUDES

- Nervous tension brought on by high level awareness.
- May accentuate unorthodoxy to the point of eccentricity.
- Selfish and dominating. Uses power for own good rather than universal benefit.
- Inability to harness power may cause feelings of inferiority.

CHART 4   THE SOUL URGE

MOTIVES

The Soul Urge is a person's inner motivation, what he really wants out of life. See Chapter 5, page 37.

His inner nature is usually revealed to others, but sometimes it is hidden within.

POSITIVE ATTITUDES

The feelings and inclinations which will be most helpful in making progress.

NEGATIVE ATTITUDES

The exaggeration or denial of the positive feelings and inclinations produces negative effects which act as deterrents to progress.

CHART **4**		**1**	INDIVIDUATION INDEPENDENCE ATTAINMENT
THE SOUL URGE			

MOTIVES

The subject would like to be as independent as possible, ideally completely free to act on his own. He wants to be the leader or organizer, free to initiate or pioneer in any venture that strikes his fancy. He prefers to take a strong individualistic stand, dominating any situation in which he's involved. He wants to be a success in large, progressive enterprises. He's concerned primarily with the broad strokes, prefers to leave the details to others. He keeps his own counsel, works with a few hand-picked employees.

POSITIVE ATTITUDES

- Ambitious, determined.
- Honest, loyal.
- Instigates action.
- Seeks opportunities to use his abilities.

NEGATIVE ATTITUDES

- Egotistical.
- Impatient, disapproving.
- Dominant, bossy.
- Headstrong, impulsive.
- Conceited.

| CHART 4 THE SOUL URGE | 2 RELATION COOPERATION |

MOTIVES

The subject would like friendship, affection, love, companionship. He usually prefers marriage to being single. He wants to work with others as part of a cooperative team, only rarely wants to lead. He will work hard to achieve a harmonious environment with sensitive, genial people.

POSITIVE ATTITUDES

- Sympathetic, concerned, devoted.
- Sensitive, diplomatic, tactful. Emotional.
- Quietly persuasive rather than forceful.
- Friendly.
- Gives love and affection.

NEGATIVE ATTITUDES

- Over-sensitive. Too delicate ego is easily hurt. May be timid or fearful.
- Not given to disciplining himself or others.
- Too easy going—may become a doormat.

CHART 4
THE SOUL URGE

3 EXPRESSION
JOY OF LIVING

MOTIVES

The subject would like to express his delight in life, his sense of joie de vivre. He wants to participate in an active social life with many close friends and diverse activities. He would like to express his artistic talents, particularly his talent with words: speaking, writing, acting, singing. He wants his home and work environment to reflect the beauty he enjoys creating.

POSITIVE ATTITUDES

- Friendly, outgoing, social.
- Rarely discouraged.
- Good mental/emotional balance.
- Intuitive. Often inspirational.
- Capable of self-expression, either in social situations or in artistic fields.

NEGATIVE ATTITUDES

- Tendency to scatter forces.
- Too easygoing and optimistic.
- Too sensitive when criticized.
- Compulsive talker, may be critical.

CHART **4** **THE SOUL URGE**	**4**	LIMITATION ORDER SERVICE

MOTIVES

The subject would like to lead a stable life. He prefers orderliness and a systematic approach in his endeavors. He wants to serve others methodically and diligently. He wants to be involved in solid, conventional, well-regulated activities. He's likely to be disturbed by innovation and erratic or sudden changes.

POSITIVE ATTITUDES

- Good at organizing, systematizing, managing. Good at establishing routine and order. Logical, thorough, exacting with details.
- Responsible, reliable.
- Honest, sincere, conscientious. Hates pretension.
- Practical and analytical.
- Self-disciplined, determined, tenacious.

NEGATIVE ATTITUDES

- Rigid, stubborn, narrow-minded.
- Hides feelings. Often, is not aware of real feelings.
- Bossy, dominant.
- May neglect large affairs because of blind involvement in details.
- Afraid to take chances.

| CHART **4** THE SOUL URGE | **5** CONSTRUCTIVE FREEDOM |

MOTIVES

The subject would like a life of freedom, excitement, unexpected happenings, unusual adventures, travel. He doesn't want to be governed by standard values or traditions. He wants to be the one to set the pace.

POSITIVE ATTITUDES

- Very adaptable and versatile.
- Natural resourcefulness, enthusiasm.
- Capable of bringing new excitement into his interests.
- Progressive approach, strong feelings.
- Good mind and imagination.

NEGATIVE ATTITUDES

- Restless and impatient. Dislikes routine and detail work.
- Jumps from interest to interest, activity to activity.
- Discards quickly to go on to the new. Rarely holds to anything.
- May have difficulty with responsibility.

CHART **4**		**6**	BALANCE
THE SOUL URGE			RESPONSIBILITY
			LOVE

MOTIVES

The subject would like to be appreciated for his ability to handle responsibility. His home and family are likely to be a strong focus in his life, one of the areas where he gives and receives friendship, love, affection. He wants to rectify and balance situations in which he is involved, to help and serve others. The subject prefers to work with others rather than by himelf. He is concerned with beauty in his surroundings and often expresses himself in creative or artistic activities.

POSITIVE ATTITUDES

- Responsible.
- Openminded, sympathetic, understanding, generous.
- Gives much friendship, affection, love. Expresses deep emotional life.
- Idealistic.
- Natural ability to serve, help and teach—capable of sacrifice if necessary.
- Artistic and creative expression.

NEGATIVE ATTITUDES

- Too emotional.
- Interfering or too protective rather than helpful.
- Often represses own needs in order to serve others—may become resentful.

CHART 4
THE SOUL URGE

7 ANALYSIS UNDERSTANDING

MOTIVES

The subject would like much time alone, much quiet and retirement from the outer world in order to develop his inner resources. He likes to dream and develop his idealistic understandings, to study and analyze to gain knowledge and wisdom, to learn the deeper truths. He prefers contemplation to activity and adventure. He prefers avoiding the business world.

POSITIVE ATTITUDES

- Good mind. Analytical approach.
- Studious, theoretical approach.
- Technical, scientific, religious or occult interests.
- Reserved.
- Seeks perfection.

NEGATIVE ATTITUDES

- Timid and withdrawn, innately shy, difficulty with casual conversation.
- Lives in dreams and fantasies.
- Difficult for others to understand. Others have difficulty showing affection.
- Represses most emotions although the emotions are often very strong.
- Secretive, selective.
- Not too adaptable.

CHART 4
THE SOUL URGE

8 MATERIAL SATISFACTION

MOTIVES

The subject wants wealth, success, status and power. He wants to excel in the business or political world, to organize, supervise or lead. He probably has substantial material needs to satisfy.

POSITIVE ATTITUDES

- Executive abilities, proceeds in businesslike manner.
- Confidence, energy and ambition.
- Analytical mind.
- Possesses good judgment. Has good sense of material values and is good judge of character.
- Capable of the imagination required for commercial success.
- Functions well in emergencies. Inspired by crises or large odds.
- Self-controlled. Emotions rarely cloud judgments.

NEGATIVE ATTITUDES

- Dominating. Too exacting.
- Thinking, straining, striving for material values, financial success—sometimes to exclusion of all else.
- Tendency to be very self-centered.
- Tendency to rigidity, stubbornness.
- Represses feelings.

| CHART 4
THE SOUL URGE | 9 SELFLESSNESS
HUMANITARIAN |

MOTIVES

The subject would like to give to others, usually in a humanitarian or philanthropic manner. Sometimes, he wants to give friendship, affection and love; sometimes, he gives of his knowledge and experience. He also would like to share his artistic or creative talents with others. These are often talents of considerable magnitude.

POSITIVE ATTITUDES

- Sympathetic, generous, kind.
- Sensitive nature. Expresses love, compassion, tolerance.
- Possesses deep, intuitive understanding of life.
- Possesses innate wisdom, good intuition, broad point of view.
- Often high ideals and an inspirational approach.
- Often self-sacrificing.
- Gives freely without being concerned about any return or reward.

NEGATIVE ATTITUDES

- May be too sensitive; very emotional with emotions being expressed strongly.
- Conflict between higher spiritual aims and personal ambitions may cause difficulties.
- May resent necessity of giving so much of the time.
- May be disappointed in lack of perfection in himself and others.
- Moody, critical.

| CHART 4 THE SOUL URGE | 11 ILLUMINATION |

MOTIVES

The subject would like to manifest his view on spiritual matters, to share his ideas of idealism, beauty and perfection. He wants to give of himself to humanity. He is often more concerned with the abstraction of giving to the world rather than specifically giving to individuals.

POSITIVE ATTITUDES

- Utopian dreamer.
- Idealistic, intuitive and inspirational.
- Religious and spiritual, possibly psychic ability.
- Much inner strength and devotion to a chosen cause, sticks to his ideals.
- Good mind.

NEGATIVE ATTITUDES

- Nervous tension brought on by high level awareness.
- Too sensitive. May be very emotional or may repress feelings altogether. In either case, the sensitivity is poorly handled.
- Strong ideas of right and wrong, often inflexible.
- Day dreams and deceives self. Impractical approach. (Often can't see these qualities in himself.)
- Often extremely selective in associations. Others may be bothered by his air of exclusivity.

CHART 4
THE SOUL URGE

22 MASTER BUILDER

MOTIVES

The subject would like to use his abilities in an important humanitarian undertaking. He wants to express the significant power he feels in a concrete manner, as a builder, engineer, diplomat, etc. In some way, he wants to make a considerable contribution to the world.

POSITIVE ATTITUDES

- Universal outlook with a practical approach.
- High intelligence.
- Unusual perceptions and awarenesses.
- Diplomatic ability.
- High ideals.
- Strong capability and leadership ability.
- Commands respect with his superior vision.

NEGATIVE ATTITUDES

- Nervous tension brought on by high level awareness.
- Too dominating.

CHART 5   THE BIRTHDAY

The Birthday is a sub-lesson to be learned in this life, a sub-focus on the Life Path. See Chapter 6, page 41.

In numerology terms, the Birthday, the day of the month on which the individual is born, is reduced to a single digit or master number. The sub-lesson of the single digit or master number is described by the related keywords.

The main emphasis of the attitudes and abilities for each Birthday is described by this single digit or master number. The master number 11 has attitudes and abilities related to its high level 11 and its reduced level 2. The master number 22 has attitudes and abilities related to its high level 22 and its reduced level 4. See Chapter 8 for a discussion of master numbers.

If the birthday falls on the 13th, 14th, 16th or 19th of the month, an additional main emphasis is added due to karmic influences. See Chapter 11 for a discussion of these influences.

The numbers behind the single digit—the 17 behind the 8, the 23 behind the 5, for instance—add minor emphases to the attitudes and abilities.

CHART 5	**1**	**INDIVIDUATION**
THE BIRTHDAY		**INDEPENDENCE**
		ATTAINMENT

1

Independent attitude.
Executive ability, good leader.
Ambitious, positive, progressive.
Self-confident.
Much will power.
Potential for achievement and financial
   reward.
Good mind.

Practical, rational.
Often original approach.

Sensitive, rarely shows feelings.

Better at starting than continuing.
Better at broad strokes than details.

   (Emphasis on 1 energy only. No sub-
   emphasis on other energies.)

10

Independent attitude.
Much energy.

Executive ability, excellent leader.
Ambitious, positive, progressive.
Self-confident.
Much will-power.
Strong potential for achievement and
   financial reward.
Compelling manner, can dominate a situa-
   tion.

Excellent mind.

Practical, rational.
Creative ideas, strongly marked originality.

Sensitive, feelings usually repressed.

Better at starting than continuing.
Better at broad strokes than details.

   (Emphasis on 1 energy only is similar
   to the 1 Birthday above, but the
   energy is more strongly expressed
   here. No sub-emphasis on other
   energies.)

19

Independence strongly desired, usually
   obstacles to overcome before dependence is
   overcome.
Executive ability.
Ambitious.
Much will power.
Creative, imaginative.
Tendency to be self-centered, inability to see
   self in relation to others.
Good mind.

Practical, rational.
Often original or unconventional approach.

Strong sensitivity may involve individual in
   dramatic situations.
Feelings usually repressed.

Better at starting than continuing.
Better at broad strokes than details.

   (Emphasis on 1 and 19/1 energy.
   Sub-emphasis on 9 energy.)

28

Independent attitude, but can work well
   with others.
Executive ability, good leader.
Organizing, managing, administrative
   capabilities.
Ambitious.
Diplomatic, uses persuasion rather than
   force.
Creative, imaginative.
Potential for achievement and financial
   reward.

Good mind.
Practical, rational.
Often original approach.

Sensitive, represses a good deal of feelings.
Affectionate.

Good at starting, capable of continuing.
Good at broad strokes, capable of taking care
   of details.
   (Emphasis on 1 energy. Sub-emphasis on 2 and 8 energy.)

CHART 5
THE BIRTHDAY

2 RELATION
COOPERATION

2

Works well with others.
Prefers partnerships to individual enterprises.

Sociable, friendly.
Diplomatic, uses persuasion rather than force.
Considerate, courteous, modest.
Cooperative, adaptable.

Much sensitivity to others' feelings, much feeling expressed.

Occasional moods of depression.
Affectionate.

Better at continuing than starting.
Good with details.

(Emphasis on 2 energy only. No sub-emphasis on other energies.)

11

11 is a master number. For this Birthday, see the description on the 11 page of this chart.

20

Works very well with others.
Prefers partnerships to individual enterprises.

Very sociable, friendly.
Much attention to family, close friends.
Diplomatic, uses persuasion rather than force.
Considerate, courteous, modest.
Cooperative, adaptable.

Extreme sensitivity to others' feelings, much feeling expressed.

Some moods of depression.
Very affectionate.

Better at continuing than starting.
Good with details.

(Emphasis on 2 energy only is similar to the 2 Birthday above, but energy is more strongly expressed here. No sub-emphasis on other energies.)

29

29 reduces to the master number 11. For this Birthday, see the description on the 11 page of this chart.

CHART **5** THE BIRTHDAY	**3** EXPRESSION JOY OF LIVING

3

Good with words—writing, speaking, singing.
Can sell or entertain.
Artistic, creative, good imagination.

Expresses joy of living.
Enthusiastic, optimistic, cheerful.
Friendly, sociable.
Good conversationalist.
Energetic.

Affectionate, loving.
Much feeling may cause occasional rapid ups and downs.

Scatters energy.
Involved with trivial or superficial matters.
Many interests, but may be bored easily.

(Emphasis on 3 energy only. No sub-emphasis on other energies.)

12

Good with words—writing, speaking, singing.
Works well alone or with others.
Original approach.
Artistic, creative, good imagination.

Expresses joy of living.
Enthusiastic, optimistic, cheerful.
Friendly, sociable.
Good conversationalist.
Energetic.

Good mind.
Practical, rational.

Very affectionate and loving. Very sensitive.
Much feeling may cause occasional rapid ups and downs.
May repress feelings in business.

Sometimes scatters energy.
Sometimes involved with trivial or superficial matters.
Many interests.
Good at broad strokes or with details.

(Emphasis on 3 energy. Sub-emphasis on 1 and 2 energy.)

21

Good with words—writing, speaking, singing.
Works well alone or with others.
Often uses original approach.
Artistic, creative, good imagination.

Expresses joy of living.
Enthusiastic, optimistic, cheerful.
Friendly, sociable.

Good conversationalist.
Energetic.

Good mind.
Practical, rational.

Very affectionate and loving. Very sensitive.
Much feeling may cause occasional rapid ups and downs.
May repress feelings in business.

Sometimes scatters energy.
Sometimes involved with trivial or superficial matters.
Many interests.
Good at broad strokes or with details.

(Emphasis on 3 energy. Sub-emphasis on 2 and 1 energy.)

30

Talent with words—writing, speaking, singing.
Can sell or entertain.
Very artistic, very creative, fine imagination.

Expresses joy of living.
Enthusiastic, optimistic, cheerful.
Very friendly and sociable.
Excellent conversationalist.
Very energetic.

Very affectionate and loving.

Strong feeling may cause upsets.

Scatters energy.
Involved with trivial or superficial matters.
Many interests, but may be bored easily.
May not take care of work or responsibility.

(Emphasis on 3 energy only is similar to the 3 Birthday above, but the energy is more strongly expressed here. No sub-emphasis on other energies.)

CHART 5
THE BIRTHDAY

4 LIMITATION
ORDER
SERVICE

4

Good organizer, manager.
Works long and hard, conscientious, dependable.
Responsible, self-disciplined.
Serious, sincere, honest.
Patient, persevering, determined.
Proceeds despite seeming limitations.

Very practical, rational.
Some rigidity or stubbornness.

Feeling generally repressed.
Shows little affection. Has difficulty attracting affection.

Patient with details, insists on accuracy.
May concentrate on details and miss the big picture.

(Emphasis on 4 energy only. No sub-emphasis on other energies.)

13

Good organizer, manager, but may dominate and irritate others.

Executive ability.
Works long, hard, energetically, dependably.
Responsible, self-disciplined, enthusiastic.
Serious, sincere, persevering.
Feels limited or restricted a good deal of the time, causing frustration or depression.

Good mind.
Very practical.

Tends to be very rigid, obstinate, dogmatic. Others may see him as unreasonable.

Feelings usually repressed.
Shows some affection. Has difficulty attracting affection.

Insists on accuracy.
Concentrates on details, often misses the big picture.

(Emphasis on 4 and 13/4 energy. Sub-emphasis on 1 and 3 energy.)

22

22 is a master number. For this Birthday, see the description on the 22 page of this chart.

31

Good organizer, manager.
Works hard, energetic, dependable, enthusiastic.
Good in the business world.
Good conversationalist.
Responsible, helpful.
Serious, sincere.
Patient, persevering, determined.

Good mind.

Very practical, rational, but some imagination shown.
Often original approach.
Some rigidity or stubbornness.

Sensitive, but feelings usually repressed.

Good with details, insists on accuracy.
Sometimes scatters energy.

(Emphasis on 4 energy. Sub-emphasis on 3 and 1 energy.)

| CHART **5** THE BIRTHDAY | **5** CONSTRUCTIVE FREEDOM |

5

Enjoys and works well with others.

Talented and versatile, good at presenting ideas.

Likes new experience, change, travel.

Entertaining, amusing, enthusiastic, progressive.

Adaptable.

Sociable, delightful companion.
Imaginative.

Quick mind, clever, analytical.

Restless, impatient, chafes at routine.
May shirk responsibility.

(Emphasis on 5 energy only. No sub-emphasis on other energies.)

14

Enjoys working with others.

Talented and versatile, can organize and systematize.

Capable of hard work at times, usually not consistently.

Desires new experience, change, travel, often with little sense of proportion.

May overindulge in eating, sensuality, liquor, drugs.

Entertaining, amusing, enthusiastic, progressive.

Usually adaptable.
Sociable.

Quick mind, clever, analytical.
Practical.
Often original approach.

Restless, impatient, somewhat erratic—tends to jump from activity to activity with little sense of accomplishment or accountability.
Often shirks responsibility.

(Emphasis on 5 and 14/5 energy. Sub-emphasis on 1 and 4 energy.)

23

Enjoys and works extremely well with others.

Sometimes spokesman or peacemaker.

Talented and versatile, good at presenting ideas.

Likes new experience, change, travel.

Entertaining, amusing, very enthusiastic, progressive.

Adaptable.

Very sociable, delightful companion.

Very imaginative, artistic, creative.
Energetic.

Quick mind, clever, analytical.
Sensitivity to others' feelings with most feelings expressed.
Affectionate.

Restless, impatient, chafes at routine.
Shirks responsibility at times.

(Emphasis on 5 energy. Sub-emphasis on 2 and 3 energy.)

CHART **5** THE BIRTHDAY	**6** BALANCE RESPONSIBILITY LOVE

6

Responsible, helpful, conscientious.
Can facilitate changes in inharmonious situations.
Sympathetic, kind, generous, understanding.
Open and honest with others.
Devoted spouse and parent, much interest in home, family.
Creative, artistic.

Good mind.
Much emotion and sensitivity.
Loving, friendly, appreciative of others.
Gives and receives much affection.
Better at continuing than starting.
Will pick up responsibilities if others falter.

>(Emphasis on 6 energy only. No sub-emphasis on other energies.)

15

Usually responsible, but independent at the same time.
Helpful, conscientious.
Can facilitate changes in inharmonious situations.
Much will-power.
Sympathetic, understanding.
Adaptable, enthusiastic.
Devoted spouse and parent, interest in home, family.
Creative, artistic, imaginative.

Potential for achievement and financial reward.
Good mind.
Practical, rational.
Emotion and sensitivity, sometimes represses feelings.
Loving, friendly, appreciative of others.
Gives and receives affection.

>(Emphasis on 6 energy. Sub-emphasis on 1 and 5 energy.)

24

Responsible, helpful, conscientious.
Sometimes spokesman or peacemaker.
Can facilitate changes in inharmonious situations.
Works well with others.
Sympathetic, kind, generous, understanding.
Devoted spouse and parent, interest in home, family.
Creative, artistic.
Good organizer, manager.
Can work long and hard, self-disciplined.
Good mind.

Practical, rational.
Much emotion and sensitivity, represses some feelings.
Loving, friendly, appreciative of others.
Gives and receives much affection.
Better at continuing than starting.
Will pick up responsibilities if others falter.
Good with details.

>(Emphasis on 6 energy. Sub-emphasis on 2 and 4 energy.)

CHART **5**	**7** ANALYSIS
THE BIRTHDAY	UNDERSTANDING

7

Not too adaptable, prefers to work alone but often feels isolated.
Needs time to rest or meditate.

Introspective, stubborn, self-centered.
Usually interested in technical, scientific, religious or occult subjects.
Likely to enjoy spiritual or psychic explorations.
Given to unique or unusual approaches or solutions.

Fine mind, good intuition.

Logical, rational approach.
Feels deeply, usually represses emotions.
Extremely sensitive, but relatively uncommunicative.
Difficulty giving or receiving affection.
Can carry work from start to finish using own approach at own pace.
Perfectionist, stickler for details.

(Emphasis on 7 energy only. No sub-emphasis on other energies.)

16

Relatively inflexible, insists on independence.
Prefers to work alone but usually feels lonely.
Needs time to rest or meditate.

Introspective, stubborn, self-centered.
Difficult to maintain permanent relations.
Interest in home, family, but strong personal needs at the same time.
Usually interested in technical, scientific, religious or occult subjects.
Likely to enjoy spiritual explorations.
Given to unique or unusual approaches.
"Different" wavelength may confuse others.
Potential for achievement and financial reward.

Fine mind, good intuition.
Logical, rational approach. Responsible.
Feels deeply, usually represses emotions.
Extremely sensitive, but usually uncommunicative.
Much difficulty giving or receiving affection.
Can carry work from start to finish using own approach at own pace.
Perfectionist, stickler for details.

(Emphasis on 7 and 16/7 energy. Sub-emphasis on 1 and 6 energy.)

25

Often not too adaptable.
Needs time to rest or meditate.

Introspective, sometimes stubborn, sometimes self-centered.
Cautiously friendly, quiet enthusiasm, sometimes peacemaker.
Cautiously enjoys new experience.
Usually interested in technical, scientific, religious or occult subjects.
Likely to enjoy spiritual or psychic explorations.
Given to unique or unusual approaches or solutions.

Fine mind, good intuition.
Logical, rational approach.
Feels deeply, often represses emotions.
Extremely sensitive, but often uncommunicative.
Some difficulty giving or receiving affection.
Better at continuing than starting, occasional restlessness.
Stickler for details.

(Emphasis on 7 energy. Sub-emphasis on 2 and 5 energy.)

CHART 5

THE BIRTHDAY

8 MATERIAL SATISFACTION

8

Very capable in business world, prefers to be in charge.
Organizational, managerial, administrative capabilities.
Can handle large projects.
Efficient, can handle money well.

Ambitious, energetic, goal-oriented.
Self-confident.
Dependable.

Seeks material satisfactions.
Practical, realistic.
Expresses little feeling.
Better at starting than continuing.
Better at broad strokes than details.

> (Emphasis on 8 energy only. No sub-emphasis on other energies.)

17

Very capable in business world, prefers to be in charge.
Independent attitude, executive ability.
Organizational, managerial, administrative capabilities.
Can handle large projects.
Efficient, can handle money well.

Ambitious, energetic, goal-oriented.
Stubborn or self-centered.
Self-confident.
Dependable.
Seeks material satisfactions.

Good mind, good intuition.
Practical, realistic.
Often original approach, unique or unusual solutions.
Sensitive, but usually represses feelings.
Difficulty giving or receiving affection.
Better at starting than continuing.
Better at broad strokes than details.

> (Emphasis on 8 energy. Sub-emphasis on 1 and 7 energy.)

26

Capable in business world, works well with others.
Organizational, managerial, administrative capabilities.
Efficient, can handle money well.

Ambitious, energetic.
Adaptable, cooperative, responsible, conscientious.
Self-confident.
Dependable.
Sociable, diplomatic. Uses persuasion rather than force.

Seeks material satisfactions.
Creative, artistic.
Good mind.
Practical, realistic.
Sensitive, expresses some of the feelings.
Affectionate, but reserved.
Good at starting and continuing.
Good at broad strokes and details.

> (Emphasis on 8 energy. Sub-emphasis on 2 and 6 energy.)

| CHART **5** THE BIRTHDAY | **9** SELFLESSNESS HUMANITARIANISM |

9

Works well with others.
Humanistic, philanthropic approach.

Broadminded, tolerant, generous.
Sympathetic, compassionate.
Idealistic, can inspire others.
Creative, imaginative.

Sensitive to others' needs and feelings.

Much feeling expressed, may be involved in many dramatic situations.
Gives much in the way of friendship, affection, love. Can sometimes be content with minimal return.

> (Emphasis on 9 energy only. No sub-emphasis on other energies.)

18

Works well with others but must preserve independence.
Humanistic, philanthropic approach, often in business situations.
Executive ability.
Organizational, managerial, administrative capabilities.

Broadminded, tolerant, generous.
Sympathetic, compassionate.
Much will-power.
Idealistic, can inspire others.
Creative, imaginative.
Potential for achievement and financial

reward.
Good mind.
Practical, rational.

Sensitive.
Some feelings expressed but much repressed, may be involved in many dramatic situations.
Gives some friendship, affection, love. Can sometimes be content with minimal return.

> (Emphasis on 9 energy. Sub-emphasis on 1 and 8 energy.)

27

Works well with others.
Needs some time to rest and meditate.
Humanistic, philanthropic approach.

Broadminded, tolerant, generous, cooperative.
Sympathetic, compassionate.
Occasional introspective or self-centered needs.
Sociable, uses persuasion rather than force.
Idealistic, can inspire others.
Creative, imaginative, unique or unusual approaches or solutions.

Good mind, logical approach.

Extremely sensitive to others' needs and feelings.
Much feeling expressed, may be involved in many dramatic situations.
Gives much in the way of friendship, affection, love. Can sometimes be content with minimal return.

> (Emphasis on 9 energy. Sub-emphasis on 2 and 7 energy.)

CHART **5** THE BIRTHDAY	**11** ILLUMINATION

11

Works well with others.
Often inspires by example.
Uses persuasion rather than force.
Spiritual, occult or psychic explorations.
Idealistic.
Creative.
Nervous tension.
Uncomfortable in business world.

Good mind, analytical ability.
Good intuition.

Very aware and sensitive, often high emotions, temperamental.

More dreamer than doer.

(Emphasis on 11 and 2 energy. No sub-emphasis on other energies.)

29

Works well with others.
Often inspires by example.
Uses persuasion rather than force.
Spiritual, occult or psychic explorations.
Idealistic.
Much creativity, imagination.
Nervous tension.
Uncomfortable in business world.

Good mind, analytical ability.
Good intuition.

Very aware and sensitive, often high emotions, temperamental.
May be involved in dramatic situations.
Gives much in the way of friendship, affection, love. Can sometimes be content with minimal return.

More dreamer than doer.

(Emphasis on 11 and 2 energy. Sub-emphasis on 9 energy.)

CHART **5**	
THE BIRTHDAY	**22** MASTER BUILDER

22	Capable of handling large scale under-takings.	Nervous tension.
	Capable of leading in new directions.	Much unusual perception and awareness.
	Extremely capable organizer.	Good intuition.
	Unorthodox approach.	Better at starting than continuing.
	Responsible, serious, sincere, works long and hard.	Better at broad strokes than details.
	Idealistic, desire to work for the good of all.	(Emphasis on 22 and 4 energy. No sub-emphasis on other energies.)
	Inner strength, often charisma.	

CHART 6   **THE ASPECTS**

This chart is different than any of the others. Rather than describe the potential characteristics and energies involved in a specific number, this chart describes the potential relation between two numbers. This relation is called an aspect.

This aspect chart indicates the potential harmony or discord of the *energies* involved. The person's *life* may be harmonious or discordant depending on (1) whether he expresses the aspect potential, rises above the aspect potential or falls below the aspect potential, (2) the use of his free will, and (3) the environment in which he finds himself.

See Chapter 7, page 49, for further discussion of the use of this chart.

Since 11 is the higher octave of 2, wherever 11 energy is involved, read both the 11 and 2 aspects.

Since 22 is the higher octave of 4, wherever 22 energy is involved, read both the 22 and 4 aspects.

The aspects are described on the page related to the *lower* number of the aspect. For instance, the 5·3 aspect (which is the same as the 3·5 aspect) would be found on the 3 page of the chart under the 3·5 heading.

The "usual" description of the aspect appears directly below each aspect heading. Sometimes, in parentheses below the usual description you'll find descriptions divergent from the "usual" description.

CHART **6** THE ASPECTS	**1**	INDIVIDUATION INDEPENDENCE ATTAINMENT

Summary of 1 aspects:

3 harmonious aspects
1 harmonious *or* discordant aspect

6 discordant aspects
1 very discordant aspect

1·1 Usually VERY DISCORDANT

Overemphasis on self and own needs. Little concern for others.

   or

Timid, afraid to stand on own two feet.

Possible approach to alleviate difficulties: The individual must work to be accepted and feel comfortable in group situations.

1·2 Usually DISCORDANT

The potential of the 1 to lead and manage

conflicts with the potential of the 2 to work along with others.

1·3 Usually HARMONIOUS

The self-centeredness of the 1 is toned down by the social awareness of the 3. The leadership potential of the 1 is enhanced by the gift

of verbal expression of the 3.

(Sometimes, the 3 expresses as a happy-go-lucky individual, conflicting with the 1's driving desire for attainment.)

1·4 Usually HARMONIOUS

The potential of the 1 to lead and manage is enhanced by the potential of the 4 for system and order.

(Sometimes, the self-centered potential of the 1 is emphasized by the 4's potential for rigidity, causing a negative approach.)

1·5 Sometimes HARMONIOUS; sometimes DISCORDANT

The attainment potential of the 1 may be enhanced by the constructive use of freedom of the 5. This combination may be extremely powerful or may produce a combination so overpowering as to work against individual's

best interests.

   or

The self-centered, goal-oriented potential of the 1 may conflict with the constant flux often seen in the 5, producing a pull in different directions.

1·6 Usually DISCORDANT

The self-centered potential of the 1 conflicts

with the potential of the 6 for responsibility and concern for others.

1·7 Usually DISCORDANT

The desire for attainment of the 1 conflicts with the introspective potential of the 7.

(Sometimes, the unique point of view of the 7 enhances the attainment potential of the 1.)

1·8 Usually HARMONIOUS

The attainment potential of the 1 is enhanced by the executive potential of the 8 for material achievement.

(Sometimes, the self-centered potential of the 1 may be emphasized by the potential of the 8 for stubbornness and rigidity, causing a negative approach.)

1·9 Usually DISCORDANT

The self-centered potential of the 1 conflicts with the potential of the 9 for giving to others.

(Sometimes, the 9's potential of giving to

others may be expressed as creative activity. In this situation, the attainment potential of the 1 may be enhanced by the creative potential of the 9.)

1·11 Usually DISCORDANT

The potential of the 1 for independence and self-centered attainment conflicts with the

potential of the 11 for idealistic or spiritual achievement.

1·22 Usually DISCORDANT

The potential of the 1 for independence and self-centered attainment conflicts with the

potential of the 22 for substantial material achievement.

CHART **6** THE ASPECTS	**2** RELATION ASSOCIATION

	Summary of 2 aspects: 5 harmonious aspects	5 discordant aspects 1 very discordant aspect
2·1	Usually DISCORDANT	
2·2	Usually VERY DISCORDANT Meddling busybody, adding confusion rather than harmony to a situation. or Difficulty in finding fulfilling place in a	group. Little patience with details or with people. Possibly withdrawn, shy and retiring. Possible approach to alleviate difficulties: the individual must work to learn system and organization.
2·3	Usually HARMONIOUS The potential of the 2 for cooperating and harmonizing is enhanced by the social awareness of the 3.	(Sometimes, the 3 expresses through frivolous activity and a dilettante's approach which may conflict with the potential of the 2 for cooperation.)
2·4	Usually HARMONIOUS The potential of the 2 for cooperation and harmonizing is enhanced by the potential of the 4 for system and order.	(Sometimes the potential for harmonizing of the 2 is stifled by the comparative fixity of approach of the 4.)
2·5	Usually DISCORDANT The potential of the 2 for cooperating and harmonizing conflicts with the strong per-	sonal desire for freedom and the state of flux of the 5.
2·6	Usually HARMONIOUS The potential of the 2 for cooperating is considerably enhanced by the potential of the 6 for responsibility. The 6's ability to show friendship, affection and love provides a very	positive side to this combination. (The 2·6 individual must take responsibility for himself as well as others. He should not be reduced to a doormat because of his desire to help others fulfill themselves.)
2·7	Usually DISCORDANT The potential of the 2 for cooperating and harmonizing conflicts with the introspective potential of the 7. The 7's appearance of being "different" makes it difficult for the 7 to work well in groups most of the time.	(Sometimes, the introspective potential of the 7 is suppressed and the potential to share wisdom and knowledge is expressed instead. This enhances the potential of the 2 for working together with others.)
2·8	Usually DISCORDANT The potential of the 2 for cooperating and harmonizing conflicts with the executive potential of the 8 for material achievement.	The 8 usually expresses a potential to lead rather than to be a cooperating member of a group.
2·9	Usually HARMONIOUS The potential of the 2 for cooperating and harmonizing is enhanced by the potential of the 9 for giving to others. (The 2·9 individual must stay aware of his own needs so that he is not completely	submerged by his desire to help others.) (The 9 often has trouble expressing its positive potential and may prefer to receive rather than give. In this case, the potential of the negative 9 would conflict with the potential of the 2.)
2·11	Usually HARMONIOUS The potential of the 2 for cooperating and harmonizing may be enhanced by the potential of the 11 for idealistic or spiritual achievement. The nervous tension of the 11 will be a	partial detriment to the 2 approach. (Sometimes, the potential of the 2 is expressing on a relatively mundane level, while the potential of the 11 is expressing on a high spiritual level, thereby causing a conflict.)
2·22	Usually DISCORDANT The potential of the 2 for being a cooperating and harmonizing member of a group conflicts with the potential of the 22 for leading the way	to substantial material achievement. The nervous tension of the 22 will act as a further detriment to the 2 approach.

CHART **6** THE ASPECTS	**3** EXPRESSION JOY OF LIVING

Summary of 3 aspects:
6' harmonious aspects

4 discordant aspects
1 very discordant aspect

3·1   Usually HARMONIOUS

3·2   Usually HARMONIOUS

3·3   Usually VERY DISCORDANT
Frivolous. Little sense of purpose. Scattering of forces.
    or
Difficulty with self-expression. May hide feelings and emotions from self and others. Seems uncomfortable in even light social situation. Often shy and withdrawn.

Possible approach to alleviate the difficulties: The individual must work to learn to accept responsibility. He has to learn what is involved in being a friend.

3·4   Usually DISCORDANT
The potential of the 3 for creative self-expression and sociability conflicts with the potential of the 4 for system and order.

(Sometimes, the self-expression of the 3 is enhanced by the constructive, systematic approach of the 4. The harmony or discord depends on whether the 4 is strong and purposeful or just rigidly set in his ways.)

3·5   Usually HARMONIOUS
The potential of the 3 for creative self-expression and sociability is enhanced by the potential of the 5 for the constructive use of freedom.

(Sometimes, the restlessness, versatility and love of change of the 5 combines with the light and joy of the 3 to produce frivolity, or in extremes, purposelessness and erratic behavior.)

3·6   Usually HARMONIOUS
The potential of the 3 for social awareness enhances the potential of the 6 for friendship and love. The potential for creative self-expression of *both* the 3 and 6 enhances the expressive capabilities.

3·7   Usually DISCORDANT
The extrovert potential of the 3 conflicts with the introvert potential of the 7. The sociability of the 3 conflicts with the "different", less adaptable approach of the 7.

3·8   Usually DISCORDANT
The potential of the 3 for creative self-expression and sociability conflicts with the executive potential of the 8 for material achievement. The adaptability of the 3 conflicts with the fixity of the 8.

3·9   Usually HARMONIOUS
The potential of the 3 for social awareness enhances the potential of the 9 for giving to others.
The potential for creative self-expression of *both* the 3 and the 9 enhances the expressive capabilities.

(The 9 often has trouble expressing its positive potential and may prefer to receive rather than give. In this case, the potential of the negative 9 would conflict with the potential of the 3.)

3·11   Usually HARMONIOUS
The potential of the 3 for creative self-expression and social awareness enhances the potential of the 11 for idealistic or spiritual achievement. The lighter tone of the 3 may be a good foil for the seriousness of the 11.

3·22   Usually DISCORDANT
The potential of the 3 for a light, less serious tone conflicts with the serious tone of the 22 and its potential for substantial material achievement.

CHART **6**		**4**	LIMITATION
			ORDER
THE ASPECTS			SERVICE

Summary of 4 aspects:

4	harmonious aspects	5	discordant aspects
1	harmonious *or* discordant aspect	1	very discordant aspect

4·1 Usually HARMONIOUS

4·2 Usually HARMONIOUS

4·3 Usually DISCORDANT

4·4 Usually VERY DISCORDANT

Feels limited, tied down, frustrated. Very rigid attitudes—stubborn, obstinate. Obsessed with system and order; loses sight of the forest because of his interest in the trees.

    or

Very disorganized. Rarely feels accountable.

Often has no sense of time or committment. Actions are often irresponsible.

Possible approach to alleviate difficulties: The individual must work to develop executive ability. He has to develop the capability of seeing things realistically, with a practical approach.

4·5 Usually DISCORDANT

The potential of the 4 for system and order conflicts with the strong desire of the 5 for freedom.

4·6 Usually HARMONIOUS

The potential of the 4 for system and order enhances the potential of the 6 for responsibility and concern.

(Sometimes, the fixity of the 4, expressed as either strength or rigidity, conflicts with the potential of the 6 for concern.)

4·7 Usually HARMONIOUS

The potential of the 4 for system and order enhances the potential of the 7 for study and research.

(Sometimes, the fixity of the 4, expressed as either strength or rigidity, combined with the introspective potential of the 7 produces a very self-centered approach and difficulty in relating to others.)

4·8 Usually DISCORDANT

The potential of the 4 for system and order combined with the executive potential of the 8 for achievement produces a self-centered person whose executive capabilities are apparent, but whose fixity stifles the potential for the use of these capabilities. This aspect tends toward a very rigid attitude—often an extremely obstinate person.

4·9 Usually DISCORDANT

The potential of the 4 for fixity of approach conflicts with the potential of the 9 for giving to others.

(Sometimes, the potential of the 4 for system and order may enhance the potential of the 9 for expression.)

4·11 Usually DISCORDANT

The potential of the 4 for system and order conflicts with the potential of the 11 for idealistic or spiritual achievement.

4·22 Sometimes HARMONIOUS; sometimes DISCORDANT.

The potential of the 4 for system and order may be enhanced by the potential of the 22 for leading the way to substantial material achievement. The fixity of the 4 is apt to conflict with the ability of the 22 to take advantage of situations with developing potential. In any case, the nervous tension of the 22 will be a partial detriment to the 4 approach.

| CHART **6** THE ASPECTS | **5** CONSTRUCTIVE FREEDOM |

Summary of 5 aspects:

1	harmonious aspect	8	discordant aspects
1	harmonious *or* discordant aspect	1	very discordant aspect

5·1   Sometimes HARMONIOUS; sometimes DIS-CORDANT.

5·2   Usually DISCORDANT

5·3   Usually HARMONIOUS

5·4   Usually DISCORDANT

5·5   Usually VERY DISCORDANT

Too much freedom used carelessly. Emphasis on freedom rather than the constructive use of freedom. Excessive pull toward food, drink, drugs, sex—physical satisfaction with little thought of other pleasures or other potentials. Forces are often scattered bringing little concrete result and much frustration.

    or

Fear of freedom and fear of taking risks produce a stagnant situation with attendant frustration. Inability to take advantage of talents and opportunities.

Possible approach to alleviate difficulties: The individual must work to be aware of individuality, to achieve independence and to attain some specific goals.

5·6   Usually DISCORDANT

The strong personal desire of the 5 for freedom conflicts with the potential of the 6 for responsibility and concern for others.

5·7   Usually DISCORDANT

The strong personal desire of the 5 for freedom conflicts with the introspective approach and potential of the 7 for study and research.

(The free-wheeling potential of the 5 for freedom may conflict with the "different", relatively inflexible potential of the 7, causing an even more discordant aspect.)

5·8   Usually DISCORDANT

The free-wheeling potential of the 5 for freedom conflicts with the fixity of approach and the executive potential of the 8 for material achievement.

5·9   Usually DISCORDANT

The strong personal desire of the 5 for freedom conflicts with the potential of the 9 for giving to others.

(Sometimes, the potential of the 5 for freedom may enhance the potential of the 9 for self-expression.)

5·11   Usually DISCORDANT

The strong personal desire of the 5 for freedom conflicts with the potential of the 11 for idealistic or spiritual achievements for all.

5·22   Usually DISCORDANT

The strong personal desire of the 5 for freedom conflicts with the potential of the 22 for substantial material achievement.

CHART 6 THE ASPECTS	6	BALANCE RESPONSIBILITY LOVE

Summary of 6 aspects:

6 harmonious aspects

4 discordant aspects
1 very discordant aspect

6·1 Usually DISCORDANT

6·2 Usually HARMONIOUS

6·3 Usually HARMONIOUS

6·4 Usually HARMONIOUS

6·5 Usually DISCORDANT

6·6 Usually VERY DISCORDANT

Overwhelmed with responsibility. Person finds it difficult to recognize and care for own needs because of the extreme and constant needs of others (parents, children, spouse particularly). Person is often reduced to a near-slave because of acceptance of so much responsibility.

or

(Rare) Inability to accept responsibility and to express friendship and love makes it difficult to have any close relation. Difficulty handling even the simplest everyday responsibilities produces a frightened individual.

Possible approach to alleviate difficulties: The individual must work on self-expression. He has to learn to see the lighter side of things, and learn to express the joy of living.

6·7 Usually DISCORDANT

The potential of the 6 for responsibility and concern for others conflicts with the introspective potential of the 7.

6·8 Usually DISCORDANT

The potential of the 6 for responsibility and concern for others conflicts with the executive potential of the 8 for material achievement.

The 8 is usually concerned with responsibility only as far as its own self-centered goals are concerned. The adaptable attitude of the 6 conflicts with the fixity of approach of the 8.

6·9 Usually HARMONIOUS

The potential of the 6 for responsibility and concern for others is enhanced by the potential of the 9 for giving to others.

(The 6 gives because of his responsibility, affection and love. The 9 gives because of the humanitarian concern. This can be an extremely strong combination, but the 6·9 individual must stay aware of his own needs so that he is not completely submerged by his desire to help others.

(The 9 often has trouble expressing its positive potential and may prefer to receive rather than give. In this case, the potential of the negative 9 would conflict with the potential of the 6.)

The potential for creative self-expression of *both* the 6 and 9 enhances the expressive capabilities.

6·11 Usually HARMONIOUS

The potential of the 6 for responsibility and concern for others is enhanced by the potential of the 11 for idealistic or spiritual achievements. The nervous tension of the 11 will be a partial detriment to the 6 approach.

(The 6 is usually concerned with home, family, friends in specific situations, while the 11 is often concerned with broader, more abstract dealings, producing the potential for conflict.)

6·22 Usually HARMONIOUS

The potential of the 6 for responsibility and concern for others is enhanced by the potential of the 22 for substantial material achievement. The nervous tension of the 22 will be a partial

detriment to the 6 approach.

(The 6 is usually concerned with home, family, friends, while the 22 is usually concerned with a larger scale of enterprise, producing the potential for conflict.)

CHART **6**		**7** ANALYSIS
THE ASPECTS		UNDERSTANDING

	Summary of 7 aspects:	8 discordant aspects
	2 harmonious aspects	1 very discordant aspect

7·1   Usually DISCORDANT

7·2   Usually DISCORDANT

7·3   Usually DISCORDANT

7·4   Usually HARMONIOUS

7·5   Usually DISCORDANT

7·6   Usually DISCORDANT

7·7   Usually VERY DISCORDANT

Extremely self-contained and inflexible. A "different" point of view that may appear to others as considerably eccentric. Difficult to get to know—purposely put others off because more comfortable keeping distance from others.

     or

Timid, shy, retiring. Very dependent on others and most resentful of that dependency. Efforts to stand alone often thwarted.

Possible approach to alleviate difficulties: The individual must work to express more freely. He has to learn to take advantage of opportunities by being more adaptable. He must also learn to express feelings honestly, rather than hiding them.

7·8   Usually DISCORDANT

The introspective potential of the 7 conflicts with the executive potential of the 8 for achievement. The inner nature of the 7 combined with the fixity of the 8 may produce a very self-centered approach and difficulty in relating to others.

(Sometimes, the potential of the 7 for study and research enhances the executive potential of the 8 for achievement.)

7·9   Usually DISCORDANT

The introspective potential of the 7 conflicts with the potential of the 9 for giving.

(Sometimes, the "different" aproach of the 7 enhances the 9's potential for self-expression.)

7·11   Usually HARMONIOUS

The potential of the 7 for study and research enhances the potential of the 11 for idealistic or spiritual achievement. The nervous tension of the 11 will be a partial detriment to the 7 approach.

(Sometimes, the introspective potential and the "different" approach of the 7 combine with the dreamy side of the 11 to produce a person somewhat removed from the realities of the world.)

7·22   Usually DISCORDANT

The introspective potential of the 7 conflicts with the potential of the 22 for substantial material achievement.

CHART **6**	**8** MATERIAL SATISFACTION
THE ASPECTS	

Summary of 8 aspects:

2	harmonious aspects	8 discordant aspects
		1 very discordant aspect

8·1 Usually HARMONIOUS

8·2 Usually DISCORDANT

8·3 Usually DISCORDANT

8·4 Usually DISCORDANT

8·5 Usually DISCORDANT

8·6 Usually DISCORDANT

8·7 Usually DISCORDANT

8·8 Usually VERY DISCORDANT

Very materialistic—obsessed with goals and achievements. Extremely rigid attitudes—stubborn and obstinate. Cold and aloof. No matter the attainment, he feels limited, tied down, frustrated.

or

Lack of concern with material things produces an unrealistic, impractical, unworkable way of approaching matters. Problems because of lack of material needs. Stubborn attitude, fixity of approach stifles potential for growth.

Possible approach to alleviate difficulties: The individual must work to see and appreciate the inherent values—including but not limited to the material values. He has to learn to study and meditate on the inner satisfactions as well as the material satisfactions.

8·9 Usually DISCORDANT

The executive potential of the 8 for material achievement conflicts with the potential of the 9 for giving.

(Sometimes, the executive potential of the 8 for material achievement may be broad enough to enhance the potential of the 9 for giving. In this instance, the 9's giving would be on a more material plane than is usually the case.)

8·11 Usually DISCORDANT

The executive potential of the 8 for material achievement conflicts with the potential of the 11 for idealistic or spiritual achievement.

8·22 Usually HARMONIOUS

The executive potential of the 8 for material achievement enhances the potential of the 22 for leading the way to substantial material achievement. The tension of the 22 will be a partial detriment. This can be an extremely powerful aspect, as long as the 8 can be flexible enough to take advantage of the opportunities.

(Sometimes, the fixity of the approach of the 8 conflicts with the 22's broad, adaptable approach.)

CHART **6** THE ASPECTS	**9** SELFLESSNESS HUMANITARIANISM

Summary of 9 aspects:
5 harmonious aspects
5 discordant aspects
1 very discordant aspect

9·1   Usually DISCORDANT

9·2   Usually HARMONIOUS

9·3   Usually HARMONIOUS

9·4   Usually DISCORDANT

9·5   Usually DISCORDANT

9·6   Usually HARMONIOUS

9·7   Usually DISCORDANT

9·8   Usually DISCORDANT

9·9   Usually VERY DISCORDANT

Overwhelmed with giving. Finds it difficult to recognize personal needs because all efforts are directed toward others. Feels discontent, trapped. Others are tired of hearing of constant sacrifice.

or

Very selfish. Concerned primarily with getting rather than giving. Insensitive to others' needs. Self-centered, usually inflexible.

Possible approach to alleviate difficulties: The individual must work to win and preserve independence. He has to learn to strive for material freedom at the same time that the humanitarian qualities are expressed.

9·11   Usually HARMONIOUS

The potential of the 9 for giving is enhanced by the potential of the 11 for idealistic or spiritual achievement.

9·22   Usually HARMONIOUS

The potential of the 9 for giving is enhanced by the potential of the 22 for significant material achievement.

CHART 6
THE ASPECTS

11 ILLUMINATION

Summary of 11 aspects:
5 harmonious aspects
5 discordant aspects
1 very discordant aspect

11·1 Usually DISCORDANT

11·2 Usually HARMONIOUS

11·3 Usually HARMONIOUS

11·4 Usually DISCORDANT

11·5 Usually DISCORDANT

11·6 Usually HARMONIOUS

11·7 Usually HARMONIOUS

11·8 Usually DISCORDANT

11·9 Usually HARMONIOUS

11·11 Usually VERY DISCORDANT

A lost dreamer. Idealistic motivations overwhelmed by impractical schemes. Aiming toward spirituality with no grasp of mundane realities. Much nervous tension.

or

Potential for accomplishment is masked in idealistic, even inspirational words, but the hidden motivation—personal power, material accomplishment, satisfaction of selfish needs—includes little perception of spiritual satisfactions.

Possible approach to alleviate difficulties: The individual must lower his sights, work to achieve a more practical, realistic view. He can try to use the enormous potential to help others.

11·22 Usually DISCORDANT

The potential of the 11 for idealistic or spiritual achievement conflicts with the potential of the 22 for leading the way to substantial material achievement. The nervous tension of both the 11 and 22 act as an additional detriment.

(Sometimes, the potential of the 11 is practical enough to enhance the potential of the 22, leading to material progress. The nervous tension is still a detriment.)

CHART **6**	**22** MASTER BUILDER
THE ASPECTS	

Summary of 22 aspects:

3 harmonious aspects
1 harmonious *or* discordant aspect
6 discordant aspects
1 very discordant aspect

22·1 Usually DISCORDANT

22·2 Usually DISCORDANT

22·3 Usually DISCORDANT

22·4 Sometimes HARMONIOUS; sometimes DIS-CORDANT

22·5 Usually DISCORDANT

22·6 Usually HARMONIOUS

22·7 Usually DISCORDANT

22·8 Usually HARMONIOUS

22·9 Usually HARMONIOUS

22·11 Usually DISCORDANT

22·22 Usually VERY DISCORDANT

Overwhelmed by extreme potential of awareness and capability plus intensified nervous tension. Difficult to amalgamate and assimilate the enormity of the potential involved in order to use talents at the desired high level. Usually, much confusion of intentions and much difficulty in organizing oneself to move in a positive direction.

or

Potential for substantial material achievement confused with personal attainment, use of personal power and self-centered material accomplishment. The achievement, though substantial, tends to overwhelm the individual who has achieved for selfish ends. He finds little of the pleasure or satisfaction he expected. The heightened nervous tension makes the path to achievement more difficult, the ultimate attainment unsatisfactory.

Possible approach to alleviate difficulties: The individual must lower his sights. He should work to achieve material freedom and the power which accompanies it, then learn to achieve the satisfaction which may be related to the material freedom at first, but is ultimately above the necessity for material attainment.

CHART 7   THE KARMIC DEBT

DESCRIPTION

The Karmic Debt is a significant difficulty in this life as payment for the misapplication of energies in a past life. See Chapter 11, page 121.

In this section, the following are discussed:

The cause of the Karmic Debt.

The characteristics manifested in this life due to the Karmic Debt.

The changes necessary in this life to reduce or remove the difficulties encountered.

The *specific* effect of the Karmic Debt on the Life Path, Expression and Soul Urge are shown below. The *specific* effect on the Birthday is already included in the description of the Birthday in CHART 5: THE BIRTHDAY.

IN THE LIFE PATH

Expression of the Karmic Debt through the Life Path.

IN THE EXPRESSION

Expression of the Karmic Debt through the Expression.

IN THE SOUL URGE

Expression of the Karmic Debt through the Soul Urge.

This chart contains pages for only 1, 4, 5 and 7 since these are the only numbers involved with Karmic Debt.

CHART 7
THE KARMIC DEBT

1 INDIVIDUATION INDEPENDENCE ATTAINMENT

DESCRIPTION

The 19/1 Karmic Debt developed from the abuse of power in a past life—acting in a completely self-centered manner, blind to everything except a selfish fulfillment of one's own desires. The 1 and 9 behind the 1 indicate the self-centered (negative 1) misused ambitions (negative 9) manifested in a previous life.

The 19/1 energy tends to exhibit the traits of the negative 1 in one of two extreme directions. (1) The subject may be completely immersed in his own concerns and may have great difficulty becoming aware of others' needs. He often undoes himself because of his inability to realistically see himself in relation to others. He is constantly surprised by others' negative reactions to his endeavors. OR (2) The subject displays an inability to act on his own. He is unhappy with his dependent nature, but finds solace by blaming the environment or other people for his inability to stand on his own two feet.

In this life, the subject will continue to meet with substantial difficulties unless (1) he can look past his own needs to the needs of others, OR (2) he can work toward independence no matter what forces are tending to keep him weak and dependent. Awareness of the Karmic Debt will produce clarity about one's own needs, others' needs and the relation between them. If, instead, the subject continues to be (1) egotistical, dominating and aggressive, OR (2) lazy, fearful and servile, the problems will be magnified.

IN THE LIFE PATH

Although the subject can see the opportunities, the path is beset with obstacles, many of his own making.

If the subject confuses independence and self-centeredness, he will find that his egotistical approach limits his awareness of the environment. His actions, commenced with positive ends in sight, will often undo the very things he hoped to accomplish, leaving him further behind than when he started. He will find himself trapped by his own misapplied energies, often exposed as the dominating, selfish person he is.

If, instead, the subject is struggling with dependence, he will find himself constantly saddled with strong pressures keeping him from breaking free. He will probably waste much time and energy because of his inability to read the realities of the environment and use them to his advantage.

IN THE EXPRESSION

The subject will probably have difficulty expressing his talents to his advantage. His dominating, self-centered approach may turn others off so that his capabilities are downgraded, OR, his weak, dependent ways will make it difficult for others to view and appreciate his abilities.

IN THE SOUL URGE

The strong motivational force of the subject's inner desires will be difficult to fulfill. Others will read his self-centered ways or his dependent weaknesses, no matter how he attempts to hide them. His innermost secrets may be exposed to his disadvantage.

The 2 page and 3 page of this chart are not applicable and are omitted.

CHART **7** THE KARMIC DEBT	**4**	LIMITATION ORDER SERVICE

DESCRIPTION

The 13/4 Karmic Debt developed from a lack of application to work requiring accomplishment in a past life—dawdling in frivolous activity, sidestepping work, burdening others with his rightful share of work. The 1 and 3 behind the 4 indicate the self-centered (negative 1), frivolous and superficial ways (negative 3) manifested in a previous life.

The 13/4 tends to exhibit the traits of the negative 4. His approach is rigid, obstinate, dogmatic. Although the subject feels limited, restricted, boxed in on all sides, he usually rationalizes his situation. He finds it extremely difficult to change his course to a more productive direction. When he complains about the limitations he feels, he accepts little of the responsibility for the pre-dicaments in which he feels trapped.

In this life, the subject will continue to meet with substantial difficulties unless he works hard, far harder than his share, a good part of the time. He must apply himself to the work at hand, be aware of the larger picture while still completing all the details. He has to accept the stringent limitations produced by his inordinate work load. Awareness of the Karmic Debt will stay the subject from looking for easier directions. This awareness can aid in finding constructive paths for development, though these paths, too, will demand much in the way of work. If, instead, the subject chooses to be lazy, indifferent, negative or involved with trivia, the problems will be magnified.

IN THE LIFE PATH

The subject will find his opportunities considerably limiting. No matter his abilities or motivation, he will seem to keep running into stone walls, boxed in with few acceptable options. The opportunities may be as restrictive as they appear to the subject. More likely, the limitations are produced or reinforced by the subject's unbending views coupled with his lack of constructive adaptability.

IN THE EXPRESSION

The subject pursues his abilities doggedly in a rigid, one-track direction. The intensity of his drive may work to his advantage, but the effect of this drive is likely to be negated by the limitations of his vision.

IN THE SOUL URGE

The subject is discontent with the limitations imposed by his significant work load. He often accomplishes the work at hand but receives little satisfaction from his achievement. He is constantly looking for easier directions to follow, and though few easier paths appear, he continues a frustrating search for them.

CHART **7**
THE KARMIC DEBT

5 CONSTRUCTIVE FREEDOM

DESCRIPTION

The 14/5 Karmic Debt developed from a misuse of freedom in a past life. The subject may have found freedom for himself at others' expense or in a manner destructive to his interests. He may have become overly involved in physical pleasures to the detriment of his development. The 1 and 4 behind the 5 indicate the self-centered (negative 1) irresponsibility and lack of accountability (negative 4) manifested in a previous life.

The 14/5 tends to exhibit the traits of the negative 5. He is apt to be somewhat erratic, jumping from activity to activity—a rolling stone with little sense of accomplishment. He tends to pleasures related to physical sensations—may overindulge in eating, sensuality, liquor, drugs. He craves the new and exciting with little sense of proportion.

In this life, the subject will continue to meet with substantial difficulties unless (1) he learns to profit from his experiences instead of repeating mistakes, and (2) he curbs his excessive appetite for physical stimulation. The difficulties encountered may take the form of delay or loss. Awareness of the Karmic Debt will allow a more constructive use of personal freedom. If, instead, the subject continues to be restless, impatient and scattering, the problems will be magnified.

IN THE LIFE PATH

The subject must learn the lesson of change—to begin and nurture an interest or relation, to experience it in full bloom, to detach from it when it is completed. This will tend to be a difficult lesson.

Instead of appreciating the beauties which enter and leave the life, the subject may be beset with disappointment at losses which are either beyond his control or caused by his lack of awareness.

IN THE EXPRESSION

The subject has an unrealistic or unclear view of the use and limitations of his talents. He is apt to meet disappointment in his work, must constantly regroup his energies to move ahead. The vague, dreamy or impractical nature of his vocational commitment adds to the difficulties.

IN THE SOUL URGE

The subject's important personal relationships may be marked by unexpected delays and interruptions. His impatience and light view of responsibility add to the problems.

The 6 page of this chart is not applicable and is omitted.

CHART 7
THE KARMIC DEBT

7 ANALYSIS UNDERSTANDING

DESCRIPTION

The 16/7 Karmic Debt developed from involvement in unusual or illicit love affairs in a past life, affairs which caused suffering to others. The 1 and 6 behind the 7 indicate the self-centered (negative 1) lack of responsibility and distortion of loving feelings (negative 6) manifested in a previous life.

The 16/7 tends to exhibit the traits of the negative 7. The subject's "differentness" is often apparent. His manner may make him difficult to approach. He is apt to be most concerned with himself—possibly self-centered but, at the least, considerably introspective. His growth will follow his own leanings—his outward actions may often not be what others expect. He may easily disconcert or confuse others, even those who feel they know him well. Permanent relations—marriage, business partnerships, etc.—tend to be difficult to maintain.

In this life, the subject will continue to meet with substantial difficulties unless he devotes himself to selfless, loving ways, subordinating his own personal needs. He is apt to meet with strangely manifesting deceptions or losses which often appear to be quirks of fate. Awareness of the Karmic Debt will provide an optimistic understanding and the ability to keep faith in himself and the universe despite adversity. If, instead, the subject expresses pride and vanity, the difficulties will be magnified.

IN THE LIFE PATH

Life is likely to provide the subject with many examples of the transient nature of reality. This impermanence is apt to be expressed in the meaningful areas in which he would like to exhibit positive growth. His status, wealth or power may change for the worse. His loving relations may shift abruptly. Other matters may end in sudden or unusual ways. The subject may be the cause of his own undoing, or may be the seeming recipient of some curious quirk of fate. Acceptance of impermanence will ease the burden.

IN THE EXPRESSION

The subject is apt to undo himself in some unexpected way in vocational matters, or may lose what he has gained due to some sudden or unusual circumstances. He should not lean too heavily on his material attributes—his wealth, status and power may prove ephemeral.

IN THE SOUL URGE

The subject's faith in his selection of friends and associates is apt to be severely tested. People on whom he relies may prove unreliable. People he trusts may act against his interests in a manner difficult for him to comprehend. Close friends may cease being close because of some sudden or unusual circumstances.

The 8, 9, 11 and 22 pages of this chart are not applicable and are omitted.

CHART 8   THE INTENSITY TABLE

See Chapter 12, page 129.

PRIME INTENSIFIER

The Prime Intensifier, the Intensity Point appearing in largest quantity, indicates strong and obvious characteristics.

INTENSITY POINT MORE THAN AVERAGE

An Intensity Point is a modifier with more than an average quantity of a number, indicates characteristics of above average intensity.

AVERAGE QUANTITY OF NUMBER

INTENSITY POINT LESS THAN AVERAGE

An Intensity Point with less than an average quantity of a number indicates characteristics of below average intensity.

MODIFIED KARMIC LESSON

A Modified Karmic Lesson is a Karmic Lesson in which the Karmic Lesson number also appears as a core element.

KARMIC LESSON

A Karmic Lesson is a modifier indicating potential weaknesses, difficulties or obstacles because the modifier energy has not been experienced in past lives.

CHART **8**	**1**	INDIVIDUATION
INTENSITY TABLE		INDEPENDENCE
		ATTAINMENT

PRIME INTENSIFIER

Important to follow own bent and get needs met. If individual has difficulty getting needs met, possibly because of conflict of core numbers, the resultant frustration is likely to be among the most obvious strong traits.

INTENSITY POINT MORE THAN AVERAGE

Five or more:
- Self centeredness and/or domination likely to be very strong and block possibilities for growth.

Four:
- Self-centered. Own interests are strong and must be satisfied.
- Lack of flexibility and adaptability. Must do things own way.
- Tends to control and dominate, but the domination usually offends others and works against the individual's best interests. Sometimes, if other numbers indicate, domination is accomplished by being weak and helpless and needing aid from others.
- Exhibits much courage, often in face of great difficulties.
- Potential to use original ideas and leadership abilities for positive ends likely to be stifled by self-centered lack of awareness.

AVERAGE QUANTITY OF NUMBER
THREE 1'S

INTENSITY POINT LESS THAN AVERAGE

One or two:
- Lack of confidence in own abilities makes it difficult to promote self. Has difficulty standing up for own rights against others' wills, often feels put down by authority.
- Still learning to be independent. Lacks consistent motivation to follow ambitions. Often makes excuses for lower position or lack of direction, or rationalizes the difficulties encountered.

MODIFIED KARMIC LESSON

- Lack of confidence in own abilities makes it difficult to promote self. Has difficulty standind up for own rights against others' wills, often feels put down by authority.
- Still learning to be independent. Lacks consistent motivation to follow ambitions. Often makes excuses for lower position or lack of direction, or rationalizes the difficulties encountered.

KARMIC LESSON

In past lives, the subject showed a lack of independence, confidence and ambition.

These qualities will play an important part in the subject's life. He will find himself in situations where he must be able to express his independence or be overwhelmed by others' dominating ways. He must learn to make decisions for himself or fall victim to others' decisions. He must develop his own ambition as a positive force for his development.

This Karmic Lesson is extremely rare and, when found, indicates a significant coloration of the core. Those people with this lesson usually have little faith in their own powers, look to others for direction, are pressured by others' decisions because of their own difficulty and/or fear in making decisions. They have great difficulty promoting their own capabilities. Life is apt to be trying until they accept the necessity of standing on their own feet.

CHART **8**
INTENSITY TABLE

2 RELATION COOPERATION

PRIME INTENSIFIER
- Extremely considerate, helpful, friendly. These are likely to be among most obvious strong traits.
- Very sensitive to others' needs.

INTENSITY POINT MORE THAN AVERAGE

Four or more:
- Feels considerate, helpful and friendly. Although manifesting, these traits tend to be negated by difficulties in distinguishing the best way to help. Good efforts often go to waste.
- Extremely sensitive. Often hurt by what they perceive to be others' insensitivity. The sensitivity may be emotionally and/or mentally draining on family and friends.
- Feelings of subservience, inferiority or fear of others may strongly mark lives.
- Very fine with detail work. May get so involved with detail that sight of the larger picture is lost.
- Appreciation of the arts.
- Emotional.

Two or three:
- Most considerate of others. Helpful, cooperative and friendly. Expresses a tactful, diplomatic manner in most situations.
- Very sensitive. As a child and young adult, apt to be shy and retiring.
- Must work to resolve:

  Feelings of subservience, OR
  Feelings of inferiority, OR
  Inner fear of others.
- Good with details.
- Appreciation of the arts.
- Emotional.

AVERAGE QUANTITY OF NUMBER ONE 2

INTENSITY POINT LESS THAN AVERAGE

Zero:

See Karmic Lesson or Modified Karmic Lesson below.

MODIFIED KARMIC LESSON

The subject will find himself in situations where sensitivity, consideration, diplomacy and concern with detail are necessary for positive development.

He is likely to have these traits developed so that they stand him in good stead.

KARMIC LESSON

In past lives, the subject showed a lack of sensitivity and consideration for others, a lack of awareness of details.

Sensitivity, consideration and detail work will play an important part in the life. The subject will find himself in situations where a sensitive nature and a diplomatic manner are imperative for positive development. His environment will include substantial work involved with detail, often presented so that the details tend to obscure the larger picture.

Most people with this Karmic Lesson are born with a great deal of sensitivity and consideration as well as a sense of the importance of detail. Those lacking the 2 who are insensitive, inconsiderate and unwilling to be bothered with detail work are likely to meet with difficulties until they choose to learn the lesson.

| CHART **8** INTENSITY TABLE | **3** EXPRESSION JOY OF LIVING |

PRIME INTENSIFIER

Artistic bent, imaginative approach and/or verbal ability are likely to be among most obvious strong traits.

INTENSITY POINT MORE THAN AVERAGE

Four or more:

- Strong indication of artistic talent—music, art, writing, etc.
- Excellent imagination.
- Strong capability with words—excellent verbal and/or written self-expression.
- Strong self-interest, possibly self-centered, even selfish.

- May scatter energies or act immoderately against own best interests.

Three:

- Artistic talent—music, art, writing, etc.
- Imaginative.
- Good verbal and/or written capabilities.
- Many interests may make it difficult to concentrate to support own best interests.

AVERAGE QUANTITY OF NUMBER
ONE or TWO 3's

INTENSITY POINT LESS THAN AVERAGE

Zero:

See Karmic Lesson or Modified Karmic Lesson below.

MODIFIED KARMIC LESSON

Problems with expression and social encounters are likely to occur. He will have to work to express his feelings and will tend to be somewhat uncomfortable in social situations. He probably isn't too good at selling himself. It's important for this subject to work to build his confidence so that he can express himself with greater facility.

KARMIC LESSON

In past lives, the subject showed little concern with expressing himself, little joie de vivre.

Difficulties with expression and problems in social encounters will play an important part in the life. Usually, the subject will lack confidence. He will rarely feel comfortable enough to express his feelings, will tend to be withdrawn or uncomfortable in social situations, will have difficulty promoting himself. His feelings of inferiority may project to others as a defeatist attitude. Unless he gains confidence in himself and improves his expressive abilities, he will find these negative traits blocking his growth.

An occasional subject will not lack in confidence or verbal ability, but the manner of expression —aggressive, over-dramatic or insensitive—will prove a stumbling block. This subject may well express his delight in the joy of living in a manner that is offensive—sometimes in a manner that puts pressure on others.

CHART **8** INTENSITY TABLE	**4**	LIMITATION ORDER SERVICE

PRIME INTENSIFIER

Practical, organized approach, ability to concentrate and work hard, capability at detail and routine are likely to be among most obvious strong traits.

INTENSITY POINT MORE THAN AVERAGE

Four or more:

- Practical, organized approach, ability to concentrate and work hard, capability at detail and routine—these traits are likely to be the basis for a significant portion of the work accomplished. The work may appear to be menial or below the individual's apparent ability, but the subject is likely to be content or comfortably rationalize the work.

Two or three:

- Practical approach.
- Very capable at organizing, systematizing.
- Ability to concentrate on work to be done, even if not particularly interested in the work.
- Good at detail and routine work.
- Hard worker when necessary.
- Tendency to be stubborn (if confirmed by other numbers).

AVERAGE QUANTITY OF NUMBER ONE 4

INTENSITY POINT LESS THAN AVERAGE

Zero:

See Karmic Lesson or Modified Karmic Lesson below.

MODIFIED KARMIC LESSON

Practicality, organization, hard work and concern with detail will play an important part in the subject's life. He will find that he can accomplish only by starting at the beginning of a task and working hard with great care and concern for detail to its completion. He is likely to innately understand this lesson because of the 4 in the core. He can probably concentrate his efforts no matter what the seeming limitations.

KARMIC LESSON

In past lives, the subject showed a lack of awareness of practicality, organization, hard work and concern with detail. These qualities will play an important part in a subject's life.

If the individual's core is strong in 2, 6 or 8 energy, he is likely to innately understand this lesson. He'll be willing and able to work long, hard and patiently, concentrating his efforts and continuing no matter what the seeming limitations.

If the individual's core is strong in 1, 3 or 5 energy, he is likely to think of hard work as a limitation. He's likely to look for easy ways out to avoid putting forth the required effort. He is apt to be severely limited in his growth until he is willing to accept the need for working hard and patiently.

CHART 8
INTENSITY TABLE

5 CONSTRUCTIVE FREEDOM

PRIME INTENSIFIER

Versatility, resourcefulness, unusual or unconventional approach, many interests are likely to be among most obvious traits. If core numbers emphasize 2, 4, 6, these characteristics are likely to be considerably reduced.

INTENSITY POINT MORE THAN AVERAGE

Seven or more:

- Extremely versatile and resourceful.
- Calls attention to self because of unusual or unconventional approach.
- Interested in everything. Tends to scatter energies.
- Must be free to do things own way. Will not allow *any* interference with personal freedom.
- Nervous temperament. Often acts impulsively.
- Tendency to abandon old ways for new, exciting avenues.

Six:

- Many interests, possibly lack of application due to restless nature.
- Versatile and resourceful.
- Unusual or unconventional approach.
- Strong interest in being free may emphasize own self-centered needs.
- Actions may stem from impulsive nature.

AVERAGE QUANTITY OF NUMBER
THREE, FOUR or FIVE 5's

INTENSITY POINT LESS THAN AVERAGE

One, two:

- Lack of adaptability.
- Limited understanding of others due to inability to benefit from experience. Probably approaches situations with mind made up and doesn't appreciate lessons to be learned from situations encountered.
- Limits experience available because of fears, insecurities or rigid approach.
- Stays with situations or people long after productiveness has been exhausted.

MODIFIED KARMIC LESSON

- Lack of adaptability.
- Limited understanding of others due to inability to benefit from experience. Probably approaches situations with mind made up and doesn't appreciate lessons to be learned from situations encountered.
- Limits experience available because of fears, insecurities or rigid approach.
- Stays with situations or people long after productiveness has been exhausted.

KARMIC LESSON

In past lives, the subject showed a lack of awareness of the uses of freedom and change. These qualities play an important part in the subject's life.

His life is likely to have significant change and uncertainty and he must learn to adapt and deal with situations with versatility. He probably has little understanding or tolerance of others' reactions because he has shown little deep interest in others, has kept himself from profiting from experience and has tended to keep away from new experiences which might prove beneficial.

This Karmic Lesson is extremely rare and, when found, indicates a significant coloration of the core.

CHART 8
INTENSITY TABLE

6 BALANCE RESPONSIBILITY

PRIME INTENSIFIER

Strong sense of responsibility, ability to balance situations and help others are likely to be among most obvious strong traits.

INTENSITY POINT MORE THAN AVERAGE

Four or more:

- Very strong sense of responsibility. May accept responsibilities even to own detriment.
- Helps others by balancing situations to produce harmony or by helping with others' responsibilities. May accept far more than own share of responsibility with little complaint.
- Rigid standards, not easily changed.
- Very strong opinions, not easily changed.

- Significant artistic ability.

Three:

- Willing to assume much responsibility.
- Helps others by balancing situations to produce harmony or by helping with others' responsibilities.
- Strong ideals.
- Strong opinions.

AVERAGE QUANTITY OF NUMBER
ONE or TWO 6's

INTENSITY POINT LESS THAN AVERAGE

Zero:

See Karmic Lesson or Modified Karmic Lesson below.

MODIFIED KARMIC LESSON

Responsibility will play an important part in the life. Subject is likely to have much responsibility to carry but be willing and able to accept. He is likely to understand that family and friends will depend on him for support, and will be there when needed.

He will be capable of balancing situations and serving others, and will show these traits strongly in marriage and parenting situations where these abilities are likely to be necessary to keep affairs running smoothly.

KARMIC LESSON

In past lives, the subject showed a lack of awareness of duties and responsibilities.

Responsibility will play an important part in the life. The subject is likely to have much responsibility to carry. He is likely to feel the pressure of caring for others who cannot or will not care for themselves. People will sense that he *can* support a heavier load than others and will lean on him or depend on him much more than he might prefer. Family and friends, instead of helping with

responsibility are apt, rather, to be the primary burden. The subject must learn, *all on his own*, how to comfortably deal with the responsibility that is his.

The subject will find much work is required to succeed in marriage (and parenthood). Much effort in balancing and serving others is necessary. Unless the individual is willing and able to learn this, marriage is likely to falter.

| CHART **8**
INTENSITY TABLE | **7** ANALYSIS
UNDERSTANDING |

PRIME INTENSIFIER

Rare.

Excellent mind, scientific or mathematical abilities and unusual viewpoint likely to be among most obvious strong traits.

INTENSITY POINT MORE THAN AVERAGE

Two or more:

- Fine mind, capable of analysis, research.
- Suppresses feelings to a large extent.
- Technical ability, scientific or mathematical talents.

- May want to search for and understand fundamentals, possibly in metaphysical studies.
- Unusual viewpoint or out-of-the-ordinary ideas.

AVERAGE QUANTITY OF NUMBER
ZERO or ONE 7

INTENSITY POINT LESS THAN AVERAGE

Zero:

See Karmic Lesson or Modified Karmic Lesson below.

MODIFIED KARMIC LESSON

An appreciation of the non-material world will play an important part in the subject's life. He's likely to understand that increasing faith in spiritual values may bring him deep and lasting peace.

KARMIC LESSON

In past lives, the subject showed a lack of awareness of the inner life, refusal to study or understand the deeper spiritual values.

Since we live in an age in which little regard is placed on spiritual values, this lesson is very common. The subject will have to learn an appreciation of the non-material world. Although faith in spiritual values may be a key to growth, it's likely to be of little interest to the individual.

CHART **8**	**8** MATERIAL SATISFACTION
INTENSITY TABLE	

PRIME INTENSIFIER

Rare.

Interest in money, status, power are likely to be among most obvious traits. These interests may lead to an unbalanced emphasis on material matters.

INTENSITY POINT MORE THAN AVERAGE

Two or more:

- Innate business ability may lead to success in commercial fields.
- Innate understanding of how to take an idea and make it into a profitable business.
- Balanced practical judgement, particularly in business matters. Can approach business affairs without being carried away with feelings.

- Probably suppresses a good deal of feelings in areas other than business.
- May place too much stress on personal achievement, may lead to exclusion of other interests or lack of concern for others' needs.
- May make difficulties for self because of need to achieve money, status, power. No matter how much is achieved, may still feel frustrated in not achieving more.

AVERAGE QUANTITY OF NUMBER
ONE 8

INTENSITY POINT LESS THAN AVERAGE

Zero:

See Karmic Lesson or Modified Karmic Lesson below.

MODIFIED KARMIC LESSON

A slightly disbalanced perspective on the relation of money to his life is likely to cause difficulties in money matters which may well affect other areas of the individual's life. Until the subject understands how to deal with money and material matters with ease, he may feel uncomfortable pressures related to financial dependence or over-balanced striving for attainment.

KARMIC LESSON

In past lives, the subject showed a lack of awareness of the practical necessities of life including the need to earn and use money.

In this life, his attitude toward money is likely to play an important part. He must learn to use and understand money so that a lack of understanding or misuse does not cause unnecessary problems. Often, a lack of awareness about the value of money may severely affect the ability to be independent (as, for instance, a long-time wife with no earning capability desiring a divorce.)

In this life, the individual must learn to handle his own material affairs and make reasonable and practical judgements. Until the subject learns how to do this with ease, he will feel significantly limited in his ability to find anything approaching complete satisfaction with himself.

| CHART 8 INTENSITY TABLE | 9 SELFLESSNESS HUMANITARIANISM |

PRIME INTENSIFIER

Strong creative capability or humanitarian concerns are likely to be among most obvious strong traits.

INTENSITY POINT MORE THAN AVERAGE

Five or more:

- High level creative ability may be expressed in artistic or literary endeavors. May have sudden flashes of intuition.
- Very emotional feelings are likely to be suppressed or expressed in poorly balanced ways.
- Overly sensitive.
- Own strong point of view held rigidly, little affected by others' position, feeling or arguments.

Four:

- High level creative ability may be expressed in artistic or literary endeavors.
- Humanitarian approach.
- Very emotional.

AVERAGE QUANTITY OF NUMBER
TWO or THREE 9's

INTENSITY POINT LESS THAN AVERAGE

One:

- Little awareness of others' feelings.
- Little sympathy or compassion shown.
- Somewhat restricted point of view.

MODIFIED KARMIC LESSON

Although a feeling and aware person, the subject is likely to have own strong needs which tend to make him self-centered and somewhat unconcerned with others' needs. Until subject becomes more selfless than self-centered, he is likely to be subject to emotional upsets.

KARMIC LESSON

In past lives, the subject showed little concern for others.

In this life, the subject is likely to be self-centered and unaware of or repressing his own feelings. He will probably be subjected to much in the way of emotional upsets, disappointments, and separations until he learns to be concerned with others—to show compassion and love, to clearly express his feelings and respond to others' feelings. This rare lesson indicates a significant coloration of the core.

CHART 8
INTENSITY TABLE

11 ILLUMINATION

PRIME INTENSIFIER

Not applicable

INTENSITY POINT MORE THAN AVERAGE

Not applicable

AVERAGE QUANTITY OF NUMBER

Not applicable

INTENSITY POINT LESS THAN AVERAGE

Not applicable

MODIFIED KARMIC DEBT

Not applicable

KARMIC DEBT

Not applicable

CHART **8** INTENSITY TABLE	**22** MASTER BUILDER

PRIME INTENSIFIER

Not applicable

INTENSITY POINT MORE THAN AVERAGE

Not applicable

AVERAGE QUANTITY OF NUMBER

Not applicable

INTENSITY POINT LESS THAN AVERAGE

Not applicable

MODIFIED KARMIC DEBT

Not applicable

KARMIC DEBT

Not applicable

CHART 9   THE CHALLENGE/THE GROWTH NUMBER

0 (Zero)

CHALLENGE

The Challenge is an obstacle encountered in the early years of life, at least, due to the emphasis placed on the negative extreme of the potential.

See Chapter 14, page 149.

CHALLENGE

In the early years, the individual is likely to have difficulty acting on his preferences. He is perfectly capable of analyzing a situation, realistically comparing possible solutions. Having sorted out alternatives, the individual has difficulty taking the requisite action. He's likely to have all sorts of excuses or rationalizations, but he effectively hinders his own development.

The individual must simply learn to have faith in himself—having indicated a preference, he *must* act. With a little practice, he's likely to find that taking action on his preference will prove as beneficial as he had hoped. Eventually, given enough practice, he can analyze, make a choice, then act with ease and comfort.

GROWTH NUMBER

The Growth Number describes the energy which will illuminate the essence of the experiences and help expand a person's development.

See Chapter 15, page 153.

GROWTH NUMBER

Not applicable

CHART **9**	**1**	INDIVIDUATION
CHALLENGE/GROWTH NO.		INDEPENDENCE
		ATTAINMENT

CHALLENGE

In the early years, the individual is likely to feel dominated by others with strong influence, probably parents or others on whom he is dependent. He's apt to feel that his desires are not being met, that his needs are being opposed. To feel less restricted, he may try to please everyone, but he'll find little satisfaction in that endeavor. He'll probably end up displeased himself, as well as confused and resentful.

The individual must learn to take stock of a situation (taking others' needs into account as well as his own), then, using the courage of his convictions, move forward in the direction of *his* choice. He must be careful not to end up dominating others, but he must remain watchful not to be dominated himself.

GROWTH NUMBER

The individual must act in an independent manner, but must not confuse independence with dominance. He has to remember that others' needs must be taken into account. He shouldn't give in to restrictive or limiting forces tending to keep him dependent, particularly in the younger years.

The individual should express his original ideas in appropriate circumstances. Shyness, fear of rejection or intimidation, especially in youth and young adulthood may make the expression of these ideas difficult. Vital opportunities may be lost because of the individual's reticence.

He should fill a leadership role when it is offered, although his leadership style may not be in the expected or commonly accepted mode.

CHART **9**		**2** RELATION COOPERATION
CHALLENGE/GROWTH NO.		

CHALLENGE

In the early years, the individual is likely to be extremely sensitive—he's likely to be fearful, timid, lacking self-confidence, brimming with feeling. It may be difficult for him to work with others because he's so afraid of being hurt by an unkind word or action or, worse yet, by being ignored. He's apt to be constantly worried about others opinions of him.

He's using his sensitivity with negative emphasis. His positive sensitivity can be an important strength, allowing him to be acutely aware of so much of which others have little inkling, to make significant connections between awarenesses which others can barely fathom. He must learn that his extreme powers of discrimination do not make him weak and inferior—but rather strong and superior.

GROWTH NUMBER

The individual must promote harmony, even if the effort tends to make his own contribution less visible. He shouldn't be so shy or self-effacing that his efforts go unnoticed. There's a very fine balance here that, particularly in the younger years, may be difficult to achieve.

The individual should practice cooperation and adaptability. He should try to take care of others' needs at the same time he is meeting his own. He should try to be as sensitive as possible to the subtle, even unspoken, nuances of those around him.

He should express friendship and affection openly and directly. Fear of rejection may, especially at first, make this expression difficult, but the acknowledgement of his feelings by others may prove to be a vital link in his personal development.

| CHART **9** | **3** EXPRESSION |
| CHALLENGE/GROWTH NO. | JOY OF LIVING |

CHALLENGE

In the early years, the individual is likely to be hiding his creativity as well as his social abilities. He's apt to feel shy, have difficulty expressing himself well, be fearful of criticism. He's likely to find it easier to hide in the background at social affairs—he may feel uncomfortable making conversation or being himself. He probably does little to develop his potential gift with words.

He's expressing himself with negative emphasis. The positive expression he can develop can be an important strength. He must develop his capability to get on well with others—to be a good conversationalist, to express his optimism and enthusiasm, to grace any social affair. His creative abilities—possibly with words; writing, singing, acting—can be developed to bring pleasure to others as well as personal satisfaction.

GROWTH NUMBER

The individual must approach his experiences with optimism and enthusiasm. His input may vitalize an endeavor with productive excitement.

He should express his creativity. Fear of rejection may make this expression difficult, particularly when he's expressing in unique or daring ways. He has to learn to offer his creative input and then let others learn to deal with it. He should express his delight in people and social activities openly and warmly.

CHART **9**	**4**	LIMITATION
CHALLENGE/GROWTH NO.		ORDER
		SERVICE

CHALLENGE

In the early years, the individual is likely to have difficulty accomplishing his work effectively. He may dislike work, avoid it if possible, or approach it in careless fashion, with little concentration or sense of practicality. Or he may approach work in a rigid manner, working hard but with little awareness of the implications of the job at hand, possibly unable or unwilling to see the forest for the trees.

He's expressing himself with negative emphasis. His positive potential, his ability to work and produce can be an important strength. He must develop his capacity to work hard and well, to accomplish his tasks with patience, understanding, practicality, to be aware of the details involved and to work within the parameters of a given schedule.

GROWTH NUMBER

The individual must work within the limitations he finds, in a positive manner. He must not succumb to frustration. He has to be careful not to be trapped because of a plodding manner or a narrow path. Learning to accept limitations is far different than falling victim to limitations, but the difference may be difficult to see at times. He must learn when the limitations can be changed rather than accepted.

He should try to be systematic and orderly, to organize with a strong awareness of the practical. The individual should be of service to others, though much hard work and patience may be required. He should concentrate on the satisfaction of the service rather than the difficulty of the work.

CHART **9**	**5** CONSTRUCTIVE FREEDOM
CHALLENGE/GROWTH NO.	

CHALLENGE

In the early years, the individual is likely to have difficulty taking full advantage of his opportunities. He's apt to be restless, impatient, impulsive, even erratic. He's likely to tire quickly of one opportunity, move on to the next as soon as it appears. In matters involving physical pleasures such as eating, sex, drink or drugs, he may limit his potential with a poor sense of proportion or timing. His need for security is likely to be poorly fulfilled by continuing to cling to some situations long after the promise has been developed.

He's using his freedom, his opportunities to expand, with negative emphasis. He must learn to pick and choose among these opportunities, develop the best of these in a responsible manner, move on only after he's accomplished what he set out to do. He must learn to curb his restlessness in the interest of achieving the lasting satisfactions he needs.

GROWTH NUMBER

The individual must expand his opportunities with his versatility and adaptability without running himself ragged and accomplishing little. He shouldn't jump erratically from exciting experience to exciting experience—he should use these opportunities for excitement along with learning. He should use his time and energy wisely—he shouldn't start unless he intends to proceed, shouldn't stick to something after the experience is completed, shouldn't jump to the new only because it's the new.

The individual should explore physical pleasures—eating, sex, drinking, drugs—as part of a balanced life, not as ends in themselves.

CHART 9 CHALLENGE/GROWTH NO.	6	BALANCE RESPONSIBILITY LOVE

CHALLENGE

In the early years, the individual is likely to have difficulty because of his insistence on his high standards. He's apt to appear authoritarian, intolerant, self-righteous. He's probably unhappy because he feels that no one measures up to his superior principles or shows any appreciation of his struggles to uplift others.

He's using his potential for balancing affairs with negative emphasis. He must, instead, develop his potentially superior skill at harmonizing situations. He must learn that his diplomatic approach will only be appreciated if others feel that their needs are met, their desires understood, their points of view respected. He must learn to allow others to set their own pace, make their own rules. He must learn to express his unconditional love and acceptance.

GROWTH NUMBER

The individual must help where help is needed. He should learn to accept the responsibilities he finds and carry through with understanding and poise. He should learn to adjust and balance the forces he finds.

He should contribute his efforts to make his home a beautiful, protected, stable and helping environment.

He must learn to give out friendship, affection and love and gracefully accept others' friendship, affection and love in return.

CHART **9**	**7** ANALYSIS
CHALLENGE/GROWTH NO.	UNDERSTANDING

CHALLENGE

In the early years, the individual is likely to have difficulty because of his discomfort with the situations he finds, situations aggravated by his reserved attitude and unexpressed feelings. He's likely to feel hopeless about bettering his situation, unable to act to relieve or change matters. He's probably a complainer, often extremely critical, with little or nothing to offer in the way of help.

He's using his potential for discrimination with negative emphasis. He must study to find the nature of wisdom. He must learn to share his knowledge and sense of discrimination with open feelings, to have faith in his abilities (rather than being afraid to use them), to respond helpfully when difficulties arise. He must learn to approach others without reserve or aloofness.

GROWTH NUMBER

The individual should retire into his very depths to find faith and peace. Peace will come from within—it will have little to do with money or material matters.

He must learn to trust his intuition to lead in directions of growth. He must wait, when necessary, with patience. He should learn the pleasure of spending time alone—studying, meditating, searching for wisdom and hidden truths.

CHART 9
CHALLENGE/GROWTH NO.

8 MATERIAL SATISFACTION

CHALLENGE

In the early years, the individual is likely to assume that satisfaction can only be gained and safeguarded by adequate material accumulation. There's likely to be considerable effort exerted to attain money, status and power, sometimes to the exclusion of almost all else.

He's using his concern with material matters with negative emphasis. He must learn to use his ability to gain money, status and power with a sense of proportion and an awareness of the relation of material affairs to other matters. He must learn to deal with the material world in a comfortable manner.

GROWTH NUMBER

The individual should aim for success with balance in the material world. He should treat the achievement of money, status and power as a means to the end of achieving understanding and pleasure. He should recognize that money, status and power are only *one* means of achieving this end, but they are significant means and should not be ignored.

The individual must learn how to accumulate money, how to handle money, how to spend money. He should learn to avoid the pressure of needing more money than is comfortably available.

| CHART **9** | **9** SELFLESSNESS |
| CHALLENGE/GROWTH NO. | HUMANITARIANISM |

CHALLENGE

Not applicable

GROWTH NUMBER

The individual must learn to give of himself for the pleasure of giving. He may give money, time, friendship, affection, love, understanding or sympathy. He should give with little expectation of return or reward and should allow the needs of others to take precedence over his personal ambitions. This seemingly difficult direction can produce the deepest of satisfactions.

CHART **9**
CHALLENGE/GROWTH NO.

11 ILLUMINATION

CHALLENGE

Not applicable

GROWTH NUMBER

The individual must learn to develop his intuition to pick up added awarenesses of the spiritual (non-material) world. He should visualize himself as a channel of special awareness.

He should spread his understandings with humility and inspire others by his example, based on the purity of his learning of the deepest spiritual truths. He should learn to communicate about these spiritual matters in a world primarily interested in material affairs, and should proceed despite the seeming discouragements.

CHART 9	
CHALLENGE/GROWTH NO.	

22 MASTER BUILDER

CHALLENGE

Not applicable

GROWTH NUMBER

The individual must learn to focus his high-level insights to develop significant material projects. The power to achieve important goals may grow from his practical yet idealistic philosophy along with his sincere desire to benefit others.

CHART **10** THE MATURITY NUMBER

See Chapter 16, page 157.

MATURITY NUMBER WITH STRONG SIMILAR ENERGY

When the Maturity Number, a sub-lesson introduced at maturity, is the same as a core element, or when the Maturity Number has the same modifier number as an Intensity Point or Karmic Lesson, the Maturity Number describes the re-evaluation of a lesson or sub-lesson on which the individual has been working in the years prior to maturity.

MATURITY NUMBER WITH NO STRONG SIMILAR ENERGY

When the Maturity Number is not the same as any core element and has a modifier number that is not matched by an Intensity Point or Karmic Lesson, the Maturity Number describes the introduction, at maturity, of a brand new sub-lesson along with the characteristics associated with that number.

The new sub-lesson is described in this chart.

THE ASSOCIATED CHARACTERISTICS ARE DESCRIBED IN THE SECOND ROW FROM THE TOP ON *CHART 2: THE LIFE PATH.* These characteristics are introduced at maturity in considerably muted form.

KARMIC MATURITY NUMBER

When the Maturity Number has a Karmic Debt behind it—13/4, 14/5, 16/7 and 19/1—additional obstacles to learning the lesson or sub-lesson are likely to be introduced at maturity. The obstacles are added whether or not the Maturity Number has strong similar energy from the core or modifiers.

<table>
<tr><td>CHART 10
MATURITY NUMBER</td><td>1</td><td>INDIVIDUATION
INDEPENDENCE
ATTAINMENT</td></tr>
</table>

MATURITY NUMBER WITH STRONG SIMILAR ENERGY

At maturity, there's likely to be a reevaluation of the meaning of independence in the subject's life. This mid-life appraisal is apt to focus on whether the individual's ability to stand on his own two feet

- has been satisfactorily achieved or whether he still feels dependent, OR
- has been achieved by taking care of his own needs, causing a lack of closeness with others, OR
- has been achieved by domination of others.

He'll also probably assess whether the independence he sought and, at least to some extent, achieved has enabled him to move on to leadership roles along with a sense of attainment of meaningful ends.

At this time in the life, the individual is likely to revise at least some attitudes and actions in regard to independence, in order to achieve a more comfortable relation with others.

MATURITY NUMBER WITH NO STRONG SIMILAR ENERGY

At maturity, a new sub-lesson is introduced: learning the meaning of independence. Since the 1 energy hasn't been a factor in the life up to this time, it's likely that there have been few problems relating to independence. The individual was probably satisfied or disinterested in his relation with others relative to dependence/independence. At maturity, there's apt to be a shift in the life, bringing problems of independence to center stage. This shift may be due to one of the following:

- a financial arrangement which allowed him to be independent may end or change, OR
- a spouse who supported him/her (financially or emotionally) may move out of the life through separation or death, or may not be able to continue the support because of sickness or financial reversal, OR
- an awareness of women's increased freedom (or children growing up) may change a woman's view of herself as well as her role in relation to her husband, OR
- a parent (or child) who previously led his/her own life may, because of illness, death or financial reversal become dependent on him.

At this time in the life, the individual is likely to face some decisions about attitudes and actions in regard to dependence/independence in order to gain more control of his own life.

19/1 KARMIC MATURITY NUMBER

The subject is likely to find obstacles in his path due to:

- his confusion of independence with self-centeredness, OR
- strong pressures keeping him from breaking out of a dependent situation in which he is involved.

| CHART **10** | **2** | RELATION |
| MATURITY NUMBER | | COOPERATION |

MATURITY NUMBER WITH STRONG SIMILAR ENERGY

At maturity, there's likely to be a reevaluation of the satisfactions derived from the subject's sensitivity. This mid-life appraisal is apt to focus on

- whether the individual has developed so that his strong sensitivity can be comfortably used, OR
- whether the individual has learned how to say and do what he needs without feeling his sensitivity compromised, OR
- whether shyness or uncertainty block him from a full expression of his sensitivity.

At this time in the life, the individual is likely to revise some attitudes and actions in order to better express his sensitivity and to better receive others' friendship and affection as a reward for that expression.

MATURITY NUMBER WITH NO STRONG SIMILAR ENERGY

At maturity, a new sub-lesson is introduced: learning the satisfaction of using sensitivity. Since the 2 energy hasn't been a factor in the life up to this time, it's likely that there have been few problems relating to sensitivity. The individual probably had little concern about his sensitivity or its expression. At maturity, there's apt to be a shift in the life bringing problems of sensitivity to center stage. This shift may be due to one of the following:

- sensitive treatment by others—family or close friends in particular—may make individual aware of the beauty of sensitivity and bring on a desire to develop personal sensitivity, OR
- insensitive treatment of individual by others (or of others by individual) may cause significant pain and spark an appraisal leading to a desire to better express sensitivity, OR
- difficulty in receiving any satisfying acknowledgement of sensitivity or contributions based on this sensitivity may trigger a desire for more contentment here.

At this time in the life, the individual is likely to face some decisions about his attitudes and actions in order to feel increased fulfillment in the expression and acknowledgment of his sensitivity.

KARMIC MATURITY NUMBER

Not applicable

CHART **10** MATURITY NUMBER

3 EXPRESSION JOY OF LIVING

MATURITY NUMBER WITH STRONG SIMILAR ENERGY

At maturity, there's likely to be a reevaluation of how well the subject has learned the joy of expression. This mid-life appraisal is apt to focus on

- whether the individual is comfortable giving of himself openly, warmly, spontaneously, OR
- whether the individual enjoys himself and is enjoyed by others at social gatherings, OR
- whether the individual enjoys expressing himself artistically and creatively.

At this time in the life, the individual is likely to revise at least some attitudes and actions in order to express himself more fully and freely.

MATURITY NUMBER WITH NO STRONG SIMILAR ENERGY

At maturity, a new sub-lesson is introduced: learning the joy of expression. Since the 3 energy hasn't been a factor in the life up to this time, it's likely that the joy of self-expression has barely been approached. Shyness, too much sensitivity, heavy responsibilities may be some of the rationalizations used to explain the lack of development in this area.

At maturity, there's apt to be a shift in the life, bringing the awareness of the lack of self-expression to center stage. This shift may be due to one of the following:

- the individual may become aware of how little he plays, how little fun he has, how rarely he can act and enjoy as he did as a child, OR
- the individual may become aware of how delightful it can be to associate with others expressing optimism, enthusiasm and fun. Comparing his own austere ways, he may seek to brighten his life, OR
- with time on his hands due to illness or loneliness, the individual may turn to creative and artistic pursuits which previously frightened or bored him.

At this time in the life, the individual is likely to face some decisions about his attitudes and actions in regard to his own self-expression in order to receive more satisfaction out of life.

KARMIC MATURITY NUMBER

Not applicable

CHART **10**		4	LIMITATION
MATURITY NUMBER			ORDER
			SERVICE

MATURITY NUMBER WITH STRONG SIMILAR ENERGY

At maturity, there's likely to be a reevaluation of the ability to live with the law of limitation. (See CHART 2: LIFE PATH, under 4 Life Path Central Focus) This mid-life appraisal is apt to focus on

- whether the individual has felt restricted and frustrated by the limitations he's encountered, OR
- whether the individual has accepted the limitations he's encountered as part of the fabric of his life, at least to some extent.

At this time in the life, the individual is likely to revise at least some attitudes and actions in regard to restrictions. He may want to become more aware of restrictions which are unknowingly self-imposed, restrictions which cannot be changed along with restrictions which can be removed or adjusted for the better.

MATURITY NUMBER WITH NO STRONG SIMILAR ENERGY

At maturity, a new sub-lesson is introduced: learning to live with the law of limitations. (See CHART 2: LIFE PATH, under 4 Life Path Central Focus) Since the 4 energy hasn't been a factor in the life up to this time, it's likely that little attention has been paid to restrictions. At maturity, there's apt to be a shift in the life, bringing the awareness of limitations to center stage. This shift may be due to one of the following:

- a free and loose approach to life has met with poor results: a broken marriage, alienated children, ruined business, lost friends, OR
- a serious, responsible approach to life, with a consistent struggle to overcome the obstacles, has met with poor results: a broken marriage, alienated children, ruined business, lost friends.

At this time in the life, the individual is likely to face some decisions about attitudes and actions toward restrictions. An awareness of the law of limitation and its practical applications may make an astonishing difference in the approach to many situations and give the subject the ability to better control his own life.

13/4 KARMIC MATURITY NUMBER

The subject is likely to find obstacles in his path due to:

- his rigid, obstinate or dogmatic ways, OR
- his lack of application to work. He may have more work to do than others, but unless he proceeds with it, it becomes an obstacle, OR
- his inability to satisfactorily take care of the details.

| CHART **10** MATURITY NUMBER | **5** CONSTRUCTIVE FREEDOM |

MATURITY NUMBER WITH STRONG SIMILAR ENERGY

At maturity, there's likely to be a reevaluation of the subject's *constructive* use of freedom. This mid-life appraisal is apt to focus on

- whether the individual has been exhilarated (or exhausted or frustrated) by the variety, change, unexpected in the life, OR
- whether the individual has been able to focus his energies so that he's been able to grow and develop by adapting to the changes which he so often finds.

At this time in the life, the individual is likely to revise at least some attitudes and actions in regard to the constructive use of freedom, so that he can make the best use of opportunities as they present themselves without being overwhelmed by them.

MATURITY NUMBER WITH NO STRONG SIMILAR ENERGY

At maturity, a new sub-lesson is introduced: learning the exhilaration of the *constructive* use of freedom. Since the 5 energy hasn't been a factor in the life up to this time, it's likely that there has been little attention paid to the possibilities for growth and development presented by the variety of opportunities opened to the individual. At maturity, there's apt to be a shift in the life, bringing an awareness of freedom to center stage. This shift may be due to one of the following:

- a breakup of one of the major stabilizing factors in the individual's life—end of marriage or business, move to another locale, death of parent(s), children leaving home, OR
- generation of freedom by significant money from business, inheritance or unexpected source, OR
- generation of freedom by abandonment of self-imposed heavy responsibilities such as high-level job pressures, OR
- developing awareness of discomfort of serious, responsible approach previously regarded as only sensible avenue.

At this time in the life, the individual is likely to face some decisions about attitudes and actions in regard to freedom in order to give himself more control of his own life as well as a sense of deeper satisfaction.

14/5 KARMIC MATURITY NUMBER

The subject is likely to find obstacles in his path due to:

- his inability to profit from his experiences instead of repeating mistakes, OR
- his excessive appetite for physical stimulation: eating, sensuality, liquor, drugs.

| CHART **10** MATURITY NUMBER | **6** BALANCE RESPONSIBILITY LOVE |

MATURITY NUMBER WITH STRONG SIMILAR ENERGY

At maturity, there's likely to be a reevaluation of the pleasure received in handling responsibility and exchanging affection. This mid-life appraisal is apt to focus on:

- whether responsibility has been handled to produce satisfaction for the individual, OR
- whether friendship, affection and love have been given and received to meet the individual's needs.

At this time in the life, the individual is likely to revise at least some attitudes and actions in regard to responsibility and affection, in order to achieve more satisfaction out of life.

MATURITY NUMBER WITH NO STRONG SIMILAR ENERGY

At maturity, new sub-lessons are introduced: (1) learning the deep pleasure in handling responsibility and (2) learning to give and receive friendship, affection and love. Since the 6 energy hasn't been a factor in the life up to this time, it's likely that there have been few problems in relation to responsibility or affection. At maturity, there's apt to be a shift in the life, bringing problems of responsibility or affection to center stage. This shift may be due to one of the following:

- economic changes which may increase personal responsibilities, OR
- marriage, separation, divorce or illness which may increase personal responsibilities for children, OR
- change of circumstances which may require assistance with aging parent(s).

Along with the change in responsibility, there's likely to be a desire for friendship, affection and love, a desire which may not have been particularly strong in the years before maturity. At this time in the life, the individual is likely to face some decisions about attitudes and actions in these areas in order to achieve more satisfaction out of life.

KARMIC MATURITY NUMBER

Not applicable

<table>
<tr><td>CHART 10
MATURITY NUMBER</td><td>7</td><td>ANALYSIS
LEADERSHIP</td></tr>
</table>

MATURITY NUMBER WITH STRONG SIMILAR ENERGY

At maturity, there's likely to be a reevaluation of the peace of mind that comes with knowing oneself. This mid-life appraisal is apt to focus on whether the subject has used his fine mind and good intuition to study and contemplate the deeper truths, and whether he's found, in the process, a deepening peace and faith as a mainstay of his existence.

At this time in the life, the individual is likely to revise at least some attitudes and actions in order to more fully experience the possibilities of peace and faith.

MATURITY NUMBER WITH NO STRONG SIMILAR ENERGY

At maturity, a new sub-lesson is introduced: learning the peace of mind that comes with knowing oneself. Since the 7 energy hasn't been a factor in the life up to this time, there's probably been little attention paid to this introspective aspect of the life. At maturity, there's apt to be a shift in the life, bringing a new awareness of spiritual matters to center stage. This shift may be due to one of the following:

- the experience of another person (or group) who has achieved peace of mind may lead the individual to search in a similar direction, OR
- a personal crisis of extraordinary magnitude may propel the individual toward spiritual explorations which haven't previously been of any concern, OR
- an awareness of the emptiness or dissatisfactions of the life or a need for more fulfillment may lead the individual to spiritual explorations.

At this time in the life, the individual is likely to face some decisions about attitudes and actions in regard to his search for peace of mind and spiritual fulfillment.

16/7 KARMIC MATURITY NUMBER

The subject is likely to find obstacles in his path due to:

- his apparent "differentness," making it difficult for others to approach, OR
- his outward actions, often not what others expect, which may be disconcerting or confusing to others, OR
- his strong introspective needs, possibly turning to or interpreted as self-centeredness.

CHART **10** MATURITY NUMBER

8 MATERIAL SATISFACTION

MATURITY NUMBER WITH STRONG SIMILAR ENERGY

At maturity, there's likely to be a reevaluation of the satisfactions obtained with the material freedom and power that has been achieved. This mid-life appraisal is apt to focus on whether the current vocation (or the position in the current vocation) meets the individual's needs for money, power and status.

For some individuals, maturity may involve a new relation to the material world because of the growth of children, divorce, separation or new feelings about themselves and their earning power. Previous material satisfactions may no longer be available because of a decreased income, or, additional material satisfactions may become available due to their own business acumen.

At this time in the life, the individual is likely to revise at least some attitudes and actions in regard to material freedom in order to achieve deeper satisfaction along with a better control of the life.

MATURITY NUMBER WITH NO STRONG SIMILAR ENERGY

At maturity, a new sub-lesson is introduced: learning the satisfactions of the material world, and the power which comes with its mastery. Since the 8 energy hasn't been a factor in the life up to this time, it's likely that the problems (and lessons) of the material world have been of little consequence. The individual was probably well-provided for (possibly by others), or at least adequately provided for so that he had no need to struggle with material problems. At maturity, there's apt to be a shift in the life, bringing the problems of the material world to center stage. This shift may be due to one of the following:

- reevaluation of the vocation, possibly in comparison to others' achievements in the same or similar vocations, OR
- desire to shift to a completely different vocation, possibly due to higher money, status, power possible in the new vocation, or desire for satisfaction above prestige, OR
- awareness of approaching retirement and need to provide adequately, OR
- economic changes which may affect financial responsibilities.

At this time in the life, the individual is likely to face some decisions about his attitudes and actions in regard to the material world in order to achieve deeper satisfaction.

KARMIC MATURITY NUMBER

Not applicable

| CHART **10**
MATURITY NUMBER | **9** SELFLESSNESS
HUMANITARIANISM |

MATURITY NUMBER WITH STRONG SIMILAR ENERGY

At maturity, there's likely to be a reevaluation of the beauty of giving of oneself for the deep satisfaction of giving, without thought of reward or return. This mid-life appraisal is apt to focus on:

- whether the individual has indeed found beauty in giving selflessly, OR
- whether the individual has even been able to approach giving selflessly, or has only operated on this high level sporadically.

At this time in the life, the individual is likely to revise at least some attitudes and actions in regard to selfless giving in order to achieve deeper satisfactions. He may prefer to give up on this lesson altogether because of its difficulty and its seeming lack of satisfaction. The numerologist can only indicate the potential satisfaction. The individual travels his own path.

MATURITY NUMBER WITH NO STRONG SIMILAR ENERGY

At maturity, a new (and difficult) sub-lesson is introduced: learning the beauty of giving of oneself solely for the deep satisfaction of giving, without thought of reward or return. Since the 9 energy hasn't been a factor in the life up to this time, it's likely that little attention has been paid to this high-level lesson. At maturity, there's apt to be a shift in the life, bringing a new awareness of selfless giving to center stage. This shift may be due to one of the following:

- a new spiritual awareness, OR
- the realization that selfishness and the resultant lack of giving has not given the individual a sense of satisfaction, OR
- an experience of selfless giving by the individual (or to the individual) that brings deep satisfaction, OR
- an experience with a humanitarian person or group which opens the eyes to a perception of the satisfaction.

At this time in the life, the individual is likely to face some decisions about attitudes and actions in regard to selfless giving in order to feel a sense of deeper satisfaction.

KARMIC MATURITY NUMBER

Not applicable

| CHART **10** MATURITY NUMBER | **11** ILLUMINATION |

MATURITY NUMBER WITH STRONG SIMILAR ENERGY

At maturity, there's likely to be a reevaluation of the importance of learning an awareness of the spiritual world and the relation of that world to the material world. This mid-life appraisal is apt to focus on:

- whether the spiritual world has even been approached, OR
- whether the awareness of the spiritual world has proved a positive influence, OR
- whether the awareness of the relation between the material and spiritual world has proved a positive influence.

At this time in the life, the individual is likely to revise at least some attitudes and actions in order to achieve deeper satisfactions. He may prefer to give up on this lesson altogether because of its difficulty and its seeming lack of satisfaction. The numerologist can only indicate the potential satisfaction. The individual travels his own path.

MATURITY NUMBER WITH NO STRONG SIMILAR ENERGY

At maturity, a new (and difficult) sub-lesson is introduced: learning the glory of the awareness of the spiritual world and the relation of that world to the material world. Since the 11 energy hasn't been a factor in the life up to this time, it's likely that little attention has been paid to this high level lesson. At maturity, there's apt to be a shift in the life, bringing a new awareness of the relation of the spiritual and material worlds to center stage. This shift may be due to one of the following:

- an enlightening experience that allows him to glimpse the beauty of the spiritual world, OR
- an experience in the material world that provides the realization that other forces may be necessary for ultimate satisfaction.

At this time in the life, the individual is likely to face some decisions about attitudes and actions in regard to his awareness of the spiritual/material worlds in order to feel a sense of deeper satisfaction. This difficult new sub-lesson may not be approached at all. The individual may prefer to ignore this sub-lesson and concentrate on the alternative 2 sub-lesson.

KARMIC MATURITY NUMBER

Not applicable

| CHART **10** | **22** MASTER BUILDER |
| MATURITY NUMBER | |

MATURITY NUMBER WITH STRONG SIMILAR ENERGY

At maturity, there's likely to be a reevaluation of the importance of the mastery achieved by combining the highest ideals with the power to achieve significant material goals. This mid-life appraisal is apt to focus on:

- whether this high-level lesson has even been approached, OR
- whether this high-level lesson seems at all attainable, OR
- whether the approach to date has been productive of at least some of its goals.

At this time in the life, the individual is likely to revise at least some attitudes and actions in order to achieve deeper satisfactions. He may prefer to give up on this lesson altogether because of its difficulty and its seeming lack of satisfaction. The numerologist can only indicate the potential satisfaction. The individual travels his own path.

MATURITY NUMBER WITH NO STRONG SIMILAR ENERGY

At maturity, a new (and difficult) sub-lesson is introduced: learning the mastery to be achieved by combining the highest ideals with the power to achieve significant material goals. Since the 22 energy hasn't been a factor in the life up to this time, it's likely that little attention has been paid to this high-level lesson. At maturity, there's a shift in the life, bringing a new awareness of the potential use of this power to center stage. This shift may be due to one of the following:

- substantial mastery of the core energies prior to maturity may spark the feeling that even more may be achieved, OR
- a desire to benefit mankind may produce the need to explore the outer limits of personal powers.

At this time in the life, the individual is likely to face some decisions about attitudes and actions in regard to his potential powers in order to feel a sense of deeper satisfaction. This difficult new sub-lesson may not be approached at all. The individual may prefer to ignore this sub-lesson and concentrate on the alternative 4 sub-lesson.

KARMIC MATURITY NUMBER

Not applicable

CHART 11 THE FIRST LETTER

The First Letter (this chart) and the First Vowel (Chart No. 12) describe the natural or innate approach, the method of response and reaction to experience.

See Chapter 20, page 185.

CHART **11**	**1**	INDIVIDUATION

CHART 11
THE FIRST LETTER

1 INDIVIDUATION INDEPENDENCE ATTAINMENT

A
First letter: 1

DYNAMIC LEADER
SENSITIVE LEADER

See Chart No. 12: The First Vowel.

J
Tenth Letter: 10 : 1

INDECISIVE LEADER

- Leader.
- Ambitious, usually in a quiet way.
- Assertive at times, only occasionally aggressive.
- Optimistic, recovers well from difficulties.
- Good mind.
- Excellent ideas.
- Original or innovative approach.
- Broad perspective may make it difficult to get started. Once started, leadership is likely to come to the fore, but progress may be plagued by indecision.

S
Nineteenth letter: 19 : 1

EMOTIONAL LEADER

- Leader.
- Very creative. Dramatic flashes of insight.
- Ambitious. Concerned with impressions made by achievements.
- Independent. Courageous.
- Expresses individuality, often dramatically.
- Very emotional. Clear thinking may be affected by the depth of feelings.
- Erratic course of action with the possibility of setbacks because of difficulty in analyzing clearly.

LETTER COMPARISON

A: Most dynamic of 1's. Only self-starter.
J: Most cautious, prudent of 1's.
S: Most emotional of 1's.

| CHART **11** | **2** RELATION |
| THE FIRST LETTER | COOPERATION |

B   SENSITIVE HELPER

Second
letter: 2

- Shy and retiring. Self-contained. Often indecisive.
- Usually more comfortable in subservient role. Prefers being a follower rather than a leader. Works better with others than alone. Very cooperative.
- Fosters and helps develop harmony in groups in which he's involved.
- Good at taking care of all the details.
- May, at times, be critical of self and others.
- Extremely sensitive and emotional. May be hurt by others' lack of sensitivity.
- Needs affection. Seeks it in own quiet way.
- May have difficulty working with others in a hurry or those who want to cut corners.

K   INTUITIVE INSPIRER

Eleventh
letter: 11/2

See 11 page of this chart.

T   EMOTIONAL HELPER

Twentieth
letter:
20 : 2

- Usually more comfortable in subservient role. Prefers being a follower rather than a leader.
- Expects much from others, but is usually patient in helping others develop to expectations.
- Generally works well with others, although likely to become anxious when problems develop. May, at times, be critical of self and others.
- Seeks higher level enlightenment.
- Extremely emotional and high strung.
- Enjoys closeness of marriage, family.
- Often self-sacrificing.

LETTER COMPARISON

B: Strong emotions usually felt and expressed. Less high level awarenesses than K or T.

K: Extreme high level awareness (operates primarily as 11 rather than as 2).

T: Extremely emotional and high-strung. Some high level awareness.

| CHART **11** THE FIRST LETTER | **3** EXPRESSION JOY OF LIVING |

C
Third letter: 3

SPONTANEOUS CREATOR

- Spontaneity of creative inspiration.
- Very verbal. Often much originality with words and ideas.
- Sensitive. Sometimes easily hurt.
- Friendly and sociable. Enjoys social activities, the lighter side of life.
- Expresses joy of living with exhilaration.
- Psychic, though often latent.

L
Twelfth letter: 12 : 3

REASONING CREATOR

- Creative abilities express slowly, surely, in a measured manner.
- Verbal. Often much originality with words and ideas.
- Sensitive.
- Friendly and sociable. Enjoys social activities, the lighter side of life.
- Expresses joy of living.
- Fine reasoning ability and powers of analysis.

U
Twenty-first letter 21 : 3

SENSITIVE RECEPTOR
CONSTRUCTIVE RECEPTOR

See Chart No. 12: The First Vowel.

LETTER COMPARISON

C: Most spontaneous and open of 3's.
L: Most mental of 3's.
U: Most receptive and self-protective of 3's.

CHART **11**	**4**	LIMITATION
THE FIRST LETTER		ORDER
		SERVICE

D   STEADY BUILDER

Fourth letter: 4

- Hard worker. Self-disciplined.
- Serious. Steady. Thorough.
- Conservative, sometimes narrow approach. Rigid attitudes may cause problems.
- Tends to show little emotion.
- Self-contained. Operates well with little deep contact with others.
- Follows instructions precisely and completely.
- Extremely well-developed approach to material, practical affairs.
- Does mundane work efficiently.
- Works steadily, efficiently to complete a project.

M   CONTROLLED BUILDER

Thirteenth letter: 13 : 4

- Hard worker. Self-disciplined.
- Serious. Steady. Thorough.
- Controlled approach. Often limited viewpoint. Usually accepts the given limits instead of expanding the potential.
- Repressed feelings may make him difficult to deal with and hard to get to know.
- May be relatively inarticulate, have difficulty explaining his approach.
- Organizational ability.
- Well-developed approach to material, practical affairs.
- Does mundane work efficiently.
- Works steadily, efficiently to complete a project.

V   INSPIRATIONAL MASTER

Twenty-second letter: 22/4

See 22 page of this chart.

LETTER COMPARISON

D: Better balanced than M.

M: More repressed, more inarticulate than D.

V: Building abilities of D,M raised to highest level with spiritual revelation (operates primarily as 22 rather than as 4).

CHART 11

THE FIRST LETTER

5 CONSTRUCTIVE FREEDOM

E
Fifth letter: 5

ADVENTUROUS ENCOUNTERER
RESTLESS ENCOUNTERER

See Chart No. 12: The First Vowel.

N
Fourteenth letter: 14 : 5

MENTAL ENCOUNTERER

- Adventurous.
- Restless. Need for change, excitement, variety.
- Adaptable.
- Imaginative.
- Seeks and enjoys confronting any and all experience.
- Generally uses strong mental approach. Good at analysis.
- Personal philosophy, based on rational approach to experience, is usually changing constantly.
- Works extremely well with people. Knows how to use others to carry through ideas.
- Restlessness shows in making decisions—often vacillates between several points of view.

W
Twenty-third letter: 23 : 5

LIMITING ENCOUNTERER

This chart describes W as consonant.
See Chart No. 12: The First Vowel for W as a vowel.

- Adventurous. Restless. Need for change, excitement, variety.
- Excellent verbal abilities. Good at selling.
- Tends to accept the given limits instead of expanding the potential.
- Seeks and enjoys confronting any and all experience.
- Often wants to express, but expression is usually limited because of more desire to experience than express.
- Works extremely well with people. Others help carry through ideas.
- Restlessness shows in making decisions—often vacillates between several points of view.

LETTER COMPARISON

E: Most capable of inspiration and accomplishment of 5's.
N: Most rational of 5's.
W: Most inexpressive, most limited aim of 5's.

CHART **11** THE FIRST LETTER	**6**	BALANCE RESPONSIBILITY LOVE

F
*Sixth
letter: 6*

STRUGGLING HARMONIZER

- Accepts much responsibility—his own and others. Responsibility is often related to home and family. Responsibility weighs heavily.
- Can protect and care for others.
- Innate desire to right wrongs.
- Attracts situations requiring much in the way of adjustment.
- Capable of much sacrifice.
- Emotional. May withdraw when upset.
- Sensitive and receptive.
- Gives affection easily. Responds to affection. Is hurt by lack of affection.

O
*Fifteenth
letter:
15 : 6*

POISED HARMONIZER
PROTECTED HARMONIZER

See Chart No. 12: The First Vowel.

X
*Twenty-
fourth letter:
24 : 6*

EMOTIONAL HARMONIZER

- Accepts much responsibility—his own and others'. Responsibility is often related to home and family. Responsibility weighs heavily.
- Can protect and care for others.
- Capable of much sacrifice, but suffers from pressures created by sacrifice.
- Extremely emotional. Must learn how to deal with his and others' feelings without being overwhelmed.
- Life often full of crises, emotional upheavals.
- Sometimes wallows in self-pity.

LETTER COMPARISON

F: Because of responsibilities, subject's life likely to be struggle.

O: Handles responsibilities well; usually expresses little feeling.

X: Because of responsibilities, subject likely to feel much emotion.

| CHART **11** THE FIRST LETTER | **7** ANALYSIS UNDERSTANDING |

G   RESERVED THINKER

Seventh letter: 7

- Reserved, introspective. Manner causes misunderstanding.
- Secretive.
- May get lost in dreams. Needs firmer grounding in and understanding of reality.
- Works best alone. Often lonely.
- Doesn't respond readily to affection. Gives little affection.
- Often anxious and lacking confidence.
- Much willpower. Keen mind. Given to thought and meditation.
- Enjoys analysis of fundamentals, philosophical speculation.

P   INEXPRESSIVE THINKER

Sixteenth letter: 16 : 7

- Reserved, introspective. Manner causes misunderstandings.
- Secretive.
- Works best alone. Often lonely.
- Feels deeply, but not always sure of or comfortable with his feelings. Expresses and shares little of his thoughts and feelings.
- Keen mind. Given to thought and meditation.
- Enjoys analysis of fundamentals, philosophical speculation.
- Usually lacks determination and willpower.

Y   UNCERTAIN THINKER

Twenty-fifth letter: 25 : 7

This chart describes Y as a consonant.
See Chart No. 12: The First Vowel for Y as a vowel.

- Reserved, introspective. Manner causes misunderstandings.
- Secretive.
- Works best alone. Often lonely. Often uncertain and vacillating.
- Feels deeply. Expresses and shares little of these feelings.
- Extremely keen mind. Given to thought and meditation.
- Enjoys analysis of fundamentals, philosophical speculation.
- Extremely perceptive. Fine intuition.
- Deep insights into higher matters.
- Strong psychic power. Must learn to trust it.

LETTER COMPARISON

G: Most willpower of the 7's.
P: Least willpower, least expressiveness of the 7's.
Y: Most insightful, most vacillating of the 7's.

| CHART **11**
THE FIRST LETTER | **8** MATERIAL SATISFACTION |

H AWARE ACHIEVER

Eighth letter: 8

- High level consciousness helps bring extreme awareness of the material world.
- Executive and leadership ability.
- Works well with others.
- Operates well in material world with strong mental capability. Uses good mind to achieve material success—money, power, status.
- Keen perceptions of people, events.
- Strong desire for advance may be blunted by changing ideas.

Q NON-CONFORMIST ACHIEVER

Seventeenth letter:
17 : 8

- Large potential power, not always used in a balanced productive manner.
- Inputs dramatic energy levels into projects with which he associates.
- Capable of superior material achievement—money, power, status—if he can proceed without being self-centered or greedy.
- Superior leadership ability. Good at directing efforts to achieve desired ends.
- Often espouses an independent, unusual (sometimes eccentric) position, no matter what opposition is created.

Z INSPIRATIONAL ACHIEVER

Twenty-sixth letter:
26 : 8

- Extremely dynamic energy.
- Self-confidence and will-power.
- Capable of leadership and attendant material achievements—money, power, status. Greed or lack of responsibility may hamper his achievements.
- Capable of inspiring others.
- Deep awareness of emotions—his own and others.
- Can work through emotional crises with understanding.
- Suffers through his own deep feelings and awarenesses.

LETTER COMPARISON

H: Best balanced of 8's.
Q: Most unusual approach of 8's.
Z: Most inspired of 8's.

| CHART **11**
THE FIRST LETTER | **9** SELFLESSNESS
HUMANITARIANISM |

I

Ninth letter: 9

EMOTIONAL HUMANITARIAN
RESTRAINED HUMANITARIAN

See Chart No. 12: The First Vowel.

R

Eighteenth letter:
18 : 9

SELFLESS HUMANITARIAN

- Humanitarian. Selfless.
- Great understanding and tolerance. Strong potential to help others. May be taken advantage of by others.
- Significant power potential.
- Idealistic. Sometimes led in impractical directions by idealistic views.
- Much emotion. Often, considerable emotional upset.
- Self-starter.
- Inspirational approach.

LETTER COMPARISON

I: More high-strung than R.
R: More selfless than I.

| CHART **11** | **11** ILLUMINATION |
| THE FIRST LETTER | |

K   INTUITIVE INSPIRER

Eleventh
letter: 11/2

- High potential for achievement.
- High nervous tension.
- Very open to spiritual awareness.
- Can inspire others.
- Receptive to others' feelings.
- Helpful. Promotes harmony. Good at detail work.
- Appreciates affection. Expresses much affection.
- Much intuitive awareness on the highest level. Can translate these awarenesses so that others can use the understanding.

- Very creative.
- Power to achieve desired ends. Best results develop when care is taken not to dominate others.
- Charisma aids in use of power.

CHART **11**	**22** MASTER BUILDER
THE FIRST LETTER	

V   **INSPIRATIONAL MASTER**

*Twenty-second
letter: 22/4*

- Inspired leader.
- Extremely receptive to spiritual revelation.
- Builder, on the highest level.
- Can envision ideas, convert ideas into practical form, organize people and resources, inspire confidence and loyalty.
- Can convert spiritual awareness to material form.
- High nervous tension.
- Hard worker. Self-disciplined.
- Serious. Steady. Thorough.
- Practical.
- Intuitive awareness is potential strong source of power.

CHART 12 THE FIRST VOWEL

The First Vowel (this chart) and the First Letter (Chart No. 11) describe the natural or innate approach, the method of response and reaction to experience.

See Chapter 20, page 185.

CHART **12** **THE FIRST VOWEL**	**1**	INDIVIDUATION INDEPENDENCE ATTAINMENT

A
*First
letter: 1*

DYNAMIC LEADER
LONG VOWEL as in *A*my, D*a*le, J*a*ne

- Leader. Ambitious. Adventurous. Progressive.
- Assertive, at the very least; often aggressive. Independent. Self-reliant.
- Strong willpower and strong opinions. Accepts advice readily only if it's in same vein as own ideas.
- Expresses individuality strongly.
- Great deal of energy. Good mind. Creative mental approach.
- Excellent ideas. Interested in new ideas but usually prefers to use own ideas.
- Original or innovative approach. Will defend his approach no matter how much opposition he faces.
- Pushes ahead with pioneering spirit. Loves to forge ahead in unknown territory.
- Interest may lag after the start. May have difficulty completing projects.

A
*First
letter: 1*

SENSITIVE LEADER
SHORT VOWEL as *A*rlene, M*a*tthew, P*a*mela

- Leader, but doesn't always care to exert power.
- Moderately adventurous. Progressive. Sometimes assertive.
- With practice, develops independence, self-reliance.
- Has own ideas, but willing to listen to others' ideas and incorporate all.
- Individuality is expressed in a subdued manner.
- Good mind. Creative mental approach. Excellent ideas.
- Original or innovative approach. Will explain his approach and is willing to struggle with the opposition, but too much opposition may wear him down.
- Pushes ahead with measured forward spirit. Enjoys moving cautiously into unknown territory.

A
*First
letter: 1*

SENSITIVE LEADER
COMBINED VOWEL as in H*a*ydn, J*oa*n, L*au*ra

- Leader.
- Some ambitions.
- Moderate independence, self-reliance.
- Individuality expressed in a subdued manner.
- Good mind. Creative mental approach. Excellent ideas.
- Original or innovative approach.

CHART 12
THE FIRST VOWEL

2 RELATION
COOPERATION

LONG VOWEL

Not applicable

SHORT VOWEL

Not applicable

COMBINED VOWEL

Not applicable

CHART **12**	**3**	EXPRESSION
THE FIRST VOWEL		JOY OF LIVING

U

*Twenty-first letter:
21 : 3*

SENSITIVE RECEPTOR
LONG VOWEL as in Hugh, Julian, Lucy

- Artistic, creative with measured approach. Although the creativity potential can be seen, there is often very little expressed.
- Usually good with words.
- Sensitive. Aware of others' feelings.
- Strong emotions.
- Friendly and sociable. Enjoys social activities, the lighter side of life.
- Idealistic, but rarely attains idealistic ends.
- Conservative approach. Rarely seeks initiative.
- Extremely intuitive.
- Indecisive approach.
- May scatter energies.

U

*Twenty-first letter:
21 : 3*

CONSERVATIVE RECEPTOR
SHORT VOWEL as in Burt, Gus, Russell

- Artistic, creative potential. If expressed at all, expressed in slow, very conservative approach.
- Capable of good communication, but often prefers not to express thoughts.
- Sensitive. Aware of others' feelings.
- Strong emotions, sometimes not expressed.
- Idealistic desires, rarely communicated or developed.
- Extremely conservative approach. Prefers not to take initiative.
- Intuitive.
- Indecisive approach.
- May scatter energies.

U

*Twenty-first letter:
21 : 3*

CONSERVATIVE RECEPTOR
COMBINED VOWEL as in Audrey, Eugene, Guy

- Artistic, creative potential, often latent.
- Either inexpressive or over-talkative. Either way, communicates little of deep thoughts.
- Sensitive.
- Deep feelings.
- Idealistic.
- Extremely conservative.
- Intuitive.
- Indecisive approach.
- May scatter energies.

CHART 12
THE FIRST VOWEL

4 LIMITATION
ORDER
SERVICE

LONG VOWEL

Not applicable

SHORT VOWEL

Not applicable

COMBINED VOWEL

Not applicable

CHART **12**	**5** CONSTRUCTIVE FREEDOM
THE FIRST VOWEL	

E
Fifth letter: 5

ADVENTUROUS ENCOUNTERER
LONG VOWEL as in Delia, Gene, Leroy

- Adventurous. Often turns life situations into adventures.
- Restless. Need for change, excitement, variety.
- Impulsive. Aggressive.
- Adaptable. Versatile.
- Needs freedom in order to develop.
- Often difficulties with marriage because of need for change, excitement. Marriage, on occasion, can provide stabilizing influence.
- Much energy.
- Much mental activity. Much stimulation.
- Keep perceptions and judgements of people, motivations, events.
- Helpful. Practical.
- Much is started, often abandoned or set aside for later time.

E
Fifth letter: 5

RESTLESS ENCOUNTERER
SHORT VOWEL as in Bernard, Emily, Kelley

- Enjoys adventure. Prefers freedom in order to develop.
- Somewhat restless. Likes change, excitement, variety.
- Adaptable. Versatile. Helpful. Practical.
- Marriage needs much work, spouse with considerable understanding in order to succeed.
- A good deal of energy, but often less energy than necessary to carry out the stimulating demands of his life.
- Mental activity. Good perceptions and judgements.
- A good deal is started, sometimes abandoned or set aside for later time, or given to others to continue and complete.

E
Fifth letter: 5

RESTLESS ENCOUNTERER
COMBINED VOWEL as in Beulah, Jeanne, Reid

- Adventurous.
- Adaptable. Versatile.
- Mental activity.
- A good deal is started, but continuity may be lacking, sometimes causing discord.

W
Twenty-third letter: 23 : 5

VACILLATING ENERGIZER
Can only be COMBINED VOWEL and follow another letter as in Howard, Seward

- Restless.
- Strong energy can be used in positive or negative direction, particularly in material affairs. With great effort, energy can be used for superior achievement; with much less effort, energy can be used to promote negative ends:
  —If core stresses egotism, domination, self-centeredness, (1,4,8 particularly), W energy tends to emphasize these negative traits.
  —If core stresses awareness or helpfulness to others (2,6,7,9,11), W energy tends to emphasize these positive traits.
  —If core stresses freedom (5 particularly), W energy stresses freedom. Rest of core and free will determine whether direction is positive or negative.
- Often vacillates between several different points of view.

CHART **12** THE FIRST VOWEL	**6**	BALANCE RESPONSIBILITY LOVE

O
Fifteenth letter:
15 : 6

POISED HARMONIZER
LONG VOWEL as in Hope, Joseph, Rose

- Takes on many responsibilities—often more than he can comfortably handle. Because he is so responsible, he may well be used by others.
- Views role in life as giving service to others: family, friends, close community.
- Attracts situations requiring much in the way of adjustment.
- Concentrates well.
- Conservative traits. Gives out little openly. Often conteht to follow traditional modes. Prefers a settled life with minimum change.
- Innately knows how to protect self from life's storms. Self-contained. Secretive.
- Deep emotions, but controlled so often not visible.
- Creative, artistic. Enjoys beautiful domestic surroundings.

O
Fifteenth letter:
15 : 6

PROTECTED HARMONIZER
SHORT VOWEL as in Dorothy, Josh, Oliver

- Responsible.
- Gives service to others; family, friends, close community.
- Attracts situations requiring much in the way of adjustment.
- Sometimes, can create balance; at other times, contributes to imbalance.
- Conservative. Traditional.
- Extremely protected. Extremely self-contained. Secretive.
- Extremely emotional, but only some of the feelings are displayed.

O
Fifteenth letter:
15 : 6

PROTECTED HARMONIZER
COMBINED VOWEL as in Boyd, Howard, Louis

- Responsible.
- Gives service.
- Attracts situations requiring much in the way of adjustment.
- Conservative. Traditional.
- Protected. Self-contained.
- Emotional. Some feelings displayed.

CHART **12**	**7** ANALYSIS
THE FIRST VOWEL	UNDERSTANDING

Y
Twenty-fifth letter:
25 : 7

UNCERTAIN THINKER
LONG VOWEL as in M*y*ron, R*y*an

- Reserved, introspective. Very secretive.
- Works best alone. Often feels isolated.
- Feels deeply. Expresses and shares little of these feelings.
- Often not understood by others.
- Extremely keen mind. Given to thought and meditation.
- Enjoys analysis of fundamentals, pursuit of wisdom, philosophical or metaphysical speculation. Extremely perceptive. Fine intuition.
- Deep insights into higher matters. Not always certain how to use these insights.
- Strong psychic power. Must learn to trust it.
- Difficulty in choosing directions, solutions. Often uncertain, vacillating. Must constantly choose path of growth or the easy way.

Y
Twenty-fifth letter:
25 : 7

DEPENDENT THINKER
SHORT VOWEL as in C*y*ril, S*y*lvia, Yvette

- Reserved, introspective. Very secretive.
- Works best alone. Often feels isolated.
- Feels deeply. Expresses and shares little of these feelings.
- Often not understood by others.
- Extremely keen mind. Given to thought and meditation. Enjoys analysis of fundamentals, pursuit of wisdom, philosophical or metaphysical speculation.
- Good perceptions. Good intuition.
- Insight into higher matters. Some psychic power. Must learn to trust it.
- Extreme difficulty in choosing directions, solutions. Usually uncertain, vacillating. Must constantly choose path of growth or the easy way.

Y
Twenty-fifth letter:
25 : 7

VACILLATOR
COMBINED VOWEL as in Bo*y*d, Fa*y*, Ra*y*mond

- Adds indecision and restlessness to the coloration of the connected vowel.
- Extreme difficulty in choosing directions, solutions. Usually uncertain. Must constantly choose path of growth or the easy way.

CHART 12
THE FIRST VOWEL

8 MATERIAL SATISFACTION

LONG VOWEL

Not applicable

SHORT VOWEL

Not applicable

COMBINED VOWEL

Not applicable

CHART **12**	**9** SELFLESSNESS
THE FIRST VOWEL	HUMANITARIANISM

I
*Ninth
letter: 9*

EMOTIONAL HUMANITARIAN
LONG VOWEL as in Clive, Ida, Michael

- Humanitarian. Giving. Serves others with love.
- Sympathetic. Deep emotional understanding of others' needs.
- Sensitive. Often too sensitive for good balance.
- Willing to sacrifice for others. At times, may be disappointed with others' response or lack of appreciation.
- Idealistic.
- Artistic, creative.
- Very intense. Much energy.
- Conservative. Prefers to work in familiar territory.
- Extremely deep feelings. The emotions rule (sometimes overwhelm) the mental faculties. Wild fluctuations in temperament possible—from joy to depression.

I
*Ninth
letter: 9*

RESTRAINED HUMANITARIAN
SHORT VOWEL as in Christy, Gilbert, Lillie

- Humanitarian. Giving.
- Quietly sympathetic.
- Sensitive.
- Often willing to sacrifice for others.
- Idealistic.
- Artistic, creative.
- Conservative. Works in familiar territory.
- Some intensity at times. A good deal of energy.
- Deep feelings, usually expressed with moderation. The emotions rule the mental faculties.

I
*Ninth
letter: 9*

RESTRAINED HUMANITARIAN
COMBINED VOWEL as in Daisy, Frieda, Neil

- Humanitarian.
- Sensitive.
- Idealistic.
- Artistic, creative.
- Conservative.
- Some intensity at times. A good deal of energy.
- Feelings expressed with moderation.

CHART **12**
THE FIRST VOWEL

11 ILLUMINATION

LONG VOWEL

Not applicable

SHORT VOWEL

Not applicable

COMBINED VOWEL

Not applicable

CHART 12
THE FIRST VOWEL

22 MASTER BUILDER

LONG VOWEL

Not applicable

SHORT VOWEL

Not applicable

COMBINED VOWEL

Not applicable